Windows Admin Scripting Little Black Book
Quick Reference

W9-CII-372

Administrative Shares

By default, Windows NT/2000 creates hidden administrative shares so that administrators can perform various tasks remotely. Table 1 lists the most common administrative shares.

Table 1   Administrative shares.

Share	Description
ADMIN$	Shares the directory Windows was installed to (for example, C:\WINNT)
DRIVE$	Shares all available drives
IPC$	Share that represents the named pipes communication mechanism
PRINT$	Share for shared printer drivers
REPL$	Shares replication directory on a server

The AT Command

The **AT** command allows you to schedule tasks from the command line. The basic syntax of the **AT** command is as follows:

```
AT \\remote ID /PARAMETERS "fullpath"
```

Here, *remote* is an optional name of a remote system on which to control tasks; *ID* specifies a task ID to modify; and *fullpath* is the complete path and file name of the item to schedule. Table 2 lists the available parameters.

Table 2   The AT command parameters.

Parameter	Description
/DELETE	Removes a scheduled job.
/EVERY:*x*	Recurrently runs the command on the specified day (*x*).
/INTERACTIVE	Sets the job to interact with the desktop. This switch must be set if you want the user to have any interactivity with the scheduled task.
/NEXT:*x*	Runs the command on the next specified date (*x*).
/YES	Combined with **/DELETE**, suppresses all jobs cancellation prompt.

The Cipher Utility

Cipher is a utility that allows you to encrypt/decrypt your files from the command line. This utility supports various command-line parameters, as shown in Table 3.

Table 3   Cipher parameters.

Parameter	Description
/A	Acts on files and folders
/D	Decrypts files and folders
/E	Encrypts files and folders
/F	Forces encryption, even on files already encrypted
/H	Includes system and hidden files
/I	Ignores errors
/K	Creates a new encryption key for the current user
/Q	Runs in silent mode
/S	Performs action on the current folder and all subfolders

Common Locations

Microsoft uses a common organized structure to store user data. By knowing the locations of these directories and the quickest way to access them, you can easily modify their contents within your scripts. Tables 4, 5, and 6 list the most common locations for Windows *9x*, Windows NT, and Windows 2000, respectively.

Table 4   Windows 9x paths.

Name	Location
Desktop	%*WINDIR*%\Desktop
Favorites	%*WINDIR*%\Favorites
NetHood	%*WINDIR*%\NetHood
PrintHood	%*WINDIR*%\PrintHood
Quick Launch	%*WINDIR*%\Application Data\Microsoft\ Internet Explorer\Quick Launch
SendTo	%*WINDIR*%\ SendTo
Start Menu	%*WINDIR*%\Start Menu

Table 5   Windows NT paths.

Name	Location
All Users Desktop	%*WINDIR*%\Profiles\All Users\Desktop
All Users Start Menu	%*WINDIR*%\ Profiles\All Users\Start Menu
Desktop	%*USERPROFILE*%\Desktop
Favorites	%*USERPROFILE*%\Favorites
NetHood	%*USERPROFILE*%\NetHood
PrintHood	%*USERPROFILE*%\PrintHood
Quick Launch	%*USERPROFILE*%\Application Data\Microsoft\ Internet Explorer\Quick Launch
SendTo	%*USERPROFILE*%\SendTo
Start Menu	%*USERPROFILE*%\Start Menu

Table 6   Windows 2000 paths.

Name	Location
All Users Desktop	%*ALLUSERSPROFILE*%\Profiles\All Users\Desktop
All Users Start Menu	%*ALLUSERSPROFILE*%\ Profiles\All Users\ Start Menu
Desktop	%*USERPROFILE*%\Desktop
Favorites	%*USERPROFILE*%\Favorites
NetHood	%*USERPROFILE*%\NetHood
PrintHood	%*USERPROFILE*%\PrintHood
Quick Launch	%*USERPROFILE*%\Application Data\Microsoft\ Internet Explorer\Quick Launch
SendTo	%*USERPROFILE*%\SendTo
Start Menu	%*USERPROFILE*%\Start Menu

Microsoft FDISK

Microsoft FDISK (Fixed DISK) is a program that allows you to create, delete, or view entries in the partition table. Microsoft FDISK supports many command-line parameters, as shown in Table 7.

Table 7   Microsoft FDISK parameters.

Parameter	Description
/ACTOK	Skips drive integrity check
/EXT:*size disk*	Creates an extended partition
/FPRMT	Skips the large drive support startup screen and sets up all partitions set up as FAT32
/LOG: *size*	Combined with **/EXT**, creates a logical partition of the specified *size*
/MBR	Creates a new Master Boot Record
/PARTN	Saves partition information to PARTSAV.FIL
/PRI:*size disk*	Creates a primary partition
/STATUS	Displays current partition information

Microsoft Script Encoder

The Microsoft Script Encoder allows you to protect your scripts using a simple encoding scheme. The default supported file types are ASA, ASP, CDX, HTM, HTML, JS, SCT, and VBS. The basic syntax of the script encoder is as follows:

```
SCRENC inputfile outputfile
```

Here, *inputfile* is the file to encode and *outputfile* is the encoded result. Microsoft Script Encoder supports many command-line parameters, as shown in Table 8.

Table 8   Microsoft Script Encoder parameters.

Parameter	Description
/E *extension*	Specifies a known *extension* for unrecognized input file types
/F	Specifies to overwrite the input file with the encoded version
/L *language*	Specifies to use the scripting language **Jscript** or **VBScript**
/S	Specifies to work in silent mode
/X1	Specifies not to include the **@language** directive in ASP files

Microsoft System Diagnostics

Microsoft System Diagnostics (MSD) is a command-line utility to display system resources and settings of a local system. The basic syntax of the MSD command is:

```
MSD /commands
```

Table 9 lists the available *commands*.

Table 9   Microsoft System Diagnostics commands.

Parameter	Description
/F *file*	Prompts for various information and then sends a complete report output to a file
/B	Runs MSD in black and white
/I	Does not attempt hardware detection
/P *file*	Sends a complete report output to a file
/S	Sends a summary report output to the default printer

Microsoft Windows Installer

The Windows Installer is a new installation and configuration service for 32-bit Windows platforms that standardizes the way programs install and uninstall. The Windows Installer supports various command-line parameters, as shown in Table 10.

Table 10   Microsoft Windows Installer parameters.

Parameter	Description
/I	Installs the program
/F	Repairs an installation
/X	Uninstalls the program
/L*V *logfile*	Logs all information to a *logfile*
/QN	Displays no user interface
/QB	Displays basic user interface
/QF	Displays full user interface
/? or **/H**	Displays some switches and copyright information
/X	Uninstalls the program

CORIOLIS
Technology Press

Windows® Admin Scripting

Little Black Book

Jesse M. Torres

President
and CEO
*Keith
Weiskamp*

Publisher
Steve Sayre

Acquisitions
Editor
*Charlotte
Carpentier*

Development
Editor
*Michelle
Stroup*

Product
Marketing
Manager
Tracy Rooney

Project Editor
*Sybil Ihrig
Helios
Productions*

Technical
Reviewer
Francis Botto

Production
Coordinator
Kim Eoff

Cover Designer
Jody Winkler

Layout Designer
April Nielsen

Windows® Admin Scripting Little Black Book

Limits of Liability and Disclaimer of Warranty

Trademarks

The Coriolis Group, LLC
14455 North Hayden Road
Suite 220
Scottsdale, Arizona 85260

(480) 483-0192
FAX (480) 483-0193
www.coriolis.com

Library of Congress Cataloging-in-Publication Data
Torres, Jesse M.
    Windows admin scripting little black book / by Jesse M. Torres.
        p.   cm.
    ISBN 1-57610-881-3
    1. Microsoft Windows (Computer file)   2. Operating systems
(Computers)   3. Programming languages (Electronic computers)   I. Title.
QA76.76.O63 T6775   2000
005.4'469–dc21   00-050858
                                                                                    CIP

Printed in the United States of America
10 9 8 7 6 5 4 3 2

The Coriolis Group, LLC • 14455 North Hayden Road, Suite 220 • Scottsdale, Arizona 85260

Dear Reader:

Coriolis Technology Press was founded to create a very elite group of books: the ones you keep closest to your machine. Sure, everyone would like to have the Library of Congress at arm's reach, but in the real world, you have to choose the books you rely on every day *very* carefully.

To win a place for our books on that coveted shelf beside your PC, we guarantee several important qualities in every book we publish. These qualities are:

- *Technical accuracy*—It's no good if it doesn't work. Every Coriolis Technology Press book is reviewed by technical experts in the topic field, and is sent through several editing and proofreading passes in order to create the piece of work you now hold in your hands.

- *Innovative editorial design*—We've put years of research and refinement into the ways we present information in our books. Our books' editorial approach is uniquely designed to reflect the way people learn new technologies and search for solutions to technology problems.

- *Practical focus*—We put only pertinent information into our books and avoid any fluff. Every fact included between these two covers must serve the mission of the book as a whole.

- *Accessibility*—The information in a book is worthless unless you can find it quickly when you need it. We put a lot of effort into our indexes, and heavily cross-reference our chapters, to make it easy for you to move right to the information you need.

Here at The Coriolis Group we have been publishing and packaging books, technical journals, and training materials since 1989. We're programmers and authors ourselves, and we take an ongoing active role in defining what we publish and how we publish it. We have put a lot of thought into our books; please write to us at **ctp@coriolis.com** and let us know what you think. We hope that you're happy with the book in your hands, and that in the future, when you reach for software development and networking information, you'll turn to one of our books first.

Keith Weiskamp
President and CEO

Jeff Duntemann
VP and Editorial Director

To my future wife, Carina:
Your love and smile mean more to me than you could ever know.
❧

About the Author

Jesse M. Torres' experience in the computer industry includes the private, corporate, and government sectors. He served six years in the Air National Guard working in computer maintenance and has since worked for large corporations such as PricewaterhouseCoopers and United Technologies. His education includes a specialist's certification in electronic switching systems from the U.S. Air Force, a B.A. in Versatile Technology from the University of Connecticut, a specialist's certification in Lotus application development, and an MCSE certification.

Jesse has extensively scripted software and OS installations and updates, inventory procedures, desktop management, maintenance, security, and more. His scripting and automation experience includes shell scripting, KiXtart, Windows Script Host (WSH), Windows Management Instrumentation (WMI), Active Directory Service Interfaces (ADSI), VBScript, JavaScript, Active Server Pages (ASP), Veritas WinINSTALL, PowerQuest DeltaDeploy, Microsoft Systems Management Server (SMS), AutoIt, and Microsoft ScriptIt. He has also written an article on WSH for *Windows 2000 Magazine's Win32 Scripting Journal*.

Currently, Jesse is working for Strategic Business Systems, LLC, a privately owned consulting firm located in Seymour, CT, and in his spare time (whenever that is), he likes to play the guitar or piano, or record his own techno music (check out his Web site **www.jesseweb.com** for audio clips). By the time this book hits the presses, he will be married to a beautiful and wonderful woman named Carina and will be relaxing somewhere in the sunny Caribbean. Kind of a nice change after writing non-stop for the past few months.

Acknowledgments

First, I would like to thank Charlotte Carpentier, acquisitions editor at The Coriolis Group. She took my small idea, helped reshape it, and fought to make it reality. Thank you, Charlotte, for your promptness and for allowing me to work with one of the leaders of the technical publishing industry.

I would also like to thank Michelle Stroup, developmental editor at The Coriolis Group. Although we worked together only a short time, thank you for your encouragement and for guiding me through the initial stages. Thanks to everyone at The Coriolis Group who worked hard on this book.

Special thanks to project editor Sybil Ihrig of Helios Productions, copyeditor Margaret Berson, and technical reviewer Francis Botto. Together you put up with my unique sense of humor and stubbornness while realizing that techies still have a life (sometimes). Thanks for adding your expertise and personal touch.

Thanks to all the software companies and developers (Rudd van Velsen, Microsoft, Sapien Technologies, Executive Software, Dave Thomas, Hidden Software, and BellCraft Technologies) for sharing information and making quality products.

Thanks to John Breyan, Ray Wise, Daniel Teplitsky, Enzo Maini, and everyone at Strategic Business Systems for your understanding and encouragement during these past few months. Special thanks to Gideon Rasmussen for his security and scripting help, regardless of his misguided devotion to Unix. Also, I would like to thank John McGowan (McGowan Consulting Group) for his support, understanding, guidance, and unfailing good humor.

Acknowledgments

Thanks to my family, whose pride in my accomplishments clearly shines through. I love you all. Special thanks to my mom and dad for supporting me and seeing the bigger picture, even when I would take apart the VCR or spend hours playing video games.

Finally, special thanks to my future wife, Carina, for giving up some of our time together so I could share this book with the world. I love you and will always be here for you, as you've been for me. Thank you for understanding.

Contents at a Glance

Table of Contents

Chapter 6
Local System Management 137

Chapter 7
Remote System Management 163

Introduction

Welcome to *Windows Admin Scripting Little Black Book*. This book is specifically designed to teach you how to quickly turn routine, repetitive, time-consuming, or complex administrative tasks into simple scripts. If you're like me, you probably don't have the time to spend thumbing through books filled with general examples that you'll never use. Because of its compact size, this book is free of generic filler material (a common trait of the larger scripting books) and comes packed with information and examples that you can actually use. Whether you're a basic Windows user or a network administrator in charge of a corporate infrastructure, this book will teach you how to use scripting to become more productive and recoup some free time from your busy schedule.

This book is a concise reference detailing various scripting methods and techniques to automate all types of administrative tasks. At its core, this book explains and illustrates the three major scripting methods: shell scripting, KiXtart, and Windows Script Host. It will also teach you the inner workings of Active Directory Service Interfaces and Windows Management Instrumentation, and how to use the provided examples to manage an enterprise. Finally, this book will show you how to use alternative methods, such as ScriptIt or AutoIt, when conventional scripting just won't cut it. Beyond the extensive scripting examples and information, this book also provides in-depth coverage of scripting for both Windows NT and Windows 2000.

Is This Book for You?

If you've read this far, chances are this is the book for you. Out of all the sites where I've worked, only a small percentage of employees have even thought about using scripting. Perhaps it's because there is a common misconception that you have to be a programmer or computer genius to write scripts. This couldn't be any further from the truth. Scripts are the simplest form of programming, and anyone who uses a computer can easily create them.

The examples and information in this book are specifically focused around the daily tasks of the IT professional. For the novice administrator or scripter, this book will guide you through the world of scripting and administration, while helping you quickly build your skill set. For the experienced administrator or scripter, this book provides a wealth of information and advanced techniques to help you manage and standardize your environment.

How to Use This Book

This book is divided into 14 chapters. Each chapter begins with a brief overview followed by a set of immediate solutions to help you automate your tasks.

Chapter 1: Scripting Workstation Setups

Chapter 1 covers how to automate hard disk setups and imaging. Immediate solutions include how to script partitioning, formatting, and boot disk creation. It also includes extensive information on how to script some of today's popular imaging utilities, such as PowerQuest Drive Image Pro and Norton Ghost.

Chapter 2: Scripting Installations and Updates

Chapter 2 covers how to automate installations and updates. Immediate solutions include how to script installations and updates using built-in switches, custom routines, and the Microsoft Windows Installer. It also includes information on how to use Microsoft ScriptIt when other scripting methods simply won't work.

Chapter 3: File Management

Chapter 3 covers how to automate file manipulation and management. Immediate solutions include how to script file renaming, replication, deletion, appending, updating, searching, and attribute modifying. It also includes information on how to use shell scripting, KiXtart, and Windows Script Host.

Chapter 4: Automating Windows and Applications

Chapter 4 covers how to automate the operating system and its applications. Immediate solutions include how to script Windows operations and settings, such as Microsoft FTP uploads, defragging, hardware devices, and Control Panel applets. It also includes information on how to script applications, such as Norton Antivirus, Microsoft Office, Internet Explorer, and Diskeeper Lite.

Chapter 5: Inside the Registry

Chapter 5 covers how to automate changes to the registry. This chapter includes in-depth information about the birth and structure of the registry while clearing up common misconceptions. Immediate solutions include how to secure, back up, restore, modify, and search the registry. It also includes information on how to modify common Windows annoyances, for example, how to disable Dr. Watson or the Welcome screens.

Chapter 6: Local System Management

Chapter 6 covers how to control and automate local system changes. Immediate solutions include how to manage shortcuts, program groups, profiles, shares, services, permissions, and more through simple scripts. It also includes information on how to script common system events, such as logging off a user or rebooting a system.

Chapter 7: Remote System Management

Chapter 7 covers how to control and automate remote systems. Immediate solutions include how to manage processes, shares, services, permissions, and more through simple scripts. This chapter includes in-depth information and examples on how to use Windows Management Instrumentation. It also includes information on how to script common system events, such as shutting down or rebooting a system.

Chapter 8: Enterprise Management

Chapter 8 covers how to automate enterprise management. Immediate solutions include how to manage user, group, and computer accounts through simple scripts. This chapter includes in-depth information and examples on how to use Active Directory Service Interfaces. It also includes information on Windows NT and Windows 2000 Enterprise networks.

Chapter 9: Managing Inventory

Chapter 9 covers how to gather inventory information without the use of expensive management systems. Immediate solutions include how to collect software and hardware information, such as battery, operating system, Network Interface Card (NIC), processor, printer, sound card, and memory information. It also includes information on how to generate inventory reports using utilities like MSD, WINMSD, MSINFO32, and SRVINFO.

Chapter 10: Security

Chapter 10 covers how to control and automate remote systems. Immediate solutions include how to manage system and domain security settings; create, apply, and export security templates; and run a security analysis through simple scripts. This chapter includes in-depth information about C2 security, authentication protocols, and common security practices. It also includes information on how to use utilities to run operations under the security context of another user, such as the RunAs or SU utility.

Chapter 11: Logging and Alerting

Chapter 11 covers how to log system events and alert users when events occur. Immediate solutions include how to manage text logs and the Windows NT/2000 event log through simple scripts. The chapter also includes information on how to script alerts to a single user, group, or user list through network alerts and email.

Chapter 12: Logon Scripts

Chapter 12 covers how to create and use logon scripts to standardize your environment. Immediate solutions include how to synchronize the system time, map drives and printers, display logon script progress, and more through simple shell, KiXtart, or WSH scripts. This chapter also includes in-depth information about the logon process and file replication services.

Chapter 13: Backups and Scheduling

Chapter 13 covers how to automate backups and scheduling tasks or scripts. Immediate solutions include how to script backups on Windows NT and Windows 2000, Emergency Repair Disks, and task scheduling. It also includes information on how to script third-party backup applications, such as Backup Exec and ARCserve.

Chapter 14: Fun with Multimedia

Chapter 14 covers how to play and control multimedia files using simple scripts. Immediate solutions include how to script the Microsoft Media Player and the RealPlayer G2. It also includes information on how to script the Microsoft Office Assistant and Microsoft Agent characters.

The *Little Black Book* Philosophy

Written by experienced professionals, Coriolis *Little Black Books* are terse, easily "thumb-able" question-answerers and problem solvers. The *Little Black Book*'s unique two-part chapter format—brief technical overviews followed by practical immediate solutions—is structured to help you use your knowledge, solve problems, and quickly master complex technical issues to become an expert. By breaking down complex topics into easily manageable components, this format helps you quickly find what you're looking for.

A Final Note

I hope this book will become your essential reference in streamlining your environment and daily tasks. I welcome your comments, questions, suggestions, tips, scripts, or anything else you would like to share. Please feel free to email me at **jesse@jesseweb.com** or visit my really cool Web site at **www.jesseweb.com** for updates.

Chapter 1

Scripting Workstation Setups

(continued)

In Brief

This chapter begins our journey into Windows Admin Scripting. In this chapter you'll learn the quickest methods to automate hard disk setups and images. You'll begin learning the secrets of Microsoft FDISK and how to create partitions from the command line. You'll also learn about the scripting limitations of Microsoft FDISK and how to use Free FDISK to script creating and deleting partitions. You'll then learn about different imaging solutions and how to script those packages to create and restore image files.

In order to implement all the examples in this chapter, you'll need to obtain the following files:

- Free FDISK (**www.23cc.com/free-fdisk/**)
- PowerQuest Drive Image Pro (**www.powerquest.com**)
- Norton Ghost (**www.symantec.com**)

NOTE: *All the DOS-related information in this chapter refers to MS-DOS 7.0.*

WARNING! This chapter contains examples on how to partition, format, and image drives. These processes will destroy any data on a disk.

Setting Up a New Hard Drive

For the typical PC, the core component to store user data and system files is the hard drive. A hard drive is like a wallet or purse—a place you can store your most valuable assets you need to access quickly. When you receive a new hard drive from the manufacturer, it is most likely low-level formatted with no data on it. After you install and configure the hard drive properly, you must partition and format it before you can put any real data on it.

Partitioning

The first step to setting up a new drive is to partition it. *Partitioning* is the act of dividing up a hard disk into logical sections, which allows one physical drive to appear as multiple drives. When you partition a new drive, a master boot record (MBR) is created on the first physical sector on the hard drive. As a computer initially powers up, it

1. Scripting Workstation Setups

calls the routines stored in the BIOS (Basic Input/Output System). These routines access the system's basic hardware devices (e.g., floppy disk, hard disk, keyboard, video). After these routines are executed, the BIOS reads and executes instructions from the MBR. The MBR contains the partition table, which contains four entries, allowing for various partition types.

Partition Types

When scripting the creation of a partition, you must know the type of partition and its dependencies beforehand. There are three different types of partitions: primary, extended, and logical. Each physical disk can have a maximum of four primary partitions, and only one can be marked active in order to boot. When a primary partition is marked active, it is automatically assigned the drive letter C.

Each primary partition can have only one extended partition. Within an extended partition, you can create up to 24 logical partitions (or 23 logical partitions if you have an active partition on the same drive). Each logical partition is assigned a drive letter (with A and B reserved for floppy drives).

NOTE: *Only one primary and one extended partition are allowed per physical disk.*

Partition Hierarchy

Partition types follow a hierarchy: primary, extended, and logical. They can only be created in this order, and can only be deleted in the opposite order. To begin scripting partitions, you must first familiarize yourself with Microsoft FDISK.

Microsoft FDISK

Microsoft FDISK (Fixed DISK) is a program that an experienced administrator can be all too familiar with. If only I had a nickel for each time I've used Microsoft FDISK, I'd be as rich as these IT salary surveys say I should be. Microsoft FDISK is the most commonly used partitioning utility for hard disks, but despite its popularity, most of its functionality remains highly undocumented. Microsoft FDISK is included in all versions of DOS and Windows. It allows you to create, delete, or view entries in the partition table. If you've ever used Microsoft FDISK to set up a new hard drive manually, you know how time-consuming it can be navigating through menus and waiting for drive integrity checks. Microsoft FDISK provides limited support for scripting from the command line.

NOTE: *If you want to change entries in the partition table, you must first delete and then recreate them.*

Scripting Limitations

Scripting Microsoft FDISK is like going to the casino—sometimes you win, sometimes you lose, but most of the time you lose. Microsoft FDISK does support many command-line options, but doesn't work well with command redirection input (for example, **FDISK < COMMANDS.TXT**). And although the menu-based portion allows for deleting partitions, there's no way to delete partitions from the command line. Just as you do when you're at the casino, you have to know when it's time to collect your chips and move on to the next table. For us, that move is to Free FDISK.

Free FDISK

If Microsoft FDISK were a used car, you could slap a new engine in it and make it run just the way you like. Well, Free FDISK does just that. Free FDISK offers enhanced functionality over Microsoft's FDISK and is the official FDISK of FreeDOS (**www.freedos.org**). Free FDISK provides the same standard Microsoft FDISK interface and command-line options, while adding even more options for batch scripting. After you partition the hard drive, formatting is the last step needed before the drive is ready for data.

Formatting

Formatting is the process of preparing a disk for reading and writing. FORMAT.COM is the executable used to format both floppy and hard disks. When you format a disk, a file allocation table (FAT) and a new root directory are created, allowing you to store and retrieve files. This, in essence, places a file system on a disk for you to use.

The FAT organizes a hard disk into clusters, grouped into 512K sectors. Clusters are the smallest units for storing data and vary in size depending on the file system. Starting with the Windows 95 OSR2 release, Windows 9*x*/2000 supports the following two file system types: FAT16 and FAT32. FAT16 is a 16-bit file system that typically stores files in 32K clusters, depending on the partition size. FAT32 is a 32-bit file system that stores files more efficiently in 4K clusters. You should choose a file system that will be compatible with the various operating systems running, provide the greatest security, and be the most efficient.

NOTE: *Windows NT does not natively support FAT32. Additionally, Windows NT/2000 support the NTFS (New Technology File System). See Chapter 6 for more information about NTFS.*

After the drive is formatted with a file system, the operating system can be loaded and made ready for deployment.

Imaging

Imaging is the process of taking an exact copy of a reference computer's hard drive or partition and storing it to an image file (usually compressed). That image can be stored on any storage medium (hard disk, CDR, ZIP) and restored to multiple computers, creating a standardized software and operating system environment. The basic principle of imaging is very similar to a simple disk copy.

Tools

For an administrator, deploying new PCs can become a large part of your job. With old PCs being retired and new PCs rolling in, finding a way to streamline the imaging process can help cut hours from your work day. And when you're dealing with more than a few PCs, automating the imaging process is not only helpful, but also essential. Imaging tools such as PowerQuest's Drive Image Pro or Norton Ghost make it easy for an administrator to re-image multiple hard drives in a matter of minutes.

PowerQuest's Drive Image Pro

Drive Image Pro (see Figure 1.1) is an imaging and software distribution solution package from PowerQuest Corporation (**www.powerquest.com**). In addition to running in standard interactive mode, this product can

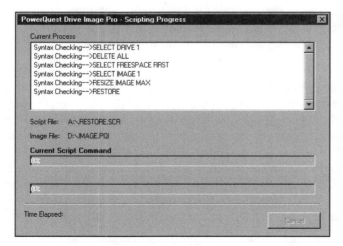

Figure 1.1   Drive Image Pro window showing automatic script syntax checking.

also be run in batch mode, allowing a script file to send commands to the main program executable (PQDI.EXE).

Drive Image Pro uses a proprietary scripting language and includes many commands and switches to image your hard disk. The most commonly used commands are:

- **SELECT DRIVE** *number*—Selects a drive according to the *number* specified

- **SELECT PARTITION** *x*—Selects a partition where *x* is:
  - A partition number
  - A drive letter
  - A disk label

- **ALL**—Selects all partitions

- **DELETE**—Deletes the partitions specified in the last **SELECT** command

- **DELETE** *x*—Deletes partitions within the currently selected drive where *x* is:
  - **ALL**—To delete all partitions
  - **EXTENDED**—To delete the extended partition (if there are no logical drives)

- **STORE**—Stores selected partitions to an image file with no compression

- **STORE WITH COMPRESSION** *x*—Stores selected partitions to an image file with compression where *x* is:
  - **OFF**—Stores images with no compression
  - **LOW**—Stores images with low compression (about 40%)
  - **HIGH**—Stores images with high compression (about 50%)

- **RESIZE IMAGE** *x*—Resizes the partitions being restored where *x* is:
  - **NO**—Turns resizing off
  - A size in megabytes (for example, 1000)
  - **PROPORTIONAL**—Resizes partitions proportionally
  - **MAX**—Resizes partitions to the maximum size possible
  - **MOST SPACE**—Resizes partitions leaving most free space

- **RESTORE**—Restores selected partitions

- **REBOOT**—Immediately reboots the computer

> **TIP:** To see a brief description of all the available switches, type "PQDI /?" at the command prompt.

Symantec's Norton Ghost

Norton Ghost from Symantec (**www.symantec.com**) is the imaging package most commonly used by IT (Information Technology) professionals. In addition to imaging, Norton Ghost includes cloning functionality, which allows disk-to-disk/partition-to-partition copying. Unlike Drive Image Pro, which mainly uses script files for automation, Norton Ghost uses only command-line switches.

The **-CLONE** switch is the main switch used to create and restore Norton Ghost image files. The basic syntax of the **-CLONE** switch is:

```
GHOST -CLONE,MODE=m,SRC=s,DST=d
```

Here, *m* is any mode parameter, *s* is any source parameter, and *d* is any destination parameter. The **MODE** parameters are:

- **COPY**—Copies one disk to another
- **LOAD**—Restores an image to disk
- **DUMP**—Creates an image from disk
- **PCOPY**—Copies one partition to another
- **PLOAD**—Restores an image to partition
- **PDUMP**—Creates an image from partition

The rest of the parameters are dependent on the selected **MODE** parameter.

The **SRC** parameters are:

- *Drive*—Specifies a drive number (**COPY/DUMP**)
- *File*—Specifies a source image file (**LOAD**)
- *Drive:partition*—Specifies a drive and partition number (**PCOPY/PDUMP**)
- **@MT***x*—Specifies a tape drive where *x* is the device number (**LOAD**)

The **DST** parameters are:

- *Drive*—Specifies a drive number (**COPY/LOAD**)
- *File*—Specifies a source image file (**DUMP/PDUMP**)

- ***Drive:partition***—Specifies a drive and partition number (**PCOPY/PLOAD**)

- **@MT*x***—Specifies a tape drive where *x* is the device number (**DUMP**)

NOTE: *Inserting spaces between the **CLONE** parameters will cause script errors.*

Immediate Solutions

Creating Partitions with Microsoft FDISK

Creating a partition with Microsoft FDISK from the command line is like scripting any program from the command line. The basic syntax to scripting a program from the command line is as follows:

```
program options
```

Here, ***program*** is the executable to be run, and ***options*** are the supported program parameters.

Creating a Primary Partition

To create a primary partition from the command line, enter the following:

```
FDISK /PRI: size disk
```

Here, ***size*** is the size of the partition in megabytes, and ***disk*** is the physical disk number.

TIP: Entering a partition size greater than the drive size will set the partition to the maximum size of the drive or the maximum size allowed by the selected file system. This is useful when creating generic scripts where you will not know the drive size in advance.

The **/PRI** option creates the primary partition and automatically sets it active. Any partition under 512MB will be set up as FAT16, and larger partitions will be set up as FAT32. To override this behavior and set up all partitions as FAT16, you can append an **O** (override) to the **/PRI** switch.

```
FDISK /PRIO: size disk
```

To have all partitions set up as FAT32, you can add the **/FPRMT** switch:

```
FDISK /FPRMT /PRI: size disk
```

Creating an Extended Partition

Scripting an extended partition creation is identical to scripting a primary partition creation, with the exception of the **/PRI** switch. To script the creation of an extended partition, enter the following:

```
FDISK /EXT: size disk
```

Here, *size* is the size of the partition in megabytes, and **disk** is the physical disk number.

The **/EXT** option creates an extended partition.

NOTE: *You must already have a primary partition created before you can create an extended partition.*

Creating a Logical Partition

To create a logical partition from the command line, enter the following:

```
FDISK /EXT: size disk /LOG: size
```

Here, *size* is the size of the partition in megabytes and must be less than or equal to the remaining free space, and **disk** is the physical disk number.

The **/EXT** switch is required in order to use the **/LOG** switch.

NOTE: *You must already have a primary and extended partition created before you can create a logical partition.*

To set up a logical partition with FAT16, you can append an **O** (override) to the **/LOG** switch.

```
FDISK /EXT: size disk /LOGO: size
```

Combining Switches

You can combine all three partition creation switches to set up a new hard drive with one line of code:

```
FDISK /PRI: size disk /EXT: size disk /LOG: size
```

NOTE: *You cannot have multiple **/LOG** switches per one line of code. If you need to create multiple logical drives, you need to add multiple lines of code.*

Rewriting the Master Boot Record

With an undocumented FDISK option, you can rewrite the master boot record without rewriting the partition table. To rewrite the MBR, proceed as follows:

```
FDISK /MBR
```

NOTE: *If you are using any utilities that write to the MBR, such as SpeedStor or PCDACS, you should consult the user manual before rewriting the MBR.*

Undocumented Microsoft FDISK Options

Even though the **/?** option is supposed to display all available command-line options, Microsoft FDISK has many undocumented options. Here are some of the most common undocumented options:

- **/ACTOK**—Skips drive integrity check
- **/EXT:*size disk***—Creates an extended partition
- **/FPRMT**—Skips the large drive support startup screen
- **/LOG:*size***—Creates a logical drive
- **/MBR**—Creates a new Master Boot Record
- **/PARTN**—Saves partition information to partsav.fil
- **/PRI:*size disk***—Creates a primary partition
- **/STATUS**—Displays current partition information

Working with Free FDISK

Free FDISK provides the same functionality as Microsoft FDISK while adding more useful features. Tasks like deleting, creating, and auto-sizing partitions are just as simple to perform as any other FDISK option.

Creating Auto-Sized Partitions

To create partitions to the maximum size, enter the following:

```
FDISK /AUTO
```

TIP: *You can create individual partitions by following the above command with a partition number.*

Deleting All Partitions

To delete all existing partitions (physical, extended, and logical), enter the following:

```
FDISK /CLEAR
```

TIP: *You can delete individual partitions by following the above command with a partition number.*

Other Free FDISK Options

Here are some of the most common options:

- **/ACTIVATE:***partition# drive#*—Sets the specified partition active
- **/C**—Checks marked bad clusters
- **/DELETE**—Deletes individual partitions
- **/FS:***filesystem*—Specifies the file system to format with
- **/ONCE**—Formats a floppy disk without prompting
- **/REBOOT**—Reboots the machine

Scripting Disk Formats

The main purpose of scripting is to streamline a process. Manual disk formats contain user prompts and pauses. Scripting a disk format allows you to control how much, if any, prompting is allowed.

Scripting a Hard Disk Format

To perform a completely hands-free drive format and label, enter the following:

```
FORMAT drive /AUTOTEST /V:label
```

Here, ***drive*** is the drive you want to format, and ***label*** is the label you want to give the drive.

The **/AUTOTEST** switch causes the **FORMAT** command to run while suppressing any prompts. The **/V** switch is used to assign a label to a disk. Disk labels can contain a maximum of eleven characters.

TIP: *You can follow this command with a **/S** to format the drive as a system drive.*

Scripting a Floppy Disk Format

Combining the **/AUTOTEST** switch with the **/V** switch does not create labels on floppy disks. Instead, you can use two separate commands:

```
FORMAT drive /AUTOTEST
LABEL drive alabel
```

Here, **drive** is the drive you want to format, and **alabel** is the label you want to give the disk.

Scripting a Faster Disk Format

If the disk has already been formatted, you can run a quick disk format that simply erases the disk address tables (not the disk data). To perform a faster disk format, start the command prompt and enter the following:

```
FORMAT drive /Q /U
```

Here, **drive** is the drive you want to format; **/Q** indicates a quick format; and **/U** indicates an unconditional format.

Other Format Options

The other commonly used options are:

- **/BACKUP**—Identical to **/AUTOTEST** except prompts for disk label
- **/C**—Checks for bad clusters

Suppressing Output When Shell Scripting

Although scripting does suppress most prompts, sometimes it does not suppress the command output. You can suppress the output of a shell command by sending the output to a **NUL** device. To suppress the output of a drive format, enter:

```
FORMAT drive /AUTOTEST > NUL
```

14

Creating Boot Disks

Any good administrator has a collection of boot disks ready and waiting in time of need. Boot disks are used when you need to bypass or perform a task before system bootup. Not only can you use scripting to create boot disks, but you can also use powerful scripts within them.

Creating a Hard Drive Setup Boot Disk

Follow these steps to create a boot disk that will automatically FDISK and format a hard disk:

1. Make a bootable DOS diskette. On Windows 9*x*, this can be done by formatting a floppy disk with the /S switch. This switch copies boot files to the floppy.

2. Copy FREE FDISK to the diskette.

3. Copy FORMAT.COM to the diskette.

4. Copy the script below to a file and save it as A:\AUTOEXEC.BAT:

```
@ECHO OFF
IF EXIST "A:\FORMAT.TXT" GOTO FORMAT
IF NOT EXIST "A:\FORMAT.TXT" GOTO FDISK

:FDISK
ECHO This system will reboot when complete.
ECHO.
ECHO Deleting all current partitions …
FDISK /CLEAR > NUL
ECHO Creating new partitions …
FDISK /AUTO > NUL
ECHO. > A:\FORMAT.TXT
GOTO REBOOT

:REBOOT
FDISK /REBOOT

:FORMAT
ECHO Formatting drive ...
FORMAT drive /AUTOTEST /V:label /S
DEL A:\FORMAT.TXT
GOTO END

:END
CLS
ECHO FINISHED FDISK AND FORMAT
```

Here, ***drive*** is the drive you want to format, and ***label*** is the label you want to give the disk.

WARNING! This disk will automatically FDISK and format all partitions. You should clearly mark this disk and store it in a secure area. TRUST ME, I KNOW!

Creating an NT Boot Disk

Nothing's worse than coming in bright and early, booting up your machine, and dealing with NTFS boot errors. An NT boot disk can be an invaluable troubleshooting asset when you are experiencing hard disk boot problems. To automate the creation of an NT boot disk, copy the following script to a BAT file:

```
FORMAT floppy: /AUTOTEST
LABEL floppy: alabel
COPY drive:\ntldr floppy:
COPY drive:\ntdetect.com floppy:
COPY drive:\boot.ini floppy:
COPY drive:\bootsect.dos floppy:
COPY drive:\ntbootdd.sys floppy:
```

NOTE: *A DOS or Windows 9x Startup disk will not work as an NT boot disk.*

Creating an NT Removal Boot Disk

To automatically remove NT from a FAT partition, proceed as follows:

1. Make a bootable DOS diskette. This can usually be done by formatting a floppy disk with the /S switch.

2. Copy RMDIR.EXE to the diskette. You can obtain RMDIR.EXE from the NT Resource Kit.

3. Copy the script below to a file and save it as A:\AUTOEXEC.BAT:

```
RMDIR /S /Q ntpath
DEL drive:\ntldr
DEL drive:\ntdetect.com
DEL drive:\boot.ini
DEL drive:\bootsect.dos
DEL drive:\ntbootdd.sys
DEL drive:\pagefile.sys
```

Here, ***ntpath*** is the full path to the Windows directory (e.g., C:\WINNT), and ***drive*** is the drive letter on which Windows was installed.

TIP: The best method of removing NT from an NTFS partition is to FDISK, format, and start over.

Scripting Drive Image Pro

Drive Image Pro provides a command interpreter to allow complete control from the command line. There are two requirements to script Drive Image Pro: a script file and a command line to run the script. The script file is a basic text file with the custom commands that control Drive Image Pro. The command line consists of various switches that control how the script will be executed. Together, they provide a way to automate all the manual tasks of Drive Image Pro.

Creating an Image

To store partition 1 on drive 1 to an image, enter the following:

```
SELECT DRIVE 1
SELECT PARTITION 1
STORE
```

To store all partitions on drives 1 and 2 to an image, enter the following:

```
SELECT DRIVE 1
SELECT PARTITION ALL
STORE
SELECT DRIVE 2
SELECT PARTITION ALL
STORE
```

*NOTE: The **SELECT** command can select only one drive or one set of partitions from a drive at a time. It cannot select two drives simultaneously, hence the need for two **STORE** commands.*

Restoring an Image

To delete all partitions on drive 1 and restore the first image to drive 1's maximum size, enter the following:

```
SELECT DRIVE 1
DELETE ALL
SELECT FREESPACE FIRST
```

```
SELECT IMAGE 1
RESIZE IMAGE MAX
RESTORE
```

To resize the second image to 500MB and restore it to the free space on drive 1, proceed as follows:

```
SELECT DRIVE 1
SELECT FREESPACE LAST
SELECT IMAGE 2
RESIZE IMAGE 500
RESTORE
```

Running a Script

To run a script, enter the following:

```
PQDI /CMD=scriptfile /IMG=imagefile /LOG=logfile ERR=errorfile
```

Here, **scriptfile** is the name of the script file, **imagefile** is the name of the image used for the **STORE** and **RESTORE** commands, **logfile** is a file that records the results of the imaging process, and **errorfile** is a file that logs any errors encountered while imaging.

NOTE: If the **/IMG** switch is omitted, the **STORE** and **RESTORE** commands will produce an error.

Scripting Norton Ghost

Norton Ghost performs all its scripting from the command line. Although it does support the use of script files, these files are nothing more than a list of switches that can be performed at the command line.

Creating an Image

To create an image of drive 1 called image.gho on a remote drive Z, enter the following:

```
GHOST.EXE -CLONE,MODE=DUMP,SRC=1,DST=Z:\IMAGE.GHO
```

To create an image of the second partition of drive 1 called image.gho on a remote drive Z, enter the following:

```
GHOST.EXE -CLONE,MODE=PDUMP,SRC=1:2,DST=Z:\IMAGE.GHO
```

Restoring an Image

To restore an image called image.gho on a remote drive Z to drive 1, enter the following:

```
GHOST.EXE -CLONE, MODE=LOAD, SRC= Z:\IMAGE.GHO, DST=1
```

To restore an image called image.gho on a remote drive Z to the second partition on drive 1, enter the following:

```
GHOST.EXE -CLONE,MODE=PLOAD,SRC= Z:\IMAGE.GHO,DST=1:2
```

Performing a Drive Copy

To copy drive 1 to drive 2, enter the following:

```
GHOST.EXE -CLONE,MODE=COPY,SRC=1,DST=2
```

Performing a Partition Copy

To copy the first partition on drive 2 to the second partition on drive 1, enter the following:

```
GHOST.EXE -CLONE,MODE=PCOPY,SRC= 2:1,DST=1:2
```

Logging Errors

Norton Ghost records all errors in a log file called ghost.err. This file is normally stored in the program's root directory, but you can change the name and location of the file per use by using the **-AFILE** switch. Here is an example of how to use the **-AFILE** switch:

```
GHOST.EXE -CLONE,MODE=PCOPY,SRC= 2:1,DST=1:2 -AFILE=filename
```

Using a Script File

Norton Ghost can also read a text file that contains all or additional command-line switches. This file must be in text format, and each command-line switch must be on a different line. Here is an example of a script file:

```
-AFILE=z:\errorlog.txt
-CLONE,MODE=PCOPY,SRC= 2:1,DST=1:2
```

To run the script file, enter the following

```
GHOST.EXE @filename
```

Here, ***filename*** is the name of the script file.

More Switches

Different versions of Norton Ghost support different switches. To see a brief description of the available switches, type "GHOST -H" at the command prompt.

Chapter 2

Scripting Installations and Updates

In Brief

In the previous chapter, you learned how to automate hard disk set-ups and images. Throughout this chapter, you will use various scripting methods to create unique scripting solutions to common administrative installations and updates. You will start by learning how to script installations from the command line. You will then learn how to use send keys to install windows and wizards using Microsoft ScriptIt.

Scripting Methods

Not all of us have the luxury of working with a centralized management system such as Systems Management Server (SMS) or WinINSTALL. With new programs, program updates, service pack updates, and hot-fixes constantly coming out, installing all of these manually can consume most of an administrator's day. Scripting provides a way to automate these tasks with little or no user intervention.

Shell Scripting

Shell scripting is running a series of commands from within a command shell. Although these commands can be run from the command line individually, they are more often stored within a script or batch file. Shell scripting has been around since the inception of MS-DOS (Microsoft Disk Operating System) and is the easiest scripting method to learn.

Microsoft Command-Line Switches

Microsoft installation and update executables support many different switches to allow for shell scripting and installation customization. Switches are not case-sensitive and, more often than not, they are not standardized. To make matters worse, Microsoft tends not to document some of the most useful switches (as you saw in Chapter 1). Here are some of the most common, and possibly undocumented, switches for Microsoft installation and update executables:

- */?*—Displays unhidden switches and usage

- */C*—Extracts files to folder specified with /T switch

- */C ID*—Used to enter a 20-digit product ID

- **/F**—Forces applications to close at shutdown
- **/K *ID***—Used to enter an 11-digit CD key
- **/N**—Does not back up files for uninstall
- **/N *name***—Used to enter a username for registration
- **/N:V**—Installs without version checking
- **/O**—Overwrites OEM files without prompting
- **/O *organization***—Used to enter an organization name for registration
- **/Q**—Runs in quiet mode, skips all prompts
- **/Q:U**—Runs in user quiet mode, shows some dialog boxes
- **/Q:A**—Runs in admin quiet mode, shows no dialog boxes
- **/R**—Reinstalls the application
- **/R:A**—Always reboots
- **/R:I**—Reboots if necessary
- **/R:N**—Does not reboot, even if necessary
- **/R:S**—Reboots without prompting
- **/T:*path***—Specifies or extracts files to a temporary working folder
- **/U**—Runs in unattended mode or uninstalls an application, prompts for shared file removal
- **/UA**—Uninstalls an application and shared files, without prompting
- **/Z**—Does not reboot when installation is complete

Windows and Wizards

Many of the tasks of an administrator involve navigating through interactive windows and wizards. Whether installing a new program or adding a new piece of hardware, these wizards guide the user through a complicated setup process. This process involves scrolling through selections, clicking check boxes, selecting tabs, browsing, entering text, and more. Although these wizards are helpful, they frequently do not support scripting.

In the past, administrators used macro recorders to deal with these unscriptable windows and wizards. The main problem with basic macro utilities is that they are great for performing linear tasks, but they choke when dealing with complex routines that require decisions. The solution is to use a send-keys utility, such as Microsoft ScriptIt.

Microsoft ScriptIt

Microsoft ScriptIt is an advanced macro utility used to send key commands to Windows objects. ScriptIt detects window titles and text and sends commands to specific windows based on that information. ScriptIt reads commands stored in a text-based script file and performs the commands on a line-per-line basis. Although you can use other scripting send-keys methods, such as Windows Script Host (WSH) or KiXtart, Microsoft ScriptIt provides the easiest way to detect windows and send keys.

Detecting Windows and Text

Sometimes multiple windows can have the same title. Luckily, Microsoft ScriptIt allows you to specify a combination of window title and window text to specify the exact window you want. Microsoft ScriptIt has two built-in functions to determine window titles and text: **/REVEAL** and **/REVEAL2**.

/REVEAL detects the currently active window in real time. To run this command, enter:

```
SCRIPTIT /REVEAL
```

For example, suppose you wanted to script the Add New Hardware Wizard window (see Figure 2.1).The **/REVEAL** switch would show the window title and text (see Figure 2.2).

Figure 2.1   The Add New Hardware Wizard window.

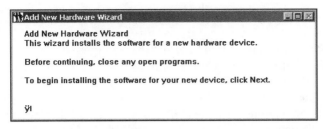

Figure 2.2   Detecting window title and text with /REVEAL.

Although this command is helpful, it does present problems when windows are hidden or forcibly maximized. To work around this, you can use the **/REVEAL2** switch:

```
SCRIPTIT /REVEAL2
```

The **/REVEAL2** switch creates a list of all window titles and text, and then refreshes the list when you click OK (see Figure 2.3).

By double-clicking on each entry in the list, you can see all the text that **/REVEAL2** detected.

Microsoft ScriptIt [SCRIPT] Section

A ScriptIt script file must contain a section called [SCRIPT]. Any commands found under this section will be executed in order. Any text found above this section will be ignored, so you can comment your script by adding text above this section.

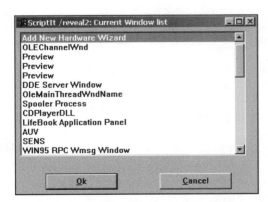

Figure 2.3   Detecting window title and text with **/REVEAL2**.

Microsoft ScriptIt [ADLIB] Section

One of the advantages that ScriptIt has over using other send-key methods, such as KiXtart or WSH, is the ability to immediately intercept windows that may occur unexpectedly. This is accomplished through an optional section called [ADLIB]. When the [ADLIB] section detects an unexpected window, the script breaks out of the [SCRIPT] section, executes the [ADLIB] command, and then returns to the [SCRIPT] section.

Microsoft ScriptIt Core Commands

Microsoft ScriptIt has five core commands: **RUN**, **RUNWAIT**, **MKFILE**, **REM**, and **TITLE+TEXT**. The **RUN** command executes the program specified:

```
RUN=program
```

The **RUNWAIT** command executes the program specified and pauses the script until the specified program closes:

```
RUNWAIT=program
```

For example, to start notepad, pause the script, and then start the script when notepad closes, you could enter:

```
RUNWAIT=notepad
```

The **MKFILE (Make File)** command appends a line to an existing text file or adds a line to a new text file:

```
MKFILE file=line to add
```

For example, if you wanted to add a line to the autoexec.bat file that removes your C:\TEMP directory, you could enter:

```
MKFILE c:\autoexec.bat=DELTREE C:\TEMP
```

The **REM (Remark)** command allows you to add comments within your script:

```
REM comments
```

The *title+text* command allows you to send key commands to the specified window:

```
title+text=commands
```

Here, *title* is the window title, *text* is any text within the window, and *commands* are the key commands being sent to the window.

The title and text are case-sensitive. In addition, both the window title and text are optional and neither needs to be typed in its entirety. For example, if you wanted to start and work with Notepad, you could enter:

```
[SCRIPT]
RUN=NOTEPAD
Untitled - Notepad=This is the full title
Untitled=This is part of the title
```

Notice that both the full and partial titles will work.

Microsoft ScriptIt Tilde Commands

Microsoft ScriptIt has nine commands that begin with a tilde (~):

- **~EXIT**—Immediately exits the script
- **~WAIT**—Pauses the script for 5 seconds
- **~WINWAITACTIVE**—Pauses the script until the specified window receives focus
- **~WINWAITCLOSE**—Pauses the script until the specified window closes
- **~WINWAITACTIVE**—Closes the currently active window and its associated application
- **~WINHIDE**—Hides the currently active window
- **~WINHIDE**—Displays the currently active hidden window
- **~WINMIN**—Minimizes the currently active window
- **~WINMAX**—Maximizes the currently active window

Microsoft Windows Installer

Before Windows 2000, installing and managing applications was a complete mess. Software companies created their own installation interfaces, each with its own set of rules, command-line options, and uninstall functions. This provided headaches for administrators who attempted to create common scripting solutions for application installations. To help reduce total cost of ownership (TCO) and provide a standardized set of installation rules, Microsoft created the Windows Installer.

The Windows Installer is a new installation and configuration service for 32-bit Windows platforms that standardizes the way programs install and uninstall. The Windows Installer is a Zero Administration Windows initiative and is required to conform to the "Designed for Microsoft Windows" logo standards. Some of the advanced features of the Windows Installer are self-repair, rollback, and install on demand. The Windows Installer comes packaged with Windows 2000, and is available as a separate download for Windows $9x$ and Windows NT.

The Windows Installer runs as a two-part installation utility that consists of a client engine and a system service. The client engine (MSIEXEC.EXE) runs with user privileges and provides the interface between the system and the installation service. MSIEXEC.EXE reads the instructions from the installation package (*.MSI) and passes them to the installation service (Windows Installer).

The installation service enables the system to keep track of all program installations and system changes, providing for cleaner uninstalls. Because the installation service runs as a system service, it can be given various privileges to allow users to install their own applications.

Self-Repair

When a program file becomes corrupted or missing, a program installed with the Windows Installer can identify these files and replace them automatically. This is a handy feature for those of us with troublesome users who like to attempt their own uninstalls.

Rollback

The Windows Installer rollback feature creates a temporary backup and script of any files changed during the installation process. If a fatal error occurs during the installation, the rollback feature immediately runs the script and returns the system to its original state. All rollback files are stored in a temporary directory called config.msi, and are automatically deleted when the installation successfully completes. Rollbacks can take a significant amount of disk space and can be disabled by an administrator.

TIP: *You can always delete the config.msi folder manually if setup fails to remove it.*

Microsoft Windows Installer Switches

The MSIEXEC.EXE supports various command-line switches, allowing you to control the installer from the command shell or batch file. Here are some of the most common command-line switches for Microsoft Windows Installer:

- **/I**—Installs the program
- **/F**—Repairs an installation
- **/X**—Uninstalls the program
- **/L*V** *logfile*—Logs all information to a *logfile*
- **/QN**—No user interface
- **/QB**—Basic user interface
- **/QF**—Full user interface
- **/?** or **/H**—Displays some switches and copyright information
- **/X**—Uninstalls the program

Immediate Solutions

Scripting a Silent Windows NT Service Pack Installation

A service pack is a combination of driver updates and hot-fixes that should be applied with every new application installation or system change. To automate a silent installation of a Windows NT service pack, proceed as follows:

1. Create a new directory to store all files included in this example.

2. Download the latest NT service pack, from **www.microsoft.com**, to the new directory.

3. Extract the service pack to the new directory.

4. Start the command prompt and enter the following:

```
new directory path\i386\update\UPDATE -F -N -O -Q
```

Here, **new directory path** is the complete path of the new folder created in step 1. Remember to change the command line if you are using a different processor type than I386.

The available command-line switches for an NT service pack are as follows:

- **-F**—Force all applications to close at shutdown

- **-N**—Do not create a service pack uninstall directory

- **-O**—Overwrite OEM files without prompting

- **-Q**—No user interaction required

- **-U**—Run UPDATE in unattended mode

- **-Z**—Do not reboot when installation is complete

Scripting a Silent Windows 2000 Service Pack Installation

The Windows 2000 service pack supports the same command-line switches as a Windows NT service pack, without forcing you to extract the files first. To automate a silent installation of a Windows 2000 service pack, proceed as follows:

1. Create a new directory to store all files included in this example.

2. Download the latest service pack, from **www.microsoft.com**, to the new directory.

3. Start the command prompt and enter the following:

```
new directory path\executable -F -N -O -Q
```

Here, ***new directory path*** is the complete path of the new folder created in step 1, and ***executable*** is the name of the service pack executable downloaded in step 2.

Scripting a Silent Windows Management Instrumentation Installation

Windows Management Instrumentation (WMI) is a management service that provides scriptable interfaces to the objects on your network. To automate a silent installation of WMI, proceed as follows:

1. Create a new directory to store all files included in this example.

2. Download the latest version of Windows Management Instrumentation, from **www.microsoft.com**, to the new directory.

3. Start the command prompt and enter the following:

```
new directory path\file /s
```

Here, ***new directory path*** is the complete path of the new folder created in step 1, and ***file*** is the name of the WMI installation executable.

Scripting an Active Directory Services Interface Installation

Active Directory Services Interfaces (ADSI) is a directory service that allows you to identify users and resources in a tree-like structure. To automate a silent installation of ADSI, proceed as follows:

1. Create a new directory to store all files included in this example.

2. Download the latest version of Active Directory Directory Services, from **www.microsoft.com**, to the new directory.

3. Start the command prompt and enter the following:

```
new directory path\file /Q:A /R:A
```

Here, ***new directory path*** is the complete path of the new folder created in step 1, and ***file*** is the name of the ADSI installation executable.

Scripting a Silent Internet Explorer Installation

Microsoft Internet Explorer is the most widely used Web browser for Windows and comes included with every Windows operating system (for now). To automate the installation of Microsoft Internet Explorer 5.x, proceed as follows:

1. Create a new directory to store all files included in this example.

2. Download the complete installation for Windows 9x, NT, ME, and 2000 from **www.microsoft.com** and store the files to the new directory.

3. Start the command prompt and enter the following:

```
new directory path\IE5SETUP /C:"IE5WZD /M:# /Q:A /R:A"
```

Here, ***new directory path*** is the complete path of the new folder created in step 1, and M:# specifies the type of installation (0=Minimal, 1=Typical, 2=Full).

TIP: You can also script an Internet Explorer 4.x installation by changing the command **IE5SETUP /C:"IE5WZD /M:# /Q:A /R:A"** to **IE4SETUP /C:"IE4WZD /M:# /Q:A /R:A"**. For more information about installing Internet Explorer from the command line, see the Microsoft TechNet Article Q200007.

Related solution:	Found on page:
Using Microsoft Internet Explorer as a Display Tool	96

Scripting a Silent Web Admin 2.0 Installation

Web Admin 2.0 is a free Web-based NT Server administration utility. This utility allows you to manage accounts, RAS, shares, sessions, servers, printers, and more over the Web. To automate the silent installation of Web Admin 2.0, proceed as follows:

1. Create a new directory to store all files included in this example.

2. Download NT Web Admin, from **www.microsoft.com/ntserver/nts/downloads/management/NTSWebAdmin/default.asp**, to the new directory.

3. Start the command prompt and enter the following:

```
new directory path\file /Q:A /R:A
```

Here, *file* is the name of the installation executable, and *new directory path* is the complete path of the new folder created in step 1.

NOTE: You must have Internet Information Server (IIS) 4 or later installed to use Web Admin 2.0. You can obtain IIS 4 from the NT Option Pack 4 CD, or download it from **www.microsoft.com/windows/downloads/contents/updates/nt40ptpk/default.asp**.

Working with INF Files

An INF (information) file is a simple text file used to store or manipulate information. A common use for an INF file is to install hardware devices. The INF file format is similar to an INI file, consisting of named sections, keys, and values. The way to install an INF file is to right-click on the file and choose Install. Although this is the intended method, you can script the installation of an INF file with a little effort.

Scripting an INF Installation

To automate an installation of an INF file, proceed as follows.

Start the command prompt and enter the following:

```
rundll32 syssetup,SetupInfObjectInstallAction DefaultInstall
128 file
```

NOTE: *The code above is one continuous statement and should be entered as a single line.*

Here, *file* is the complete path and name of the INF file to install.

Scripting a Silent TweakUI Installation

To automate the installation of TweakUI, proceed as follows:

1. Remove the line from the [TweakUI.Add.Reg] section of the tweakui.inf file to prevent the installation from pausing on the TweakUI help file:

   ```
   HKLM,%SMWCV%\RunOnce\Setup,%ITWEAK%,,"WINHLP32.EXE -i Main
   %18%\TWEAKUI.HLP"
   ```

NOTE: *The code above is one continuous statement and should be entered as a single line.*

2. Start the command prompt and enter the following:

   ```
   rundll32 syssetup,SetupInfObjectInstallAction DefaultInstall
   128 filepath\tweakui.inf
   ```

NOTE: *The code above is one continuous statement.*

Here, *filepath* is the complete path of the TweakUI installation files.

Scripting a Silent Norton AntiVirus 2000 Installation

Norton AntiVirus 2000 is the latest version of antivirus protection from Symantec (**www.symantec.com**). To automate a silent installation of Norton AntiVirus 2000, proceed as follows.

Start the command prompt and enter the following:

```
file path\SETUP -S
```

Here, *file path* is the complete path of the Norton AntiVirus 2000 installation files, and **-S** specifies a silent install.

Scripting a Silent pcANYWHERE 9.0 Installation

PcANYWHERE 9.0 is the latest version of remote control from Symantec (**www.symantec.com**). To automate a silent installation of pcANYWHERE 9.0, proceed as follows.

Start the command prompt and enter the following:

```
file path\SETUP -S
```

Here, *file path* is the complete path of the pcANYWHERE 9.0 installation files.

Scripting a Silent LiveUpdate Installation

LiveUpdate is a free Symantec application used to automatically update its other software applications. To automate a silent installation of LiveUpdate, proceed as follows.

Start the command prompt and enter the following:

```
file path\LUSETUP -S
```

Here, *file path* is the complete path of the LiveUpdate installation files.

Scripting a Silent Diskeeper Lite 1.1 Installation

Windows NT does not include any defragmentation utility. Diskeeper Lite is a free, slimmed-down version of Executive Software's (**www.execusoft.com**) Diskeeper (a defragmentation utility). This utility is free because it does not include the scripting or scheduling capability of the full version. To automate the installation of Diskeeper Lite 1.1, proceed as follows:

1. Create a new directory to store all files included in this example.

2. Download the Diskeeper Lite 1.1 installation executable (DKLITE_i.EXE), from **www.execusoft.com**, to the new directory.

3. Download and extract Microsoft ScriptIt, from **www.microsoft.com**, to the new directory.

4. Select Start|Run and enter "*new directory path*\scriptit *scriptfile*".

Here, ***new directory path*** is the complete path of the new folder created in step 1, and ***scriptfile*** is a text file that contains the following:

```
REM To automate the installation of Diskeeper Lite 1.1
[SCRIPT]
RUN=dklite_i.exe
Diskeeper Lite=~WINWAITACTIVE#{ENTER}
Welcome+Welcome to the Diskeeper Lite Setup =~WINWAITACTIVE#!N
Diskeeper Lite+Diskeeper Lite works on =~WINWAITACTIVE#!N
Software License Agreement=~WINWAITACTIVE#!Y
Choose Destination Location=~WINWAITACTIVE#!N
Diskeeper Lite+HOW TO REACH US=~WINWAITACTIVE#!N
Information+Diskeeper Lite is now=~WINWAITACTIVE#{ENTER}

[ADLIB]
REM Used to prevent installation from unexpectedly ending
Exit Setup+Setup is not complete=!R

REM Used to exit the script if a severe error is detected
Severe+Could not find value of={ENTER}#~exit
```

Scripting a Silent WinZip 8.0 Installation

WinZip is the most popular Windows compression utility for the ZIP format. To automate the installation of WinZip 8.0, proceed as follows:

1. Create a new directory to store all files included in this example.

2. Download the WinZip 8.0 installation executable (WINZIP80.EXE), from **www.winzip.com**, to the new directory.

3. Download and extract Microsoft ScriptIt, from **www.microsoft.com**, to the new directory.

4. Select Start|Run and enter "*new directory path*\scriptit *scriptfile*".

Here, ***new directory path*** is the complete path of the new folder created in step 1, and ***scriptfile*** is a text file that contains the following:

```
REM To automate the installation of WinZip 8.0
[SCRIPT]
RUN=WINZIP80.EXE
WinZip 8.0 Setup=~WINWAITACTIVE#!S
WinZip Setup+Setup will install=~WINWAITACTIVE#{ENTER}


License Agreement=~WINWAITACTIVE#!Y
WinZip Setup+WinZip Quick Start=~WINWAITACTIVE#!N
WinZip Setup+Select=~WINWAITACTIVE#!C!N
WinZip Setup+Click=~WINWAITACTIVE#!N
WinZip Setup+Installation is complete.=~WINWAITACTIVE#{ENTER}


[ADLIB]
REM Used for the evaluation installation
WinZip Setup+Thank you for installing={ENTER}


REM Used to prevent installation from unexpectedly ending
WinZip Self-Extractor+Abort unzip operation?=!N
WinZip+Setup is not complete.=!N
WinZip Self-Extractor+This self-extracting Zip file={ENTER}


REM Used for upgrading from older version
Setup Complete 1={ENTER}
Setup Complete message 2={ENTER}


REM Used to exit script if still running
WinZip Tip of the Day=!C#~exit
```

Working with the Windows Installer

The Windows Installer replaces the ACME installer, adding more features and functionality. This new installer provides a standard method for application installations and an easy way for administrators to script installations.

Scripting a Silent Windows 2000 Resource Kit Installation

The Windows 2000 resource kit provides many tools and utilities that allow you to perform powerful administrative and system tasks. To automate a silent installation of a Windows 2000 resource kit, start the command prompt and enter the following:

```
MSIEXEC /I DRIVE:\W2000RKPRO.MSI /QN
```

NOTE: *Using the **/QB** switch may cause the installer to prompt that it is uninstalling the resource kit when in fact it is installing it.*

Here, **DRIVE** is the CD-ROM drive letter containing the Windows 2000 resource kit CD.

TIP: *You can script a silent Microsoft TechNet installation using the same install syntax and replacing the name of the msi file.*

Scripting the Windows Installer Installation

Although the Windows Installer redistributable files usually come packaged with a program that uses the Windows Installer, they can be downloaded and installed individually. To automate the installation of the Windows Installer, proceed as follows:

1. Create a new directory to store all files included in this example.

2. Download the Windows Installer redistributable from **www.microsoft.com/msdownload.platformsdk/ instmsi.htm**.

3. Select Start|Run and enter "*new directory path\wiexe* /Q:A /R:A".

Here, **new directory path** is the complete path of the new folder created in step 1, and **wiexe** is the name of the Windows Installer redistributable executable.

Scripting a Silent NAI VirusScan 4.5x Installation

VirusScan 4.5x is the latest version of antivirus protection from Network Associates (**www.nai.com**). To automate a silent installation of VirusScan 4.5x, start the command prompt and enter the following:

```
file path\SETUP /Q /L*V ADDLOCAL=ALL REBOOT=F
USEADMINONLYSECURITY=1 /I
```

NOTE: *The code above is one continuous statement.*

Here, *file path* is the complete path of the NAI VirusScan 4.5x installation files.

Scripting Microsoft Office 2000

Microsoft Office 2000 was one of the first applications released by Microsoft to utilize the new Windows Installer. Although the following examples are focused toward Microsoft Office 2000, they can be applied to any application that utilizes the new Windows Installer.

Removing Older Versions

The Microsoft Office Removal Wizard can be used to remove older versions of Microsoft Office before installing Microsoft Office 2000. To automate the removal of older versions of Microsoft office, start the command prompt and enter the following:

```
SETUP /S /Q /R /L log file
```

Here, *log file* records all activity of the removal process.

NOTE: *The Microsoft Office Removal Wizard is included in the Microsoft Office 2000 Resource Kit.*

Scripting a Silent Installation

Microsoft Office 2000 is the latest version of the Office products. To automate the installation of Microsoft Office 2000, start the command prompt and enter the following:

Start the command prompt and enter the following:

```
file path\SETUP /QN /L*V install log COMPANYNAME="company"
```

Here, ***file path*** is the complete path of the Office installation files, ***install log*** is the file to store all errors and output, and ***company*** is the name of the company registered for Office.

TIP: *For more information about Office 2000 command-line switches, see the Microsoft TechNet Article Q202946.*

Scripting an Uninstall
To automate the uninstallation of Microsoft Office 2000, start the command prompt and enter the following:

```
file path\SETUP /QN /X msifile
```

Here, ***file path*** is the complete path of the Office installation files originally used to install Office, and ***msifile*** is the name of the msi package to uninstall.

Scripting a Repair
To automate the repair of a Microsoft Office 2000 installation, start the command prompt and enter the following:

```
file path\SETUP /FOCUMS msifile
```

Here, ***file path*** is the complete path of the Office installation files originally used to install Office, and ***msifile*** is the name of the msi package to repair.

Scripting a Reinstallation
To automate the reinstallation of Microsoft Office 2000, start the command prompt and enter the following:

```
file path\SETUP /FECUMS msifile
```

Here, ***file path*** is the complete path of the Office installation files originally used to install Office, and ***msifile*** is the name of the msi package to reinstall.

Advertising
Instead of installing an application, you can simply set up the Start menu shortcuts that, when activated, will install the application on

first use. This setup method is called *advertising*. To advertise Microsoft Office 2000, start the command promt and enter the following:

```
file path\SETUP /QN /JU msifile
```

Here, ***file path*** is the complete path of the Office installation files originally used to install Office, and ***msifile*** is the name of the msi package to advertise.

Disabling Windows Installer Rollbacks

To disable the Windows Installer rollback feature during an installation, start the command prompt and enter the following:

```
file path\SETUP DISABLEROLLBACK=1
```

Here, ***file path*** is the complete path of the installation files used in the original installation.

Installing the Windows Installer Clean Up Utility

Microsoft has created a utility that allows you to delete Windows Installer registry entries from a system. This is useful when you have had corrupted installations that are preventing you from successfully installing a program. Although the utility's installer states that it supports the standard Microsoft installation switches, they do not work. To automate the installation of the Windows Installer Clean Up Utility, proceed as follows:

1. Create a new directory to store all files included in this example.

2. Download the Windows Installer Clean Up Utility from Microsoft.

   For Windows 9*x*:

   ```
   download.microsoft.com/download/office2000pro/util22/1/W9X/
   EN-US/msicu.exe
   ```

NOTE: *The code above is one continuous statement.*

   For Windows NT/2000:

   ```
   download.microsoft.com/download/office2000pro/util20/1/NT4/
   EN-US/msicuu.exe
   ```

NOTE: *The code above is one continuous statement.*

2. Scripting Installations and Updates

3. Download and extract Microsoft ScriptIt, from **www.microsoft.com**, to the new directory.

4. Select Start|Run and enter "*new directory path*\scriptit *scriptfile*".

Here, ***new directory path*** is the complete path of the new folder created in step 1, and ***scriptfile*** is a text file that contains the following:

```
REM To automate the install of the Windows Installer Clean Up
Utility
[SCRIPT]
RUN=executable
Windows Installer+It is strongly=~WINWAITACTIVE#!N
Windows Installer+License=~WINWAITACTIVE#!A!N
Windows Installer+Start=~WINWAITACTIVE#!N
REM The two lines below should be one continuous line
Windows Installer+Windows Installer Clean Up has been
successfully installed=~WINWAITACTIVE#!F

[ADLIB]
REM Used to prevent installation from unexpectedly ending
Windows Installer+Setup is not complete=!R
REM The two lines below should be one continuous line
Windows Installer+Windows Installer Clean Up was
interrupted={ENTER}

REM Used for uninstallation
Windows Installer+This will remove=!N
REM The two lines below should be one continuous line
Windows Installer+Windows Installer Clean Up has been
successfully uninstalled=!F#~EXIT

REM Used if wrong version installation is attempted
Installer Information=!O
Fatal Error={ENTER}#~EXIT
```

Here, ***executable*** is the name of the Windows Installer Clean Up executable.

NOTE: *For more information about the Windows Installer Clean Up utility, see the Microsoft TechNet article Q238413.*

Chapter 3

File Management

(continued)

In Brief

Files are the backbone of any information system. They hold the data you work with and make up the programs you use. As a computer user, everything you do involves interacting with files. Finding, deleting, creating, and modifying files are actions you do every day, often without even noticing it.

As administrators, we've all dealt with users who tried to back up their entire system to the server or start their own MP3 (Motion Pictures Experts Group Layer-3 Audio) server with their user directory. Although Windows 2000 provides disk quota management, it does not include a method to target and remove the offending files. In addition to eating a disk's free space, users also have a tendency to save files with strange names and extensions while storing the data anywhere they please.

And while users are slowly tearing at the file system, the system is also filling the disk with temp files, orphaned files, and system logs. With more user data and application files being placed on a system daily, keeping the file system healthy is a constant race that never ends. In this chapter, you will learn how to use shell scripting, KiXtart, and Windows Script Host to clean up your file system and perform file-related tasks.

Shell Scripting Limitations

Because my scripting roots date back to the good old days of MS-DOS (Microsoft Disk Operating System), I hate to admit it, but shell scripting is a limited language. Shell scripting is not a collective language, but rather a language consisting of various individual executables. It has limited logical statements, no debugging capabilities, limited error-handling capabilities, and no access to ActiveX objects. Although shell scripting continues to improve over the years, it is best used for simple scripting tasks that do not require complex calculations or extensive file manipulation. To perform more powerful file management tasks, you should turn to another scripting method, such as KiXtart or Windows Script Host.

KiXtart

KiXtart is an easy-to-use scripting tool that comes included in both the Windows NT and 2000 Resource Kits. Some of the advanced features of KiXtart are built-in debugging, the ability to modify the registry, and the ability to shut down or reboot systems. Although primarily used for logon scripting, KiXtart can be used as a standalone scripting solution to automate everyday tasks.

KiXtart Files

The KiXtart package consists of five files:

- *KIX32.EXE*—The main program file
- *KX32.DLL*—32-bit Dynamic Link Library (DLL) used to connect to NETAPI.DLL on Windows 9*x* systems
- *KX16.DLL*—16-bit DLL used to connect to NETAPI.DLL on Windows 9*x* systems
- *KXRPC.EXE*—A Windows NT service to support Windows 9*x* systems running KX95.DLL
- *KX95.DLL*—32-bit DLL used to connect to the KiXtart Remote Procedure Call (RPC) service

Limitations of Windows 9*x*

When working with Windows 9*x*, KiXtart cannot obtain certain network information (for example, user Security ID [SID], local groups, home directories) without a little modification. KiXtart provides two methods to compensate for this limitation: DLLs and an RPC service. Windows 9*x* uses a 16-bit DLL called NETAPI.DLL for network management functions. KX16.DLL and KX32.DLL are used to retrieve information from the NETAPI.DLL.

The KiXtart RPC service is a client/server mechanism to retrieve certain networking information not available from the NETAPI.DLL. The KX95.DLL, loaded on the Windows 9*x* client, retrieves and reports the information to the RPC service, which is loaded on a Windows NT system.

NOTE: *The RPC service can be run on any NT system, but it must be a member of the domain where the logon script resides. For more information on configuring KiXtart for Windows 9x, please consult the KiXtart manual.*

KiXtart Components

There are three basic components to KiXtart: commands, functions, and macros. KiXtart commands are instructions that perform simple tasks, such as the RUN or SHELL commands. KiXtart functions perform complex tasks and usually require parameters, similar to functions in other scripting languages. KiXtart macros provide various system and user information by accessing Windows Application Programming Interfaces (APIs).

KiXtart Variables

Most KiXtart functions return codes that indicate the success or failure of the completed operation. Variables are used extensively in KiXtart to store values or return codes. KiXtart variables names consist of a $ sign followed by text, and should not be the same as any of the built-in KiXtart component names. Optionally declaring a variable and assigning a value is identical to doing so in VBScript:

```
DIM $MYVARIABLE
$MYVARIABLE = "SOME VALUE"
```

Windows Script Host

Microsoft's Windows Script Host is a language-independent scripting host for 32-bit windows operating systems. It provides the most powerful functionality of all the scripting methods discussed so far. Windows Scripting Host works seamlessly with all scriptable objects available to Windows, allowing you to create complex, scripted applications. By providing extensive scripting capabilities combined with support for multiple scripting languages, WSH is quickly becoming the scripting method of choice.

CSCRIPT and WSCRIPT

Windows Script Host is controlled by two executables, CSCRIPT and WSCRIPT. CSCRIPT is the command-line host utility that is commonly used to run tasks in the background or in a command prompt. WSCRIPT is the graphical host utility commonly used to interact with the user. These two executables support many command-line parameters, as shown in Table 3.1.

Table 3.1   Windows Script Host parameters.

Parameter	Description
//B	Disables command prompt user input.
//D	Enables active debugging.
//E:*engine*	Uses the specified engine at script execution
//H:CSCRIPT	Sets CSCRIPT as the default execution host.
//H:WSCRIPT	Sets WSCRIPT as the default execution host.
//I	By default, enables command prompt user input.
//JOB	Executes a WSC job.
//LOGO	By default, displays logo at script execution.
//NOLOGO	Suppresses logo at script execution.
//U	For CSCRIPT only, specifies to use UNICODE for I/O operations
//S	Saves options on a per user basis
//T:*seconds*	Specifies the maximum time, in *seconds*, a script is allowed to run.
//X	Executes the current script within the debugger
//?	Displays help context

What in the World Is an API?

Before you can start scripting with Windows Script Host, you should have a basic understanding of APIs. An Application Programming Interface (API) is a collection of functions that the operating system or application can call on to perform many different tasks. By using a common set of code, applications can perform operations identical to those that the operating system performs. These APIs are normally stored in DLL files. Although programmers can access DLLs through compiled applications, scripters need to find another method of access.

Working with Objects

Objects provide a way for scripters to access API functions. An *object* is simply a collection of functions that perform similar tasks. These objects are normally stored in OCX (OLE custom control) or DLL files. To gain access to an object, you use the **CreateObject** function to load an object into memory, connect to the object, and set this connection to a variable. This is called *instantiating* an object and is performed as follows:

```
Set variable = CreateObject("object")
```

Once the instance is created, you can use this variable throughout your script to access all the methods within the object.

The Windows Script Host object model (see Figure 3.1) is a hierarchal, organized collection of objects, mostly stored in a file called WSHOM.OCX located in the Windows\System or Winnt\System32 directories. Each of the core objects contains its own methods and properties to perform specific tasks.

The Wscript Object

The **Wscript** object is the core scripting object. It allows you to collect information about your script, work with arguments, and call other ActiveX objects. The **Wscript** object contains the methods to instantiate other objects and is automatically instantiated every time a script is run. The most commonly used **Wscript** method is the **Echo** method, which sends output to the screen:

```
Wscript.Echo "Some Output"
```

The WshNetwork Object

The **WshNetwork** object provides access to Windows network functions. You can use this object to work with network connections and perform various network-related tasks. The most common tasks used with this function are mapping printers and drives, and obtaining a computer's network information.

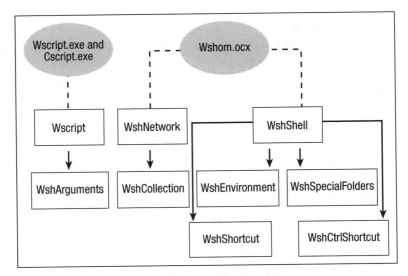

Figure 3.1   The Windows Script Host object model.

The WshShell Object

The **WshShell** object provides direct access to Windows and registry functions. You can use this object to work with shortcuts, display messages to users, manipulate the registry and environment variables, and run external commands.

The FileSystemObject Object

Is there an echo in here? Although not actually a part of the Windows Script Object model, the **FileSystemObject** object, contained in SCRRUN.DLL, can be used to access and manipulate the file system. Through this object, you can perform almost any file management task that you perform manually.

Now that you are familiar with the Windows Script Host Object model, you can start using subroutines to organize your scripts.

Subroutines

Imagine if you had to perform a series of 20 steps on more than 1,000 files. What a pain it would be to rewrite those steps so many times! This is why developers created subroutines. Throughout this chapter, you will find various subroutines reused in examples. *Subroutines* allow you to take a section of repeated code and make it accessible by simply calling it. Subroutines accept multiple parameters, allowing you to pass arguments to the subroutine for manipulation. Windows Script Host provides two types of subroutines: sub procedures and functions.

Sub Procedures

A sub procedure performs a series of actions without returning any data. A typical use of a sub procedure is to perform file manipulation, working with text files, or to display user prompts. A sub procedure is structured as follows:

```
Sub SubName (arguments)
   Code
End Sub
```

Here, *SubName* is the name given to the sub procedure; *arguments* are the parameters passed to the sub procedure (separated by commas); and *code* is the script action(s) to perform.

NOTE: *Any variables used within a sub procedure will not be accessible outside of the sub procedure, unless they are explicitly declared beforehand.*

Functions

A function is similar to a sub procedure except that it can return data. A typical use of a function is to perform calculations, create objects, or return error codes. A function is structured as follows:

```
Function FunctionName (arguments)
   Code
End Function
```

Here, ***FunctionName*** is the name given to the function; ***arguments*** are the parameters passed to the function (separated by commas); and ***Code*** is the script action(s) to perform. To return a value outside of the function, from within your function name a variable with the same name as your function and set a value to it.

Immediate Solutions

Working with the File System

Files and folders are the building blocks of any system. They contain the data we treasure, the operating system we use, and the applications we work with. Shell scripting, KiXtart, and Windows Script Host provide many ways of working with the file system. Although the tasks these scripting methods perform are similar, the commands, syntax, and limitations of each method differ.

Manipulating the File System Using Shell Scripting

Shell scripting provides limited functionality for manipulating the file system. Although Resource Kit utilities extend the capabilities of shell scripting, it still cannot compare to the more powerful functions of KiXtart and Windows Script Host. So, why use shell scripting? Shell scripting comes built into every operating system, and you will run into situations where shell scripting is your only alternative.

Deleting Files Depending on Extension

The Windows NT/2000 DELETE command supports many options that the Windows $9x$ command does not. To remove files based on extension in Windows NT/2000, start the command prompt and enter the following:

```
DEL *.ext /F /Q /S
```

Here, *ext* is the file extension of the files to delete; the **/F** switch forces the deletion of read-only files; the **/Q** switch removes prompts; and the **/S** switch performs deletions not only in the current directory, but in the subdirectories as well.

Deleting Folders and Subfolders

As ridiculous as this may sound, Windows NT does not include a command to delete folders. Microsoft has created a Resource Kit utility called RMDIR.EXE (Remove Directory), included in Windows 2000, that mimics the Windows 9*x* DELTREE.EXE (Delete Tree) command. To delete a root folder and all its subfolders with RMDIR, start the command prompt and enter the following:

```
RMDIR /Q /S directory
```

Here, **directory** is the name of the directory to delete; the **/Q** switch removes prompts; and the **/S** switch performs the deletion of all files and subdirectories.

Determining File Versions

FILEVER.EXE is a Resource Kit utility to display file versions from the command line. To determine a file version, start the command prompt and enter the following:

```
FILEVER filename
```

Here, **filename** is the path and name of file to determine the file version.

NOTE: *Remember, only application files have versions.*

Updating Program Files Depending on Version

REPLACE.EXE is a Windows NT/2000 command that can be used to update older files with newer file versions. To update a file with a newer version, start the command prompt and enter the following:

```
REPLACE /R /S /U source destination
```

Here, **source** is the path and name of the source file; **destination** is the directory to start the replacement; the **/R** switch allows for read-only file replacement; the **/S** switch performs the replacement in the current directory and all subdirectories; and the **/U** switch specifies to only replace files with a newer version.

3. File Management

Replicating Files and Directories

You can tell users to back up their files to the server, but whether the users actually do back the files up is a different story. ROBOCOPY is a Resource Kit utility to copy, move, or replicate files from the command line. To replicate files, start the command prompt and enter the following:

```
ROBOCOPY /MIR /ETA /NP /LOG+:logfile source destination
```

Here, the **/MIR** mirrors a directory tree; the **/ETA** switch displays the estimated time of arrival of copied files; the **/NP** switch causes no copy progress to be displayed; the **/LOG+:*logfile*** outputs the status to the *logfile*; and *destination* is the location to replicate the *source* to.

NOTE: *Version 1.95 of ROBOCOPY was designed for Windows NT/2000 and does not work in Windows 9x.*

Appending Text Files

Collecting information from log files can be a time-consuming task. Often, these files are properly formatted but simply need to be collected to a central file. To append the contents of one text file to another, start the command prompt and enter the following:

```
TYPE file1 >> file2
```

Here, *file1* is the file whose contents you want to append to *file2*.

Manipulating the File System Using KiXtart

KiXtart is a scripting language that is best used when you know the exact file or directory you want to manipulate. KiXtart provides poor directory parsing capabilities with its limited DIR command and lack of recursive support. To compensate, you can call external commands for indirect file management and KiXtart commands for direct file management.

Using External Commands

KiXtart provides two statements to run an external 16- or 32-bit application or command: **SHELL** and **RUN**. The **SHELL** statement will wait for the external command to complete, but the **RUN** statement will not. Both the **SHELL** and **RUN** statements have the same syntax:

```
statement "command"
```

Here, *statement* is the **RUN** or **SHELL** statement, and *command* is the command to run. To delete all the files in the temp directory using the **RUN** statement, you would enter:

```
RUN "%COMSPEC% /C DEL C:\TEMP\*.* /F /Q /S"
```

NOTE: %COMSPEC% /C *is used to run commands from the DOS environment.*

Renaming a File or Folder

KiXtart does not contain a function to rename a file or folder. Instead, you can copy the current item to a new item with the desired name, and then delete the old item. To rename a file or folder, proceed as follows:

1. Create a new directory to store all files included in this example.

2. Download and extract the latest version of KiXtart from **www.microsoft.com** to the new directory.

3. Select Start|Run and enter "kix32 *scriptfile*".

Here, *scriptfile* is the full path of the new directory from step 1 and the file name of a script file that contains the following:

```
$Root = "rootdir"
$File = "oldfilefolder"
$Name = "newfilefolder"

Copy "$Root\$File" "$Root\$Name" /H
Del "$Root\$File"
```

Here, *rootdir* is the root directory name of the file or folder to rename (without the last \); *oldfilefolder* is the name of the file or folder to rename; *newfilefolder* is the name to rename the *oldfilefolder* to; and **/H** specifies to include system and hidden files.

Displaying File or Folder Attributes

The KiXtart command **GetFileAttr** allows you to display file or folder attributes. To display the attributes of a file or folder, proceed as follows:

1. Create a new directory to store all files included in this example.

2. Download and extract the latest version of KiXtart, from **www.microsoft.com**, to the new directory.

3. Select Start|Run and enter "kix32 *scriptfile*".

Here, *scriptfile* is the full path of the new directory from step 1 and file name of a script file that contains the following:

```
$File = "filefolder"
GoSub FileAttribs
GoSub DisplayAttribs

:FileAttribs
  $ReadOnly = 0      $Hidden = 0       $System = 0
  $Dir = 0           $Archive = 0      $Encrypt = 0
  $Normal = 0        $Temp = 0         $Sparse = 0
  $Reparse = 0       $Compress = 0     $Offline = 0

  If GetFileAttr($File) & 1 $ReadOnly = 1 EndIf
  If GetFileAttr($File) & 2 $Hidden = 1 EndIf
  If GetFileAttr($File) & 4 $System = 1 EndIf
  If GetFileAttr($File) & 16 $Dir = 1 EndIf
  If GetFileAttr($File) & 32 $Archive = 1 EndIf
  If GetFileAttr($File) & 64 $Encrypt = 1 EndIf
  If GetFileAttr($File) & 128 $Normal = 1 EndIf
  If GetFileAttr($File) & 256 $Temp = 1 EndIf
  If GetFileAttr($File) & 512 $Sparse = 1 EndIf
  If GetFileAttr($File) & 1024 $Reparse = 1 EndIf
  If GetFileAttr($File) & 2046 $Compress = 1 EndIf
  If GetFileAttr($File) & 4096 $Offline = 1 EndIf
Return

:DisplayAttribs
  ? "File: " + $File
  ? ""
  ? "ReadOnly: " + $ReadOnly
  ? "Hidden: " + $Hidden
  ? "System: " + $System
  ? "Directory: " + $Dir
  ? "Archive: " + $Archive
  ? "Encrypted: " + $Encrypt
  ? "Normal: " + $Normal
```

```
? "Temporary: " + $Temp
? "Sparse: " + $Sparse
? "Reparse: " + $Reparse
? "Compressed: " + $Compress
? "Offline: " + $Offline
Sleep 5
Return
```

Here, *filefolder* is the file or folder that contains the attributes you want to get.

NOTE: *Windows 2000 adds several new file attributes with NTFS 5. For more information, see Chapter 17 of the Windows 2000 Professional Resource Kit.*

Setting File or Folder Attributes

The KiXtart command **SetFileAttr** allows you to set file or folder attributes. To display the attributes of a file or folder, proceed as follows:

1. Create a new directory to store all files included in this example.

2. Download and extract the latest version of KiXtart, from **www.microsoft.com**, to the new directory.

3. Select Start|Run and enter "kix32 *scriptfile*".

Here, *scriptfile* is the full path of the new directory from step 1 and file name of a script file that contains the following:

```
$File = "filefolder"

$ReadOnly = 0 $Hidden = 0    $System = 0
$Archive = 0  $Normal = 0    $Temp = 0
$Offline = 0

GoSub SetAttribs

:SetAttribs
  $Rcode = SetFileAttr($File,128)
  $Attribs = 0
  If $ReadOnly = 1 $Attribs = $Attribs + 1 EndIf
  If $Hidden = 1 $Attribs = $Attribs + 2 EndIf
  If $System = 1 $Attribs = $Attribs + 4 EndIf
  If $Archive = 1 $Attribs = $Attribs + 32 EndIf
  If $Temp = 1 $Attribs = $Attribs + 256 EndIf
  If $Offline = 1 $Attribs = $Attribs + 4096 EndIf
  $Rcode = SetFileAttr($File,$Attribs)
Return
```

Here, *filefolder* is the file or folder that contains the attributes you want to set. To modify *filefolder*'s attributes, change the value of the corresponding variable names (*$ReadOnly*, *$Hidden*, *$System*, *$Archive*, *$Normal*, *$Temp*, *$Offline*) to 1 to enable, or 0 to disable.

Appending Text Files

To append the contents of one text file to another, proceed as follows:

1. Create a new directory to store all files included in this example.
2. Download and extract the latest version of KiXtart, from **www.microsoft.com**, to the new directory.
3. Select Start|Run and enter "kix32 *scriptfile*".

Here, *scriptfile* is the full path of the new directory from step 1 and file name of a script file that contains the following:

```
$File1 = "file1"
$File2 = "file2"

$Rcode = Open(1,$File1)
$Rcode = Open(2,$File2,5)

$File1 = ReadLine(1)
While @Error=0
  If $File1
    $Rcode = WriteLine(2,$File1 + Chr(13) + Chr(10))
  EndIf
$File1 = ReadLine(1)
Loop

$Rcode = Close(1)
$Rcode = Close(2)
```

Here, *file1* is the file whose contents you want to append to *file2*.

Searching and Replacing Lines within Files

Replacing specific lines within the AUTOEXEC.BAT, CONFIG.SYS, or other text files is a common administrative task. To search and replace a line within a text file, proceed as follows:

1. Create a new directory to store all files included in this example.
2. Download and extract the latest version of KiXtart, from **www.microsoft.com**, to the new directory.
3. Select Start|Run and enter "kix32 *scriptfile*".

Here, **scriptfile** is the full path of the new directory from step 1 and file name of a script file that contains the following:

```
$File = "somefile"
$DLine = 'searchline'
$RLine = 'replaceline'
$TempFile = $File + ".TMP"
$LineNum = 0

$Rcode = OPEN (1, $File, 2)
DEL $TempFile
$Rcode = OPEN (2, $TempFile, 5)

$Line = READLINE(1)
WHILE @Error = 0
  $LineNum = $LineNum + 1
  IF $Line = $DLine
    $Rcode = WRITELINE(2, $RLine + Chr(13) + Chr(10))
  ELSE
    $Rcode = WRITELINE(2, $Line + Chr(13) + Chr(10))
  ENDIF
  $Line = READLINE(1)
LOOP

$Rcode = CLOSE(1)
$Rcode = CLOSE(2)
COPY $TempFile $File
DEL $TempFile
```

Here, **somefile** is the file to parse, and **replaceline** is the text to replace the **searchline** with.

Searching and Replacing within an INI File

INI files, or initialization files, are text files that were originally created to store configuration information for 16-bit applications. KiXtart is the easiest scripting method for modifying an INI file because it has two built-in INI functions (**READPROFILESTRING** and **WRITE PROFILESTRING**). To search and replace a value in an INI file, proceed as follows:

1. Create a new directory to store all files included in this example.

2. Download and extract the latest version of KiXtart, from **www.microsoft.com**, to the new directory.

3. Select Start|Run and enter "kix32 *scriptfile*".

Here, **scriptfile** is the full path of the new directory from step 1 and file name of a script file that contains the following:

```
$LoadKey = ReadProfileString("inifile", section, key)
If $LoadKey = oldvalue
  WriteProfileString("inifile ", section, key, newvalue)
EndIf
```

Here, **inifile** is the complete name and path of the INI file; **section** is the name of the INI section to search (without the brackets); **key** is the name of the key to search; **oldvalue** is the value to find; and **newvalue** is the value to replace it with.

NOTE: WriteProfileString in this example replaces the old value with a new value surrounded by double quotes. If you wish to clear the value, the new value should be a space surrounded by double quotes. Simply supplying double quotes (no space) would delete the entire key and value from the INI file.

Manipulating the File System Using Windows Script Host

Many of the file management tasks administrators would like to script are too complex or cannot be done with shell scripting or KiXtart. Windows Script Host (WSH) provides direct access to the file system, allowing you to create complex and unique file management scripts.

Accessing the **FileSystemObject**

The **FileSystemObject** stores all the functions that allow you to manipulate the file system through a script file. To create an instance of the **FileSystemObject**, proceed as follows:

```
Set FSO = CreateObject("Scripting.FileSystemObject")
```

Going through Subfolders

This subroutine will work through the subfolders of a main directory, calling another subroutine called **MainSub**:

```
Sub GoSubFolders (objDIR)
  If objDIR <> "\System Volume Information" Then
    MainSub objDIR
    For Each eFolder in objDIR.SubFolders
      GoSubFolders eFolder
    Next
  End If
End Sub
```

NOTE: *The System Volume Information directory is a Windows 2000 system directory that causes script errors when attempting access to it.*

Connecting to a File

Before performing certain WSH actions on a file, you must first connect to it using the **GetFile** method. Here is a function to connect to a file:

```
Function GetFile(sFILE)
  On Error Resume Next
  Set GetFile = FSO.GetFile(sFILE)
  If Err.Number <> 0 Then
    Wscript.Echo "Error connecting to: " & sFILE & VBlf & _
    "[" & Err.Number & "] " & Err.Description
    Wscript.Quit Err.Number
  End If
End Function
```

TIP: On Error Resume Next *allows the script to continue to the next statement if an error occurs. This allows you to perform error checking and alerting.*

In this script, a connection to a file is attempted, and the user is prompted if any errors occur.

Connecting to a Folder

Before performing certain WSH actions on a folder, you must first connect to it using the **GetFolder** method. Here is a function to connect to a folder:

```
Function GetFolder(sFOLDER)
  On Error Resume Next
  Set GetFolder = FSO.GetFolder(sFOLDER)
  If Err.Number <> 0 Then
```

```
      Wscript.Echo "Error connecting to folder: " & sFOLDER & _
      VBlf & "[" & Err.Number & "] " & Err.Description
      Wscript.Quit Err.Number
   End If
End Function
```

Generating a Directory Listing

To generate a directory list, proceed as follows:

1. Create a new directory to store all files included in this example.

2. Download and install the latest version of Windows Script Host, from **www.microsoft.com**, to the new directory.

3. Select Start|Run and enter "cscript *scriptfile*.vbs".

Here, ***scriptfile*** is the full path and file name of a script file that contains the following:

```
Set FSO = CreateObject("Scripting.FileSystemObject")
sDIR = "directory"

Set objDIR = GetFolder(sDIR)
GoSubFolders objDIR

Sub ListFiles (objDIR)
    For Each efile in objDIR.Files
      Wscript.Echo efile
    Next
End Sub

Sub GoSubFolders (objDIR)
  If objDIR <> "\System Volume Information" Then
    ListFiles objDIR
    For Each eFolder in objDIR.SubFolders
      Wscript.Echo eFolder
      GoSubFolders eFolder
    Next
  End If
End Sub
```

Here, ***directory*** is the root folder containing the files and folders to list. The subprocedure ListFiles rotates through all the files within the current directory and lists their names.

NOTE: *You need to append the **GetFolder** routine, listed earlier in this chapter, to this script in order for it to run.*

TIP: *If you want to send the directory list to a text file, you can use the DOS append command (>>) when running the script from the command line (for example, **cscript scriptfile.vbs >> textfile.txt**).*

Deleting a File

To delete a file with WSH, you can use the **DeleteFile** method. Here is a subroutine to delete a file:

```
Sub DelFile(sFILE)
  On Error Resume Next
  FSO.DeleteFile sFILE, True
  If Err.Number <> 0 Then
    Wscript.Echo "Error deleting file: " & sFILE
  End If
End Sub
```

In this script, a file deletion is attempted, and the user is prompted if any errors occur.

Deleting All Files within a Folder

To delete all files within a root folder and its subfolders, proceed as follows:

1. Create a new directory to store all files included in this example.

2. Download and install the latest version of Windows Script Host, from **www.microsoft.com**, to the new directory.

3. Select Start|Run and enter "cscript *scriptfile*.vbs".

Here, ***scriptfile*** is the full path and file name of a script file that contains the following:

```
Set FSO = CreateObject("Scripting.FileSystemObject")
sDIR = "directory"
Set objDIR = GetFolder(sDIR)
GoSubFolders objDIR
```

3. File Management

```
Sub MainSub (objDIR)
  For Each efile in objDIR.Files
    DelFile efile
  Next
End Sub
```

Here, **directory** is the root folder containing the files to delete.

NOTE: *You need to append the **GoSubFolders, DelFile,** and **GetFolder** routines, listed earlier in this chapter, to this script in order for it to run.*

Deleting Files Depending on Size

It happens to all of us, but every now and then a user chooses to upload hundred meg files to a public share. To delete all files within a root folder and its subfolders depending on size, proceed as follows:

1. Create a new directory to store all files included in this example.

2. Download and install the latest version of Windows Script Host, from **www.microsoft.com**, to the new directory.

3. Select Start|Run and enter "cscript *scriptfile*.vbs".

Here, **scriptfile** is the full path and file name of a script file that contains the following:

```
Set FSO = CreateObject("Scripting.FileSystemObject")
sDIR = "directory"
lSIZE = lowersize
uSIZE = uppersize

Set objDIR = GetFolder(sDIR)
GoSubFolders objDIR

Sub MainSub (objDIR)
  For Each efile in objDIR.Files
    If lSIZE = Null and uSIZE = Null Then
      If efile.Size = 0 Then
        DelFile efile
      End If
    ElseIf lSIZE <> Null and uSIZE = Null Then
      If efile.Size < lSIZE Then
        DelFile efile
      End If
    ElseIf lSIZE = Null and uSIZE <> "" Then
```

```
          If efile.Size > uSIZE Then
            DelFile efile
          End If
        ElseIf lSIZE = uSIZE Then
          If efile.Size = lSIZE Then
            DelFile efile
          End If
        Else
          If efile.Size > lSIZE and _
          efile.Size < uSIZE Then
            DelFile efile
          End If
        End If
      Next
End Sub
```

Here, **directory** is the folder containing the files to delete, **lowersize** is the lower size limit, and **uppersize** is the upper size limit. If both limits are null, the script will delete all empty files. If just the upper limit is null, the script will delete files smaller than the lower limit. If just the lower limit is null, the script will delete files larger than the upper limit. If both limits are not null but equal, the script will delete files equal to the limit. If both limits are not null and not equal, the script will delete files within the two limits.

NOTE: *You need to append the **GoSubFolders**, **DelFile**, and **GetFolder** routines, listed earlier in this chapter, to this script in order for it to run.*

Deleting Files Depending on Date

A common administrative task is deleting old files from public shares. To delete all files within a root folder and its subfolders depending on last modified date, proceed as follows:

1. Create a new directory to store all files included in this example.

2. Download and install the latest version of Windows Script Host, from **www.microsoft.com**, to the new directory.

3. Select Start|Run and enter "cscript *scriptfile*.vbs".

Here, **scriptfile** is the full path and file name of a script file that contains the following:

```
Set FSO = CreateObject("Scripting.FileSystemObject")
sDIR = "directory"
lDATE = "lowerdate"
uDATE = "upperdate"
```

```
1DATE = CDate(1DATE)
uDATE = CDate(uDATE)
Set objDIR = GetFolder(sDIR)
GoSubFolders objDIR

Sub MainSub (objDIR)
  For Each efile in objDIR.Files
    If 1DATE = Null and uDATE = Null Then
      If efile.DateLastModified = Date Then
        DelFile efile
      End If
    ElseIf 1DATE <> Null and uDATE = Null Then
      If efile.DateLastModified < 1DATE Then
        DelFile efile
      End If
    ElseIf 1DATE = Null and uDATE <> Null Then
      If efile.DateLastModified > uDATE Then
        DelFile efile
      End If
    ElseIf 1DATE = uDATE Then
      If efile.DateLastModified = 1DATE Then
        DelFile efile
      End If
    Else
      If efile.DateLastModified > 1DATE and _
      efile.DateLastModified < uDATE Then
        DelFile efile
      End If
    End If
  Next
End Sub
```

Here, *directory* is the folder containing the files to delete, *lowerdate* is the lower date limit, and *upperdate* is the upper date limit. If both limits are null, the script will delete files last modified today. If just the upper limit is null, the script will delete files smaller than the lower limit. If just the lower limit is null, the script will delete files larger than the upper limit. If both limits are not null but equal, the script will delete files equal to the limit. If both limits are not null and not equal, the script will delete files within the two limits.

NOTE: *You need to append the **GoSubFolders**, **DelFile**, and **GetFolder** routines, listed earlier in this chapter, to this script in order for it to run.*

Deleting Files Depending on Name

From hacker tools to new viruses, deleting files with a specific name is a common administrative task. To delete all files with a specific name within a root folder and its subfolders, proceed according to the steps on the next page.

1. Create a new directory to store all files included in this example.

2. Download and install the latest version of Windows Script Host, from **www.microsoft.com**, to the new directory.

3. Select Start|Run and enter "cscript *scriptfile*.vbs".

Here, **scriptfile** is the full path and file name of a script file that contains the following:

```
Set FSO = CreateObject("Scripting.FileSystemObject")
sDIR = "directory"
sFILE = "filename"

Set objDIR = GetFolder(sDIR)
GoSubFolders objDIR

Sub MainSub (objDIR)
  For Each efile in objDIR.Files
    If LCase(efile.Name) = LCase(sFILE) Then
      DelFile efile
    End If
  Next
End Sub
```

Here, **directory** is the folder containing the files to delete, and **filename** is the name of the file to search for.

NOTE: *You need to append the **GoSubFolders**, **DelFile**, and **GetFolder** routines, listed earlier in this chapter, to this script in order for it to run.*

Deleting Files Depending on Extension

Cleaning a system of specific file types, such as TMP (Temporary), MP3 (Motion Picture Experts Group Layer 3 Audio), AVI (Audio Video Interleave), and other file types, is a very common administrative task. To delete all files with a specific extension within a root folder and its subfolders, proceed as follows:

1. Create a new directory to store all files included in this example.

2. Download and install the latest version of Windows Script Host, from **www.microsoft.com**, to the new directory.

3. Select Start|Run and enter "cscript *scriptfile*.vbs".

Here, ***scriptfile*** is the full path and file name of a script file that contains the following:

```
Set FSO = CreateObject("Scripting.FileSystemObject")
sDIR = "directory"
sEXT = "EXT"

Set objDIR = GetFolder(sDIR)
GoSubFolders objDIR

Sub MainSub (objDIR)
  For Each efile in objDIR.Files
    fEXT = FSO.GetExtensionName(efile.Path)
    If LCase(fEXT) = LCase(sEXT) Then
      DelFile efile
    End If
  Next
End Sub
```

Here, ***directory*** is the folder containing the files to delete, and ***ext*** is the file extension to search for. The sub procedure **MainSub** rotates through every file within the current directory, checks the file extension, and deletes the file if specified.

NOTE: *You need to append the **GoSubFolders**, **DelFile**, and **GetFolder** routines, listed earlier in this chapter, to this script in order for it to run.*

Deleting a Folder

To delete a folder with WSH, you can use the **DeleteFolder** method. Here is a subroutine to delete a folder:

```
Sub DelFolder(sFOLDER)
  On Error Resume Next
  FSO.DeleteFolder sFOLDER, True
  If Err.Number <> 0 Then
    Wscript.Echo "Error deleting folder: " & sFOLDER
  End If
End Sub
```

Deleting All Subfolders

To delete all subfolders within a directory, proceed as follows:

1. Create a new directory to store all files included in this example.

2. Download and install the latest version of Windows Script Host, from **www.microsoft.com**, to the new directory.

3. Select StartIRun and enter "cscript *scriptfile*.vbs".

Here, **scriptfile** is the full path and file name of a script file that contains the following:

```
Set FSO = CreateObject("Scripting.FileSystemObject")
sDIR = "directory"
Set objDIR = GetFolder(sDIR)
GoSubFolders objDIR

Sub GoSubFolders (objDIR)
  If objDIR <> "\System Volume Information" Then
    For Each eFolder in objDIR.SubFolders
      DelFolder eFolder
    Next
  End If
End Sub
```

Here, **directory** is the folder containing the subfolders to delete.

NOTE: *You need to append the **GoSubFolders**, **DelFile**, and **GetFolder** routines, listed earlier in this chapter, to this script in order for it to run.*

Deleting Folders Depending on Size

By maintaining public shares, you get to notice all the bad habits of a typical user. One of these habits includes leaving empty folders spread throughout the public share. To delete all folders depending on size within a root folder and its subfolders, proceed as follows:

1. Create a new directory to store all files included in this example.

2. Download and install the latest version of Windows Script Host, from **www.microsoft.com**, to the new directory.

3. Select StartIRun and enter "cscript *scriptfile*.vbs".

3. File Management

Here, **scriptfile** is the full path and file name of a script file that contains the following:

```
Set FSO = CreateObject("Scripting.FileSystemObject")
sDIR = "directory"
lSIZE = lowersize
uSIZE = uppersize

Set objDIR = GetFolder(sDIR)
GoSubFolders objDIR

Sub MainSub (objDIR)
  If objDIR <> "\System Volume Information" Then
    For Each eFolder in objDIR.SubFolders
      If lSIZE = Null and uSIZE = Null Then
        If efolder.Size = 0 Then
          DelFolder efolder
        End If
      ElseIf lSIZE <> Null and uSIZE = Null Then
        If efolder.Size < lSIZE Then
          DelFolder efolder
        End If
      ElseIf lSIZE = Null and uSIZE <> Null Then
        If efolder.Size > uSIZE Then
          DelFolder efolder
        End If
      ElseIf lSIZE = uSIZE Then
        If efolder.Size = lSIZE Then
          DelFolder efolder
        End If
      Else
        If efolder.Size > lSIZE and _
        efolder.Size < uSIZE Then
          DelFolder efolder
        End If
      End If
    Next
  End If
End Sub
```

Here, **directory** is the root folder containing the subfolders to delete, **lowersize** is the lower size limit, and **uppersize** is the upper size limit. If both limits are null, the script will delete all subfolders with a size of 0. If just the upper limit is null, the script will delete subfolders smaller than the lower limit. If just the lower limit is null, the script will delete subfolders larger than the upper limit. If both limits are not null but equal, the script will delete subfolders equal to the limit. If both limits are not empty and not null, the script will delete subfolders within the two limits.

NOTE: *You need to append the **GoSubFolders**, **DelFile**, and **GetFolder** routines, listed earlier in this chapter, to this script in order for it to run.*

Deleting Folders Depending on Date

If you let them, users will leave files and folders forever on a public share. To delete all folders depending on last modified date within a root folder and its subfolders, proceed as follows:

1. Create a new directory to store all files included in this example.
2. Download and install the latest version of Windows Script Host, from **www.microsoft.com**, to the new directory.
3. Select Start|Run and enter "cscript *scriptfile*.vbs".

Here, ***scriptfile*** is the full path and file name of a script file that contains the following:

```
Set FSO = CreateObject("Scripting.FileSystemObject")
sDIR = "directory"
lDATE = "lowerdate"
uDATE = "upperdate"

lDATE = CDate(lDATE)
uDATE = CDate(uDATE)
Set objDIR = GetFolder(sDIR)
GoSubFolders objDIR

Sub MainSub (objDIR)
   If objDIR <> "\System Volume Information" Then
      For Each eFolder in objDIR.SubFolders
         If lDATE = Null and uDATE = Null Then
            If efolder.DateLastModified = 0 Then
               DelFolder efolder
            End If
         ElseIf lDATE <> Null and uDATE = Null Then
            If efolder.DateLastModified < lDATE Then
               DelFolder efolder
            End If
         ElseIf lDATE = Null and uDATE <> Null Then
            If efolder.DateLastModified > uDATE Then
               DelFolder efolder
            End If
```

```
      ElseIf lDATE = uDATE Then
        If efolder.DateLastModified = lDATE Then
          DelFolder efolder
        End If
      Else
        If efolder.DateLastModified > lDATE and _
          efolder.DateLastModified < uDATE Then
            DelFolder efolder
        End If
      End If
    Next
  End If
End Sub
```

Here, **directory** is the root folder containing the subfolders to delete, **lowerdate** is the lower date limit, and **upperdate** is the upper
date limit. If both limits are null, the script will delete subfolders last
modified today. If just the upper limit is null, the script will delete
subfolders smaller than the lower limit. If just the lower limit is null,
the script will delete subfolders larger than the upper limit. If both
limits are not null but equal, the script will delete subfolders equal to
the limit. If both limits are not null and not equal, the script will delete
subfolders within the two limits.

NOTE: You need to append the **GoSubFolders**, **DelFile**, and **GetFolder** routines, listed earlier
in this chapter, to this script in order for it to run.

Deleting Folders Depending on Name
Any user public folder called GAMES or QUAKE is most likely not
work-related, unless you have a better job than I do. To delete all
folders with a specific name within a root folder and its subfolders,
proceed as follows:

1. Create a new directory to store all files included in this example.

2. Download and install the latest version of Windows Script Host,
   from **www.microsoft.com**, to the new directory.

3. Select Start|Run and enter "cscript *scriptfile*.vbs".

Here, **scriptfile** is the full path and file name of a script file that contains the following:

```
Set FSO = CreateObject("Scripting.FileSystemObject")
sDIR = "directory"
sFOLDER = "foldername"
```

```
Set objDIR = GetFolder(sDIR)
GoSubFolders objDIR

Sub MainSub (objDIR)
  If objDIR <> "\System Volume Information" Then
    For Each eFolder in objDIR.SubFolders
      If LCase(eFolder.Name) = LCase(sFOLDER) Then
        DelFolder efolder
      End If
    Next
  End If
End Sub
```

Copying a File

To copy a file with WSH, you can use the **CopyFile** method. Here is a subroutine to copy a file:

```
Sub CopyFile(sFILE, sDIR)
  If Right(sDIR,1) <> "\" Then sDIR = sDIR & "\"
  On Error Resume Next
  FSO.CopyFile sFILE, sDIR, True
  If Err.Number <> 0 Then
    Wscript.Echo "Error copying file: " & sFILE
  End If
End Sub
```

Here, **sFILE** is the file to copy, and **sDIR** is the location to copy the file to.

Copying a Folder

To copy a folder with WSH, you can use the **CopyFolder** method. Here is a subroutine to copy a folder:

```
Sub CopyFolder(sFOLDER, sDIR)
  If Right(sFOLDER,1) = "\" Then
    sFOLDER = Left(sFOLDER,(Len(sFOLDER)-1))
  End If
  If Right(sDIR,1) <> "\" Then sDIR = sDIR & "\"
  On Error Resume Next
  FSO.CopyFolder sFOLDER, sDIR, True
  If Err.Number <> 0 Then
    Wscript.Echo "Error copying folder: " & sFOLDER
  End If
End Sub
```

Here, **sFOLDER** is the folder to copy, and **sDIR** is the location to copy the folder to.

Moving a File

To move a file with WSH, you can use the **MoveFile** method. Here is a subroutine to move a file:

```
Sub MoveFile(sFILE, sDIR)
  If Right(sDIR,1) <> "\" Then sDIR = sDIR & "\"
  On Error Resume Next
  FSO.MoveFile sFILE, sDIR
  If Err.Number <> 0 Then
    Wscript.Echo "Error moving file: " & sFILE
  End If
End Sub
```

Here, **sFILE** is the file to move, and **sDIR** is the location to move the file to.

Moving Files with Specific Extensions to a Central Directory

Although certain file types, such as MP3s, do not belong in the public share, you may want to keep them for your own purposes. To move files with a specific extension to a central directory, proceed as follows:

1. Create a new directory to store all files included in this example.

2. Download and install the latest version of Windows Script Host, from **www.microsoft.com**, to the new directory.

3. Select Start|Run and enter "cscript *scriptfile*.vbs".

Here, **scriptfile** is the full path and file name of a script file that contains the following:

```
Set FSO = CreateObject("Scripting.FileSystemObject")
sEXT = "extension"
sDIR = "startdir"
sNEW = "enddir"

Set objDIR = GetFolder(sDIR)
GoSubFolders objDIR

Sub MainSub (objDIR)
    For Each efile in objDIR.Files
        fNAME = efile
        fEXT = FSO.GetExtensionName(efile.Path)
        If LCase(fEXT) = LCase(sEXT) Then
```

```
    sEXIST = sNEW & efile.Name
        If ((FSO.FileExists(sEXIST)) AND _
      (efile <> sEXIST)) Then
            DelFile sEXIST
        End If
        On Error Resume Next
        MoveFile efile, sNEW
      End If
    Next
End Sub
```

Here, ***extension*** is the name of the extension to search for, ***startdir*** is the name of the directory to start the search, and ***enddir*** is the directory to store all files.

NOTE: *You need to append the **GoSubFolders**, **DelFile**, and **GetFolder** routines, listed earlier in this chapter, to this script in order for it to run.*

Moving a Folder

To move a folder with WSH, you can use the **MoveFolder** method. Here is a subroutine to move a folder:

```
Sub MoveFolder(sFOLDER, sDIR)
  If Right(sFOLDER,1) = "\" Then
    sFOLDER = Left(sFOLDER,(Len(sFOLDER)-1))
  End If
  If Right(sDIR,1) <> "\" Then sDIR = sDIR & "\"
  On Error Resume Next
  FSO.MoveFolder sFOLDER, sDIR
  If Err.Number <> 0 Then
    Wscript.Echo "Error moving folder: " & sFOLDER
  End If
End Sub
```

Here, ***sFOLDER*** is the folder to move, and ***sDIR*** is the location to move the folder to.

Renaming a File

To rename a file, proceed as follows:

1. Create a new directory to store all files included in this example.

2. Download and install the latest version of Windows Script Host, from **www.microsoft.com**, to the new directory.

3. Select Start|Run and enter "cscript *scriptfile*.vbs".

Here, ***scriptfile*** is the full path and file name of a script file that contains the following:

```
Set FSO = CreateObject("Scripting.FileSystemObject")
sFILE = "filename"
sNAME = "newname"
Set gFILE = GetFile sFILE

gFILE.name = sNAME
```

Here, ***filename*** is the name of the file to rename, and ***sname*** is the name to rename the file.

NOTE: *You need to append the **GetFile** routine, listed earlier in this chapter, to this script in order for it to run.*

Renaming Specific File Extensions

I don't know what planet of bad habits this came from, but some users like to name files with their own personal extensions. Although this might be beneficial to them when searching for their files, it becomes an administrator's nightmare when these files are being shared. Unfortunately, the DOS RENAME command does not have the ability to act through subdirectories. To rename files with specific extensions with a new extension, proceed as follows:

1. Create a new directory to store all files included in this example.

2. Download and install the latest version of Windows Script Host, from **www.microsoft.com**, to the new directory.

3. Select Start|Run and enter "cscript *scriptfile*.vbs".

Here, ***scriptfile*** is the full path and file name of a script file that contains the following:

```
Set FSO = CreateObject("Scripting.FileSystemObject")
sEXT = "oldext"
sNEW = "newext"
sDIR = "directory"

Set objDIR = GetFolder(sDIR)
GoSubFolders objDIR
```

```
Sub MainSub (objDIR)
  For Each efile in objDIR.Files
    fEXT = FSO.GetExtensionName(efile.Path)
    If LCase(fEXT) = LCase(sEXT) Then
      fNAME=Left(efile.name,(Len(efile.Name)-Len(fEXT)))+sNEW
      efile.name = fNAME
    End If
  Next
End Sub
```

Here, *oldext* is the name of the extension to search for, *newext* is the name of the extension to replace with, and *directory* is the name of the directory to start the search.

NOTE: *You need to append the **GetFolder** and **GoSubFolders** routines, listed earlier in this chapter, to this script in order for it to run.*

Renaming Files with Short File Names

To rename a file with its short DOS 8.3 name, proceed as follows:

1. Create a new directory to store all files included in this example.

2. Download and install the latest version of Windows Script Host, from **www.microsoft.com**, to the new directory.

3. Select Start|Run and enter "cscript *scriptfile*.vbs".

Here, *scriptfile* is the full path and file name of a script file that contains the following:

```
Set FSO = CreateObject("Scripting.FileSystemObject")
sFILE = "filename"
Set gFILE = GetFile sFILE

ShortName = gFILE.shortname
gFILE.name = ShortName & "SN"
gFILE.name = ShortName
```

Here, *filename* is the name of the file to rename. An important thing to know is that you can't rename a file from a long file name to its short name directly because Windows sees long and short file names collectively, and you can't name a file the same name as another file in the current directory. In this example, we first append an SN to the file name and then change the file name to its short name.

NOTE: *You need to append the **GetFile** routine, listed earlier in this chapter, to this script in order for it to run.*

Related solution:	Found on page:
Using SCANDSKW.EXE to Convert Long File Names to Short	90

Updating Program Files Depending on Version

To update a program file with a newer version, proceed as follows:

1. Create a new directory to store all files included in this example.

2. Download and install the latest version of Windows Script Host, from **www.microsoft.com**, to the new directory.

3. Select Start|Run and enter "cscript *scriptfile*.vbs".

Here, *scriptfile* is the full path and file name of a script file that contains the following:

```
Set FSO = CreateObject("Scripting.FileSystemObject")
sDIR = "directory"
sFILE = "filename"

Set nFILE = GetFile(sFILE)
Set objDIR = GetFolder(sDIR)
GoSubFolders objDIR

Sub MainSub (objDIR)
  For Each efile in objDIR.Files
    fVER = FSO.GetFileVersion(efile)
    nVER = FSO.GetFileVersion(sFILE)
    If LCase(efile.Name) = LCase(nFILE.Name) Then
      If fVER = nVER Then
        CopyFile nFILE, efile.ParentFolder
      End If
    End If
  Next
End Sub
```

Here, *directory* is the folder containing the files to update, and *filename* is the file used to update the older file versions.

NOTE: *You need to append the **GetFile**, **GetFolder**, **GoSubFolders**, and **CopyFile** routines, listed earlier in this chapter, to this script in order for it to run. Remember, only program files have versions.*

Getting File Attributes

To display the attributes of a file, proceed as follows:

1. Create a new directory to store all files included in this example.

2. Download and install the latest version of Windows Script Host, from **www.microsoft.com**, to the new directory.

3. Select Start|Run and enter "cscript *scriptfile*.vbs".

Here, ***scriptfile*** is the full path and file name of a script file that contains the following:

```
Set FSO = CreateObject("Scripting.FileSystemObject")
fNAME = "filename"

Set gFILE = GetFile(fNAME)
gATTRIB = gFILE.Attributes

If gATTRIB and 1 Then ReadOnly = 1 Else ReadOnly = 0
If gATTRIB and 2 Then Hidden = 1 Else Hidden = 0
If gATTRIB and 4 Then System = 1 Else System = 0
If gATTRIB and 5 Then Volume = 1 Else Volume = 0
If gATTRIB and 16 Then Directory = 1 Else Directory = 0
If gATTRIB and 32 Then Archive = 1 Else Archive = 0
If gATTRIB and 64 Then Alias = 1 Else Alias = 0
If gATTRIB and 128 Then Compressed = 1 Else Compressed = 0

Wscript.Echo "FILE: " & UCase(fNAME) & vblf & vblf & _
   "Readonly:  " & vbtab & ReadOnly & vblf & _
   "Hidden:    " & vbtab & Hidden & vblf & _
   "System:    " & vbtab & System & vblf & _
   "Volume:    " & vbtab & Volume & vblf & _
   "Directory: " & vbtab & Directory & vblf & _
   "Archive:   " & vbtab & Archive & vblf & _
   "Alias:     " & vbtab & vbtab & Alias & vblf & _
   "Compressed:" & vbtab & Compressed
```

Here, ***filename*** is the file that contains the attributes you want to get.

NOTE: *You need to append the **GetFile** routine, listed earlier in this chapter, to this script in order for it to run.*

Related solution:	Found on page:
Getting File or Folder Details	106

Setting File Attributes

To set the attributes of a file, proceed as follows:

1. Create a new directory to store all files included in this example.

2. Download and install the latest version of Windows Script Host, from **www.microsoft.com**, to the new directory.

3. Select Start|Run and enter "cscript *scriptfile*.vbs".

Here, **scriptfile** is the full path and file name of a script file that contains the following:

```
Set FSO = CreateObject("Scripting.FileSystemObject")
fNAME = "filename"
ReadOnly = 0
Hidden = 0
System = 0
Archive = 0

Set gFILE = GetFile(fNAME)
gFILE.Attributes = 0
Attribs = 0
If ReadOnly = 1 Then Attribs = Attribs + 1
If Hidden = 1 Then Attribs = Attribs + 2
If System = 1 Then Attribs = Attribs + 4
If Archive = 1 Then Attribs = Attribs + 32
gFILE.Attributes = Attribs
```

Here, **filename** is the file that contains the attributes you want to set. To modify **filename**'s attributes, change the value of the corresponding variable names (**ReadOnly**, **Hidden**, **System**, **Archive**) to 1 to enable, or 0 to disable.

NOTE: You need to append the **GetFile** routine, listed earlier in this chapter, to this script in order for it to run.

Setting Attributes to All Files within Folders

Corrected in Windows 2000, Windows 9*x*/NT does not recursively apply file attributes through the file properties page. This missing feature can become extremely annoying when you attempt to work with read-only files copied from a CD. To set the attributes of all files within a folder and its subfolders, proceed as follows:

1. Create a new directory to store all files included in this example.

2. Download and install the latest version of Windows Script Host from **www.microsoft.com** to the new directory.

3. Select Start|Run and enter "cscript *scriptfile*.vbs".

Here, *scriptfile* is the full path and file name of a script file that contains the following:

```
Set FSO = CreateObject("Scripting.FileSystemObject")
sDIR = "directory"
sReadOnly = 0
sHidden = 0
sSystem = 0
sArchive = 0


Set objDIR = GetFolder(sDIR)
GoSubFolders objDIR

Sub MainSub (objDIR)
  For Each efile in objDIR.Files
    Set gFILE = GetFile(efile)
    gFILE.Attributes = 0
    Attribs = 0
    If sReadOnly = 1 Then Attribs = Attribs + 1
    If sHidden = 1 Then Attribs = Attribs + 2
    If sSystem = 1 Then Attribs = Attribs + 4
    If sArchive = 1 Then Attribs = Attribs + 32
    gFILE.Attributes = Attribs
  Next
End Sub
```

Here, *directory* contains the files whose attributes you want to set. To modify the attributes, change the values of the corresponding variable names (**ReadOnly**, **Hidden**, **System**, **Archive**) to 1 to enable, or 0 to disable.

NOTE: *You need to append the **GetFile** routine, the **GetFolder** routine, and the **GoSubFolders** routine listed earlier in this chapter to this script in order for it to run.*

Appending Text Files

To append the contents of one text file to another, proceed as follows:

1. Create a new directory to store all files included in this example.

2. Download and install the latest version of Windows Script Host, from **www.microsoft.com**, to the new directory.

3. Select Start|Run and enter "cscript *scriptfile*.vbs".

Here, **scriptfile** is the full path and file name of a script file that contains the following:

```
Set FSO = CreateObject("Scripting.FileSystemObject")
File1 = "1stfile"
File2 = "2ndfile"

Set txtFile1 = FSO.OpenTextFile(File1, 1)
Set txtFile2 = FSO.OpenTextFile(File2, 8)

Do While txtFile1.AtEndOfline <> True
  txtFile2.WriteLine(txtFile1.Readline & vbcr)
Loop

txtFile1.close
txtFile2.close
```

Here, **1stfile** is the file whose contents you want to append to **2ndfile**.

Chapter 4

Automating Windows and Applications

In Brief

In this chapter, you will first learn how to script applications, Control Panel applets, Windows, and wizards from the command line. You will then learn about automation and how to script the Windows shell and most common applications (for example, Word, Excel, Internet Explorer). Finally, you will learn how to use send-keys to automate applications that do not easily support conventional scripting methods. In later chapters, you will learn how to automate Windows and applications to perform more specific tasks (such as adding shares, controlling services, or performing backups).

Automation

Automation was originally created as a method for applications to easily access and control one another. Application automation originally developed from Dynamic Data Exchange (DDE), grew to Object Linking and Embedding (OLE), developed into OLE automation, and eventually turned into just Automation. Automation interfaces with applications through Component Object Model (COM) objects. COM objects are ActiveX controls that contain isolated sections of reusable code. Through automation, you can create documents, save files, play sounds, and even control the operating system, depending on whether it has an object model.

Visual Basic for Applications

Microsoft Office applications support a scripting language called Visual Basic for Applications (VBA). VBA, which is based on Visual Basic, is the standard programming language to control Microsoft Office application functions remotely. Application developers can use VBA to call other application functions from within their projects.

NOTE: *Applications that support VBA are known as "customizable applications."*

A common method to produce easy VBA code is to record a macro and edit it in the built-in Visual Basic editor. To record a new macro, start an Office application and select Tools|Macro|Record New Macro. After you have started recording, perform the functions you would like to code and then stop the macro recording. Next, start the Visual Basic Editor by selecting Tools|Macro|Visual Basic Editor. After the

```
Microsoft Visual Basic - Normal - [NewMacros (Code)]
File  Edit  View  Insert  Format  Debug  Run  Tools  Add-Ins  Window  Help
(General)                              Macro1
    Sub Macro1()
        Selection.Font.Bold = wdToggle
        Selection.TypeText Text:="Hello There"
        Selection.TypeParagraph
        ActiveDocument.Shapes.AddLine(72#, 90#, 549#, 90#).Select
        Selection.ShapeRange.IncrementTop 9#
        Selection.ShapeRange.IncrementTop -9#
        Selection.MoveDown Unit:=wdLine, Count:=2
        Selection.TypeParagraph
        Selection.MoveUp Unit:=wdLine, Count:=1
        Selection.Delete Unit:=wdCharacter, Count:=1
        Selection.MoveDown Unit:=wdLine, Count:=1
        Selection.EndKey Unit:=wdLine
        Selection.TypeParagraph
        Selection.Font.Bold = wdToggle
        Selection.TypeText Text:="This is our sample report"
    End Sub
```

Figure 4.1   Editing a recorded Office macro.

editor opens, select Tools|Macro, highlight your macro, and click Edit. In Figure 4.1, you can see the VBA code of all the functions you have just recorded.

Through Windows Script Host, you can use VBScript to call many VBA functions to automate Office applications. There are three steps to automating an application through Automation: accessing the application object, controlling the application, and closing the application object.

Accessing the Application Object

The application object is the top-level object, which allows you to send data to an application object and manipulate a program through it. As you learned in the previous chapter, in order to gain access to an object, you must first use the **CreateObject** method and set it to a variable:

```
Set variable = CreateObject("object.Application")
```

Once the instance is created, you can use this variable throughout your script to access all the methods within the object. Here is a list of the most common automation identifiers:

- **Access.Application**—Used to automate Microsoft Access
- **Excel.Application**—Used to automate Microsoft Excel
- **InternetExplorer.Application**—Used to automate Microsoft Internet Explorer
- **Outlook.Application**—Used to automate Microsoft Outlook

85

- **PowerPoint.Application**—Used to automate Microsoft PowerPoint
- **Shell.Application**—Used to automate Microsoft Windows
- **Word.Application**—Used to automate Microsoft Word

Microsoft Office contains help files on how to use automation with the various Microsoft Office applications. To view these files, run the Office setup and install the help files for Visual Basic. Run the application's help feature and search for "VBA HELP".

Changing the Application Visibility

After you've instantiated an application object, most of the objects start in hidden mode. This allows you to manipulate the object and perform various tasks before making the object visible. To make the object visible, set the object's visible state to true:

```
Variable.Visible = True
```

Similarly, you can hide the object by setting the visible state to **False**.

Closing the Application Object

After you are finished with the application object, you should close it to free up system resources. To close an application object, proceed as follows:

```
Variable.Quit
```

If an application object is not closed properly, that application will remain in memory regardless of its visibility or use. You should leave objects open only if you plan to use them at a later moment, such as using Microsoft Outlook to send admin alerts.

ScriptIt vs. AutoIt

Unfortunately, not everything you want to script has an automation object. In Chapter 2, you learned how to script installations using Microsoft ScriptIt. Microsoft ScriptIt is a utility that reads a script file of simple text commands to send keys to the currently active window. AutoIt is an application you can use in place of Microsoft ScriptIt to create more powerful scripts.

Limitations of Microsoft ScriptIt

Microsoft ScriptIt is an 808KB utility that does nothing more than send keys to active windows. It is not a scripting language and does not contain scripting statements such as **IF** or **GOTO**. ScriptIt does not have the capabilities to move windows, send mouse clicks, edit INI files or the registry, display messages, accept user input, and more. On top of all that, Microsoft does not provide any support or updates for Microsoft ScriptIt.

AutoIt to the Rescue!

AutoIt is a 59K free automation tool available from HiddenSoft (**www.hiddensoft.com/autoit**) that picks up where ScriptIt left off. In addition to providing all the functionality of ScripIt, AutoIt adds some of the following features:

- Access to the clipboard
- Built-in variables to determine the OS, date, and script information
- The capability to script the following actions:
  - Disable mouse and keyboard input
  - Display message boxes and accept user input
  - Manipulate DOS variables
  - Manipulate text and INI files
  - Manipulate the registry
  - Move and manipulate windows
  - Move the mouse pointer and perform mouse clicks
  - Send ASCII characters
  - Send key commands such as PrintScreen, Break, and the Windows key
  - Shut down Windows and force window closes
- Silent usage option
- Subroutines, looping, and conditional statements

NOTE: *For more information and details on usage, see the AutoIt documentation included in the program install.*

Convert Script Files to EXEs

Included in the AutoIt installation package is a utility called AUT2.EXE to convert AutoIt script files into standalone executables. By converting your scripts, you can prevent users from reading your code and modifying your scripts. The conversion utility is menu-based and allows you to set your own executable icon, provided that it is 32 by 32 pixels in 16 colors.

Scripting the AutoIt ActiveX Control

You can use the scriptable ActiveX control version of AutoIt with Windows Script Host. To gain access to the AutoIt object, you must first use the **CreateObject** function and set it to a variable:

```
Set variable = CreateObject("AutoItX.Control")
```

NOTE: *For more information and details on usage, see the AutoIt ActiveX control documentation included in the program install.*

Immediate Solutions

Automating Applications from the Command Line

Most Windows applications support some level of shell scripting. This was originally intended for backward compatibility with DOS batch files, but is slowly dying with the birth of automation objects. Controlling applications from the command line is extremely useful when you need to perform simple tasks from within DOS batch files or Windows shortcuts.

Scripting Windows 9*x* Scandisk

Microsoft 9*x* includes a Scandisk utility based on Norton Disk Doctor. This utility checks for and repairs disk errors, usually caused by Windows lockups or incorrect shutdowns. The Windows graphical interface for Scandisk is SCANDSKW.EXE, which calls DISK-MAINT.DLL to run the scans. SCANDSKW.EXE supports the following command-line options:

- **/ALLFIXEDDISKS**—Scans all local drives
- **/NONINTERACTIVE**—Starts scan automatically
- **/OLDNFS**—Removes long file names
- **/PREVIEW**—Runs Scandisk in preview mode
- **/SILENT**—Does not display summary screens

Scripting a Windows 9x System Scan

To automate a Scandisk scan of all system drives, select Start|Run and enter the following:

```
SCANDSKW /ALLFIXEDDISKS /NONINTERACTIVE /SILENT
```

TIP: *To automate a Scandisk of a single drive, enter "scandskw drive /NONINTERACTIVE". Here, **drive** is the drive to be scanned.*

Using SCANDSKW.EXE to Convert Long File Names to Short

To convert long file names to short file names, select Start|Run and enter the following:

```
SCANDSKW /OLDNFS
```

WARNING! *This conversion is irreversible and is not recommended on system drives.*

Scripting Windows 9*x* Defrag

When a file or folder is created or modified, pieces of that file or folder are scattered throughout the hard disk. This is known as disk fragmentation. Although this behavior occurs naturally, fragmentation does slow down data access time. Reorganizing these files or folders contiguously improves performance and is known as defragmentation. Microsoft 9*x* includes a scriptable defragmentation utility based on Norton Speed Disk. The command-line options are:

- **/ALL**—Defrags all local drives
- **/CONCISE**—Displays the Hide Details view
- **/DETAILED**—Displays the Show Details view
- ***drive*:**—Drive to be defragged
- **/F**—Defrags files and free space
- **/NOPROMPT**—Unattended mode (no prompts)
- **/P**—Optimizes system and hidden files
- **/Q**—Defrags free space only
- **/U**—Defrags files only

Scripting a Windows 9x System Defrag

The following command automatically defrags all system drives:

```
DEFRAG /ALL /P /CONCISE /NOPROMPT
```

Scripting Norton Antivirus 2000

Although Norton Antivirus 2000 is a Windows graphical antivirus scanner, it does provide support for being scripted from the command line. The basic syntax for command-line scripting is as follows:

```
NAVW32.EXE path options
```

Here, ***path*** is any drive, folder, file, or combination of these to be scanned; and ***options*** are any valid command-line switches passed to NAVW32.EXE. Here is a list of the available switches:

- **/A**—Scan all drives except drives A and B. Network drives will be scanned if the Allow Network Scanning option is selected.

- **/L**—Scan all local drives except drives A and B.

- **/S**—Scan all subfolders specified in the path.

- **/M*option***—Enable or disable memory scanning. Here, ***option*** is + for enabling, and - for disabling.

- **/MEM**—Scan only memory.

- **/B*option***—Enable or disable boot sector scanning. Here, ***option*** is + for enabling, and - for disabling.

- **/BOOT**—Scan only boot sectors.

- **/NORESULTS**—Do not display scan results.

- **/DEFAULT**—Reset settings to default.

- **/HEUR:*option***—Sets the heuristic scanning sensitivity. Here, ***option*** can be values 0–4 where 4 is the highest and 0 is disabled.

Scripting FTP

FTP (File Transfer Protocol) is a common method for transferring files between two locations. Although you could use a third-party FTP client (such as CuteFTP), Microsoft FTP is a more than adequate file transfer tool that supports command-line switches, commands, and script files. FTP command line switches control how the FTP client starts. The most common command line switches are:

- **-i**—Interactive mode, turns off interactive prompting during multiple file transfers

- **-n**—Prevents automatic logon

- **-s: *script***—Specifies an FTP ***script*** to run

- **-v**—Verbose mode, turns on transfer data statistics and responses

To start an FTP client in verbose and interactive more, start a command prompt and enter the following:

```
ftp -v -i
```

Once the FTP client is active, you can enter various commands to list, delete, put, retrieve and files. The most common FTP commands are:

- **ascii**—Selected by default, sets the file transfer type to ASCII (shar, uu)

- **binary**—Sets the file transfer site to binary (z, arc, tar, zip)

- **bye**—Terminates the current FTP session and exits the FTP program

- **cd** *directory*—Changes the *directory* on the remote system

- **close**—Terminates the current FTP session

- **delete** *file*—Deletes a remote *file*

- **get** *file*—Retrieves a single *file* from the remote system

- **lcd** *directory*—Changes the *directory* on the local system

- **mdelete** *files*—Deletes remote *files*

- **mget** *files*—Retrieves multiple *files* from the remote system

- **mput** *files*—Uploads local *files* to a remote system

- **open** *host*—Establishes a connection to the *host* name specified

- **password** *password*—Specifies the *password* for the account name specified

- **prompt**—Toggles interactive prompting

- **put** *file*—Uploads a local *file* to a remote system

- **user** *name*—Specifies the account *name* to connect to the remote system

---

TIP: *To see the available FTP switches, enter "FTP -?" at the command line.*

Scripting an FTP Upload

A common administrative task is uploading daily files to an FTP server. To script an FTP upload, select Start|Run and enter "FTP -I -S:*scriptfile*".

Here, **-I** turns off prompting during multiple file copies; **-S:** specifies a script file to use; and ***scriptfile*** is the full path and file name of a script file that contains the following:

```
OPEN ftpserver
Username
Password
```

```
CD ftpdirectory
LCD filedirectory
MPUT files
BYE
```

Here, ***ftpserver*** is the server to connect to; ***username*** and ***password*** are the logon credentials; ***ftpdirectory*** is the directory to upload the files to on the FTP server; ***filedirectory*** is the local directory where the files reside; and ***files*** are the multiple files to upload (such as ***.***, ***.txt, daily.***).

---

*TIP: To upload a single file, change the **MPUT** command to **PUT**.*

Scripting an FTP Download

A common administrative task is downloading files from an FTP server. To script an FTP download, select Start|Run and enter "FTP -I -S:*scriptfile*".

Here, **-I** turns off prompting during multiple file copies; **-S:** specifies a script file to use; and ***scriptfile*** is the full path and file name of a script file that contains the following:

```
OPEN ftpserver
Username
Password
CD ftpdirectory
LCD filedirectory
MGET *.*
BYE
```

Here, ***ftpserver*** is the server to connect to; ***username*** and ***password*** are the logon credentials; ***ftpdirectory*** is the directory to download files from an FTP server; and ***filedirectory*** is the local directory where the files reside.

Scripting an FTP Download of Norton Antivirus Update Files

Many administrators maintain a share that stores the latest version of antivirus updates and then point their user's antivirus program to the share. This ensures that the administrator can first test the update, as opposed to simply directing the user's antivirus to the vendor. To download Norton antivirus update files to a central share using FTP and shell scripting, proceed as follows:

1. Create a new directory to store all files included in this example.
2. Select Start|Run and enter "*scriptfile*.bat".

Here, **scriptfile** is the full path and file name of a script file that contains the following:

```
@Echo Off
Net Use Z: \\server\share
ftp -n -s:ftpscript >> logfile
Net Use Z: /Delete
```

Here, **server** is the system containing the network share to store the antivirus update files; **logfile** is the full path and file name of a text file to log the FTP transfer, and **ftpscript** is the full path and file name of a script file containing the following:

```
open ftp.symantec.com
user anonymous
youremail@yourdomain.com
lcd Z:\
cd \public\english_us_Canada\antivirus_definitions\
norton_antivirus\static
bin
get sarci32.exe
bye
```

NOTE: *The highlighted code above must be entered on one line.*

Scripting an FTP Download of McAfee Antivirus Update Files

To download McAfee antivirus update files to a central share using FTP and shell scripting, proceed as follows:

1. Create a new directory to store all files included in this example.
2. Select Start|Run and enter "*scriptfile*.bat".

Here, **scriptfile** is the full path and file name of a script file that contains the following:

```
@Echo Off
Net Use Z: \\server\share
ftp -n -s:ftpscript >> logfile
Net Use Z: /Delete
```

Here, *server* is the system containing the network share to store the antivirus update files; *logfile* is the full path and file name of a text file to log the FTP transfer, and *ftpscript* is the full path and file name of a script file containing the following:

```
open ftp.nai.com
user anonymous
youremail@yourdomain.com
lcd Z:\dats
cd \pub\antivirus\datfiles\4.x
prompt
bin
mget *
bye
```

NOTE: *The script above obtains antivirus updates for McAfee VirusScan 4.x. You can change the highlighted code above to obtain updates for your specific version.*

Scripting Control Panel Applets

CONTROL.EXE, located in your Windows directory, is essentially the Windows Control Panel. To open the Control Panel, select Start|Run and enter "control". Using this executable, you can start any Control Panel applet.

Control Panel applets are stored as CPL (Control Panel) files. To call an applet, select Start|Run and enter "control *applet*". One CPL file can actually store multiple applets. To call various applets within one CPL file, select Start|Run and enter "control *applet*, @#". Here, **#** is the number of the applet to call. If you do not specify an applet number, CONTROL.EXE will automatically open the first one (0).

For applets that contain multiple tabs, you can open the exact tab you want by selecting Start|Run and entering "control *applet*, , #". Here, **#** is the number of the tab to open. If you do not specify a tab number, CONTROL.EXE will automatically open the first one (0).

So, what's the big deal about starting a Control Panel applet? After you start an applet, you can use a send-keys utility to perform the task you want.

NOTE: *To find all the applets and functions on your system, search for CPL files and experiment opening the different applets and tabs.*

Modifying Mouse Properties

Here is a quick example to show the use of scripting Control Panel applets combined with using send-keys. To change a mouse to use left-handed button properties, proceed as follows:

1. Create a new directory to store all files included in this example.

2. Download and extract Microsoft ScriptIt, from **www.microsoft.com**, to the new directory.

3. Select Start|Run and enter *"new directory path\scriptit scriptfile"*.

Here, ***new directory path*** is the complete path of the new folder created in step 1, and ***scriptfile*** is a text file that contains the following:

```
[SCRIPT]
RUN=CONTROL MOUSE.CPL
Mouse=~WINWAITACTIVE#!L{ENTER}
```

Scripting Wizards and Dialog Boxes

RUNDLL32.EXE is a 32-bit command-line utility that allows you to call functions from DLL files designed to accept calls from it. You can incorporate these calls in your scripts and combine them with send-keys to complete specific tasks. Table 4.1 shows the most common RUNDLL32 calls.

Automating Applications through an Application Object

Most new applications include a scriptable automation object model, allowing user and other applications to script them.

Using Microsoft Internet Explorer as a Display Tool

Other than dialog boxes and a DOS window, Windows Script Host really doesn't have a method to display output to the user. You can use Microsoft Internet Explorer to display information to the user or

Table 4.1   Wizards and dialog boxes.

Task	RUNDLL32 calls
Add new printer	RUNDLL32.EXE SHELL32.DLL, SHHelpShortcuts_RunDLL AddPrinter
Cascade windows	RUNDLL32.EXE USER.DLL,cascadechildwindows
Copy a floppy disk	RUNDLL32.EXE DISKCOPY.DLL,DiskCopyRunDll
Create new briefcase	RUNDLL32.EXE SYNCUI.DLL,Briefcase_Create
Create new dialup connection	RUNDLL32.EXE RNAUI.DLL,RnaWizard @1
Create new share	RUNDLL32.EXE NTLANUI.DLL,ShareCreate
Disable keyboard	RUNDLL32.EXE KEYBOARD,disable
Disable mouse	RUNDLL32.EXE MOUSE,disable
Disconnect network drive	RUNDLL32.EXE USER.DLL,wnetdisconnectdialog
Format a disk	RUNDLL32.EXE SHELL32.DLL,SHFormatDrive
Install new modem	RUNDLL32.EXE SHELL32.DLL,Control_RunDLL modem.cpl, ,add
Logoff Windows	RUNDLL32.EXE SHELL32.DLL,SHExitWindowsEx 0
Manage a share	RUNDLL32.EXE NTLANUI.DLL,ShareManage
Map network drive	RUNDLL32.EXE USER.DLL,wnetconnectdialog
Open fonts folder	RUNDLL32.EXE SHELL32.DLL, SHHelpShortcuts_RunDLL FontsFolder
Open printers folder	RUNDLL32.EXE SHELL32.DLL, SHHelpShortcuts_RunDLL PrintersFolder
Open with …	RUNDLL32.EXE SHELL32.DLL,OpenAs_RunDLL *extension*
Print Test Page	RUNDLL32.EXE SHELL32.DLL, SHHelpShortcuts_RunDLL PrintTestPage
Reboot	RUNDLL32.EXE SHELL32.DLL,SHExitWindowsEx 2
Refresh	RUNDLL32.EXE USER.DLL,repaintscreen
Shut down Windows	RUNDLL32.EXE USER.DLL,ExitWindows
Shut down Windows	RUNDLL32.EXE SHELL32.DLL,SHExitWindowsEx 1
Shut down Windows (Force)	RUNDLL32.EXE KRNL386.EXE,exitkernel
Swap mouse buttons	RUNDLL32.EXE USER.DLL,swapmousebutton
Tile windows	RUNDLL32.EXE USER.DLL,tilechildwindows

4. Automating Windows and Applications

to generate HTML documents. To display the contents of C:\TEMP in Microsoft Internet Explorer, proceed as follows:

1. Create a new directory to store all files included in this example.

2. Download and install the latest version of Windows Script Host, from **www.microsoft.com**, to the new directory.

3. Select Start|Run and enter "cscript *scriptfile*.vbs".

Here, **scriptfile** is the full path and file name of a script file that contains the following:

```
Set FSO = CreateObject("Scripting.FileSystemObject")
Set MSIE = CreateObject("InternetExplorer.Application")
sDIR = "C:\TEMP"
sTITLE = "Generating Directory List ..."

Set objDIR = GetFolder(sDIR)
SetupMSIE
MSIE.Document.Write "<HTML><TITLE>" & sTitle & _
  "</TITLE><BODY bgcolor=#C0C0C0><FONT FACE=ARIAL>"
MSIE.Document.Write "<B>Displaying the contents of " & _
  sDIR & ":</B><BR><BR><table border=0 width=100% " & _
  "cellspacing=0 cellpadding=0>"
GoSubFolders objDIR
MSIE.Document.Write "</table><BR><B>End of List</B>" & _
  "</FONT></BODY>"

Sub SetupMSIE
  MSIE.Navigate "About:Blank"
  MSIE.ToolBar = False
  MSIE.StatusBar = False
  MSIE.Resizable = False

  Do
  Loop While MSIE.Busy

  SWidth = MSIE.Document.ParentWindow.Screen.AvailWidth
  SHeight = MSIE.Document.ParentWindow.Screen.AvailHeight
  MSIE.Width = SWidth/2
  MSIE.Height = SHeight/2
  MSIE.Left = (SWidth - MSIE.Width)/2
  MSIE.Top = (SHeight - MSIE.Height)/2

  MSIE.Visible = True
End Sub
```

```
Sub ListFiles (objDIR)
    For Each efile in objDIR.Files
        MSIE.Document.Write "<tr><td>" & efile & "</td>" & _
            "<td> </td><td align=right>" & efile.size & _
            "</td></tr>"
    Next
End Sub

Sub GoSubFolders (objDIR)
  If objDIR <> "\System Volume Information" Then
    ListFiles objDIR
    For Each eFolder in objDIR.SubFolders
        MSIE.Document.Write "<tr><td>" & _
            efolder & "</td><td>&lt;DIR&gt;</td><td " & _
            "align=right>" & efolder.size & "</td></tr>"
        GoSubFolders eFolder
    Next
  End If
End Sub
```

NOTE: *You need to append the **GetFolder** routine, listed earlier in Chapter 3, to this script in order for it to run. In this example, the window will not be updated until the directory listing is complete.*

Creating Detailed Reports in Microsoft Word

You can script Microsoft Word to create logs and reports through Windows Script Host. To delete all temp files from your system and record the actions in a Microsoft Word document, proceed as follows:

1. Create a new directory to store all files included in this example.

2. Download and install the latest version of Windows Script Host, from **www.microsoft.com**, to the new directory.

3. Select Start|Run and enter "cscript *scriptfile*.vbs".

Here, ***scriptfile*** is the full path and file name of a script file that contains the following:

```
Set FSO = CreateObject("Scripting.FileSystemObject")
Set WordApp = CreateObject("Word.Application")
sDIR = "C:\"
sEXT = "TMP"
sTITLE = "Deleting Files"
```

```
WordApp.Documents.Add
WordApp.Visible = True
WordApp.Caption = sTITLE
WordApp.Selection.Font.Bold = True
WordApp.Selection.TypeText "Deletion Log:" & sEXT & _
   " Files: "
WordApp.Selection.InsertDateTime
WordApp.Selection.Font.Bold = False
WordApp.Selection.TypeText vblf & vblf

Set objDIR = GetFolder(sDIR)
GoSubFolders objDIR
WordApp.Selection.Font.Bold = True
WordApp.Selection.TypeText vblf & "**END OF LOG**"

Sub MainSub (objDIR)
  For Each efile in objDIR.Files
    fEXT = FSO.GetExtensionName(efile.Path)
    If LCase(fEXT) = LCase(sEXT) Then
      DelFile efile
    End If
  Next
End Sub

Sub DelFile(sFILE)
  On Error Resume Next
  FSO.DeleteFile sFILE, True
  If Err.Number <> 0 Then
    WordApp.Selection.TypeText "Error deleting: " & _
      sFILE & vblf
  Else
    WordApp.Selection.TypeText "Deleted: " & sFILE & vblf
  End If
End Sub
```

4. Automating Windows and Applications

NOTE: *You need to append the **GetFolder** routine, listed in Chapter 3, to this script in order for it to run.*

Creating Detailed Spreadsheets in Microsoft Excel

You can script Microsoft Excel to create spreadsheets through Windows Script Host. To delete all temp files from your system and record the actions in a Microsoft Excel spreadsheet, proceed as follows:

1. Create a new directory to store all files included in this example.

2. Download and install the latest version of Windows Script Host, from **www.microsoft.com**, to the new directory.

3. Select Start|Run and enter "cscript *scriptfile*.vbs".

Here, **scriptfile** is the full path and file name of a script file that contains the following:

```
Set FSO = CreateObject("Scripting.FileSystemObject")
Set ExcelApp = CreateObject("Excel.Application")
Row = 1
Column = 1
ExcelApp.Workbooks.Add
ExcelApp.Visible = True

sDIR = "C:\"
sEXT = "TMP"
sTITLE = "Deleting Files"

ExcelApp.caption = sTITLE
ExcelApp.Range("A1").Select
ExcelApp.Selection.Font.Bold = True
ExcelApp.Cells(Row,Column).Value = "Deletion Log:" & sEXT & _
  " Files"
Row = Row + 1
Set objDIR = GetFolder(sDIR)
GoSubFolders objDIR
ExcelApp.Selection.Font.Bold = True
Row = Row + 1
ExcelApp.Cells(Row,Column).Value = "**END OF LOG**"

Sub MainSub (objDIR)
  For Each efile in objDIR.Files
    fEXT = FSO.GetExtensionName(efile.Path)
    If LCase(fEXT) = LCase(sEXT) Then
      DelFile efile
    End If
  Next
End Sub

Sub GoSubFolders (objDIR)
  If objDIR <> "\System Volume Information" Then
    MainSub objDIR
    For Each eFolder in objDIR.SubFolders
      GoSubFolders eFolder
```

```
      Next
    End If
  End Sub

  Sub DelFile(sFILE)
    On Error Resume Next
    FSO.DeleteFile sFILE, True
    If Err.Number <> 0 Then
      ExcelApp.Cells(Row,Column).Value = "Error deleting: " & _
        sFILE
    Else
      ExcelApp.Cells(Row,Column).Value = "Deleted: " & sFILE
    End If
    Row = Row + 1
  End Sub
```

NOTE: *You need to append the **GetFolder** routine, listed in Chapter 3, to this script in order for it to run.*

Scripting the Windows Shell

Windows has its own automation object called **shell.automation**. Although you might assume that you can completely automate every Windows function, in reality you can control only a limited set of objects available to scripting. To access the Windows shell, you must instantiate the shell object as follows:

```
Set variable = CreateObject("Shell.Application")
```

Controlling System Windows

When an item is opened in Microsoft Windows, it is opened in a system window. The standard window controls include minimize and maximize functions. You can script these Windows commands and more through the Windows shell object. The following is a list of the window objects and their functions:

- **CascadeWindows**—Cascade open windows

- **MinimizeAll**—Minimize open windows

- **TileHorizontally**—Tile open windows horizontally

- **TileVertically**—Tile open windows vertically

- **UndoMinimizeAll**—Restore minimized windows

To call any of these methods, proceed as follows:

```
Set Shell = CreateObject("Shell.Application")Shell.Method
```

Browsing for Folders

Using the **BrowseForFolder** method, you can incorporate the common Browse For Folder Windows dialog box used in most Windows applications. To call the dialog box, proceed as follows:

1. Create a new directory to store all files included in this example.

2. Download and install the latest version of Windows Script Host, from **www.microsoft.com**, to the new directory.

3. Select Start|Run and enter "cscript *scriptfile*".

Here, *scriptfile* is the full path and file name of a script file that contains the following:

```
Set Shell = CreateObject("Shell.Application")
Set Folder = Shell.BrowseForFolder (handle, "Title", options,
RootFolder)
Wscript.Echo "FOLDER: " & Folder.Title & vblf & _
     "PARENT: " & Folder.ParentFolder
```

Here, ***RootFolder*** can be a directory path or a special folder constant.

Table 4.2 lists the special folder constants.

Table 4.2   Special folder constants.

Constant	Folder or directory path
&H0	All Users Desktop
&H2	All Users Program folder
&H3	Control Panel
&H4	Printers Folder
&H5	Personal Folder
&H6	Favorites Folder
&H7	Startup Folder
&H8	Recent Folder
&H9	SendTo Folder
&Ha	Recycle Bin
&Hb	Start Menu

(continued)

4. Automating Windows and Applications

Table 4.2   Special folder constants *(continued)*.

Constant	Folder or directory path
&H10	Desktop Directory
&H11	Drives (My Computer)
&H12	Network Neighborhood
&H13	Fonts Folder
&H14	Templates Folder
&H15	Common Start Menu
&H16	Common Programs Folder
&H17	Common Programs Folder
&H18	Common Startup Folder
&H19	Common Desktop Directory
&H1a	Application Data Folder
&H1b	PrintHood Folder
&H1c	Local Application Data Folder
&H1d	Alt Startup Folder
&H1e	Common Alt Startup Folder
&H1f	Common Favorites Folder
&H20	Common Internet Cache Folder
&H21	Common Cookies Folder
&H22	History Folder
&H23	Common Application Data Folder
&H24	Windows Folder
&H25	System Folder
&H26	Program Files Folder
&H27	My Pictures Folder
&H28	Profile Folder

Running a Control Panel Applet

The Control Panel contains various applets you can use to perform various tasks. These applets have .cpl extensions and reside in your system directory. To call a Control Panel applet through the shell automation object, proceed as follows:

```
Set Shell = CreateObject("Shell.Application")
Shell.ControlPanelItem "applet.cpl"
```

Ejecting a PC
To undock a notebook through the shell automation object, proceed as follows:

```
Set Shell = CreateObject("Shell.Application")
Shell.EjectPC
```

Exploring a Folder
To explore a folder through the shell automation object, proceed as follows:

```
Set Shell = CreateObject("Shell.Application")
Shell.Explore RootFolder
```

Here, ***RootFolder*** can be a directory path or a special folder constant.

Opening a Folder
To open a folder through the shell automation object, proceed as follows:

```
Set Shell = CreateObject("Shell.Application")
Shell.Open RootFolder
```

Here, ***RootFolder*** can be a directory path or a special folder constant.

Calling System Dialog Boxes
System dialog boxes are windows that require user input, such as the Find Files or Run dialog box. You can call one of these dialog boxes within your script, and combine it with send-keys to perform regular user tasks. To call a system dialog box through the shell automation object, proceed as follows:

```
Set Shell = CreateObject("Shell.Application")
Shell.SysDialog
```

Here, **SysDialog** consists of the following methods:

- **FileRun**—Calls the Start|Run dialog box
- **FindComputer**—Calls the Start|Find/Search|Computer dialog box
- **FindFiles**—Calls the Start|Find/Search|File or Folders dialog box

- **SetTime**—Calls the Date/Time dialog box
- **ShutdownWindows**—Calls the Start|Shutdown dialog box
- **TrayProperties**—Calls the Tray Properties dialog box

Refreshing the Start Menu

To refresh the contents of the Start menu, proceed as follows:

```
Set Shell = CreateObject("Shell.Application")
Shell.RefreshMenu
```

Suspending a Computer

Most laptops have a feature called suspend, used to place the computer in lower power mode when not in use. To suspend a computer through the shell automation object, proceed as follows:

```
Set Shell = CreateObject("Shell.Application")
Shell.Suspend
```

Connecting to a Folder Name Space

In Chapter 2, you learned how to connect to a folder using the **GetFolder FileSystemObject** method. To connect to a folder through shell automation, use the **NameSpace** method and proceed as follows:

```
Set Shell = CreateObject("Shell.Application")
Set Folder = Shell.NameSpace(RootFolder)
```

Getting File or Folder Details

Although Windows NT/9x simply stores basic file and folder information, Windows 2000 stores many more pieces of information. You can use the folder object's **GetDetailsOf** method on either operating system to obtain information about the file or folder specified. To connect to a folder through shell automation, use the **NameSpace** method and proceed as follows:

```
Set Shell = CreateObject("Shell.Application")
Set Folder = Shell.NameSpace(RootFolder)
For Each Item in Folder.Items
  Summary = "Name: " & Item.Name & vblf
  For Count = 1 to 37
    On Error Resume Next
    Detail = Folder.GetDetailsOf(Item,Count)
    If Detail <> "" Then
      Summary = Summary & Folder.GetDetailsOf(0,Count) & _
              ": " & Folder.GetDetailsOf(Item,Count) & vblf
```

```
    End If
  Next
  Wscript.Echo Summary
Next
```

Here, *RootFolder* can be a directory path or a special folder constant. The output of the script may appear similar to Figure 4.2.

Copying and Moving Files and Folders

Whenever you copy or move a file in Windows, graphical dialog boxes appear displaying progress meters and confirmation windows (see Figure 4.3).

Although the **FileSystemObject** can perform file management operations, it does not display any of these dialog boxes. To use these dialog boxes in your scripts, you can use the shell automation object. To copy or move files and folders to another folder, proceed as follows:

```
Set Shell = CreateObject("Shell.Application")
Set Folder = Shell.NameSpace(RootFolder)
Folder.Method "Files", Flags
```

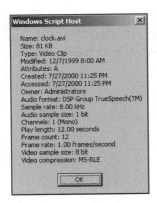

Figure 4.2 **GetDetailsOf** file and folder output.

Figure 4.3 Windows file operating dialog box.

Here, **RootFolder** can be a directory path or a special folder constant; **Method** is the **CopyHere** or **MoveHere** folder method; **Files** are the files or folders to copy or move; and **Flags** are the optional parameters that control the file operation. You can concatenate multiple parameters using the + character.

NOTE: You can use the FOF_SILENT flag to suppress the progress dialog box. For more information on the file operation flags, search Microsoft's Web site for SHFILEOPSTRUCT.

Accessing the Context Menu

Every time you right-click on a file (on a right-handed mouse), you call the context menu. This menu is full of tasks added to the menu by the system, the media, and any programs you may have installed (see Figure 4.4).

You can access these tasks by clicking on them or entering the quick key combination (ALT+the underlined letter). Through shell automation, you activate any of these tasks:

```
Set Shell = CreateObject("Shell.Application")
Set Folder = Shell.NameSpace("RootFolder")
Set File = Folder.ParseName("File")
File.InvokeVerb("Task")
```

Here, **RootFolder** can be a directory path or a special folder constant; **File** is any file within the **RootFolder**; and **Task** is any task listed in the context menu.

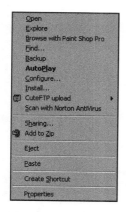

Figure 4.4   Windows context menu.

There are two important things to note about the InvokeVerb **Task**. The first is that if the task contains a quick key, you must precede that letter with an ampersand (&). For example, to run the Open task for Figure 4.4, you would enter "&Open". The second is that if the command pulls up a system window (such as a properties window), that window will close as soon as the script ends.

Automating Applications through Send-Keys

Some applications have been specifically designed without command-line options or automation object models. Without a scriptable back door to send commands to, another alternative to scripting the unscriptable is by using send-keys.

Scripting a Diskeeper Lite Drive Defrag

When Diskeeper Lite detects any attempt to be scripted (running from a batch file or called directly in a script), the program immediately shuts down. An alternative method to scripting Diskeeper Lite is using send-keys. When you use send-keys, the application thinks the user, and not a script, is performing these commands. To automate a drive defrag with Diskeeper Lite, proceed as follows:

1. Create a new directory to store all files included in this example.
2. Download and install Diskeeper Lite 1.1 (see Chapter 2 for details).
3. Download and install AutoIt, from **www.hiddensoft.com/ autoit**.
4. Select Start|Run and enter "*autoit2 scriptfile*".

Here, *autoit2* is the complete path and name of the autoit executable, and *scriptfile* is a text file that contains the following:

```
SEND, {LWIN}R
SEND, "installdir"{ENTER}
WINWAITACTIVE, Diskeeper Lite+Tree View+Fragmented Files
SEND, {ALTDOWN}D{ALTUP}D
WINWAITACTIVE, Select Drive To Defragment
SEND, {ALTDOWN}O
WINWAITACTIVE, Defragmentation Completed
SEND, {ALTDOWN}O
```

```
WINWAITACTIVE, Diskeeper Lite+Tree View+Fragmented Files
SEND, {ALTDOWN}F{ALTUP}X
```

Here, ***installdir*** is the install directory for Diskeeper Lite.

NOTE: *Notice that we did not run DKLITE.EXE directly, but instead ran it through the Windows RUN command.*

Scripting a Windows 2000 Drive Defrag

Windows 2000 includes a special, slimmed-down version of Executive Software's Diskeeper, made specifically for Windows 2000. Like Diskeeper Lite, the Windows 2000 defrag utility does not include the scripting or scheduling capability of the full version. To script a Windows 2000 drive defrag, proceed as follows:

1. Download and install AutoIt, from **www.hiddensoft.com/autoit**.

2. Select Start|Run and enter *"autoit2 scriptfile"*.

Here, ***autoit2*** is the complete path and name of the autoit executable, and ***scriptfile*** is a text file that contains the following:

```
Run, defragmmc
Winwaitactive, Disk Defrag
Send, {ALTDOWN}A{ALTUP}D
Winwaitactive, Defragmentation Complete
Send, {TAB}{ENTER}
Winwaitactive, Disk Defrag
Send, {ALTDOWN}{F4}{ALTUP}
```

Here, ***defragmmc*** is the full path to DFRG.MSC, usually found in the Winnt\system32 directory.

Changing Internet Explorer's Default Start Page

To change the default start page for Internet Explorer, proceed as follows:

1. Download and install AutoIt, from **www.hiddensoft.com/autoit**.

2. Select Start|Run and enter *"autoit2 scriptfile"*.

Here, ***autoit2*** is the complete path and name of the autoit executable, and ***scriptfile*** is a text file that contains the following:

```
Run, control.exe inetcpl.cpl
WinWaitActive, Internet Properties
Send, http://www.jesseweb.com{Enter}
```

Changing Network Identification Settings (Windows 9*x* Only)

To change the network identification settings in Windows 9*x*, proceed as follows:

1. Download and install AutoIt, from **www.hiddensoft.com/autoit**.

2. Select Start|Run and enter "*autoit2 scriptfile*".

Here, *autoit2* is the complete path and name of the autoit executable, and *scriptfile* is a text file that contains the following:

```
Run, control.exe netcpl.cpl
WinWaitActive, Network
Send, {Ctrldown}{Tab}{Ctrlup}
Send, NewComputerName{Tab}
Send, NewWorkGroup{Tab}
Send, NewDescription{Enter}
```

Browsing the Internet

Whether you have an Internet provider that consistently disconnects you or a program that feeds off active Internet connections, you may need to have continually active Internet activity. To repeatably browse Internet sites, proceed as follows:

1. Download and install AutoIt, from **www.hiddensoft.com/autoit**.

2. Select Start|Run and enter "*autoit2 scriptfile*".

Here, *autoit2* is the complete path and name of the autoit executable, and *scriptfile* is a text file that contains the following:

```
SetTitleMatchMode, 2
Run, C:\\Program Files\\Internet Explorer\\Iexplore.exe
WinWaitActive, Microsoft Internet Explorer
Repeat
  Send, {ALTDOWN}D{ALTUP}www.jesseweb.com{Enter}
    Sleep, 10000
  Send, {ALTDOWN}D{ALTUP}www.fightclub.com{Enter}
    Sleep, 10000
  Send, {ALTDOWN}D{ALTUP}www.tylerandjacks.com{Enter}
    Sleep, 10000
  Send, {ALTDOWN}D{ALTUP}www.napster.com{Enter}
    Sleep, 10000
  Send, {ALTDOWN}D{ALTUP}www.audiofind.com{Enter}
    Sleep, 10000
EndRepeat
```

4. Automating Windows and Applications

Clearing the Microsoft Internet Explorer Cache

Internet Explorer caches Web pages and previously entered usernames, passwords, and form entries. To delete these items using the
AutoIt ActiveX control, proceed as follows:

1. Download and install AutoIt, from **www.hiddensoft.com/autoit**.

2. Select Start|Run and enter "cscript *scriptfile*.vbs".

Here, *scriptfile* is a text file that contains the following:

```
Set Shell = WScript.CreateObject("WScript.Shell")
Set AIT = WScript.CreateObject("AutoItX.Control")

Shell.Run "control.exe inetcpl.cpl", 1, FALSE
AIT .WinWaitActive "Internet Properties", ""
AIT .Send "{ALTDOWN}F{ALTUP}"
AIT .WinWaitActive "Delete Files", ""
AIT .Send "{TAB}{ENTER}"
AIT .WinWaitActive "Internet Properties", ""
AIT .WinClose "Internet Properties", ""

Shell.Run "control.exe inetcpl.cpl, ,2", 1, FALSE
AIT .WinWaitActive "Internet Properties", ""
AIT .Send "{ALTDOWN}U{ALTUP}"
AIT .WinWaitActive "AutoComplete Settings", ""
AIT .Send "{ALTDOWN}C{ALTUP}"
AIT .WinWaitActive "Internet Options", ""
AIT .Send "{ENTER}"
AIT .WinWaitActive "AutoComplete Settings", ""
AIT .Send "{ALTDOWN}L{ALTUP}"
AIT .WinWaitActive "Internet Options", ""
AIT .Send "{ENTER}{ESC}"
AIT .WinWaitActive "Internet Properties", "
AIT .Send "{ESC}"

WScript.Quit
```

Chapter 5

Inside the Registry

In Brief

Most administrators go out of their way to avoid working with the registry, and I don't blame them. The registry is one of those aspects of Windows you are constantly being warned not to mess with. With the frequent threats of virtual nuclear destruction combined with the lack of documentation, the registry is a dark and scary place. In this chapter, you will learn the basics of the registry, how to modify it safely, and the hidden tricks and goodies the registry has to offer.

Holy INI Files, Batman!

In the old days of 16-bit Windows, all settings were stored in initialization files. The two main files for storing settings were the SYSTEM.INI and WIN.INI files. As each application was installed, it stored its settings in these two files. Unfortunately, these applications could store only a limited set of entries because of the restrictive 64K size of INI files. To counteract this, application developers started using their own INI files. Although this might have seemed a good idea at first, as the number of applications grew, so did the number of INI files; and as each INI file grew, the system would often slow down.

And Then Came the Registry

The registry was born simultaneously with the birth of Windows NT in 1993 and is the answer to Windows INI files. The registry is a hierarchal, relational database that holds system information, OLE (Object Link Embedding) and Automation information, application settings, operating system configuration data, and more. The information stored includes everything from your display settings to your hardware configuration. To speed access time, the registry is stored in binary format and is composed of multiple files.

Windows 9*x* Registry Files

On Windows 9*x* systems, the registry consists of two hidden files: user.dat and system.dat. These files are stored in the WINDOWS directory. User.dat consists of all individual user-related settings. System.dat consists of settings for the entire machine.

Windows NT/2000 Registry Files

Under Windows NT/2000, user-related settings are stored in a file called ntuser.dat. This file is stored in the user's profile directory located in the *%WINDIR%*\Profiles directory. System settings are stored in the SYSTEM32\CONFIG directory and consist of the following five files:

- *Default* (HKEY_USERS\DEFAULT)—Stores default settings for new users

- *SAM* (HKEY_LOCAL_MACHINE\SAM)—Stores system security information

- *Security* (HKEY_LOCAL_MACHINE\Security)—Stores network security information

- *Software* (HKEY_LOCAL_MACHINE\Software)—Stores specific application and operating system information

- *System* (HKEY_LOCAL_MACHINE\System)—Stores device driver and system information

NOTE: *Windows 9x, NT, and 2000 registries are incompatible with each other. You cannot import a registry file from one operating system to another. Windows 2000 can import Windows NT registry entries.*

The Registry Hierarchy

The registry consists of top-level keys called hives:

- HKEY_CLASSES_ROOT
- HKEY_CURRENT_USER
- HKEY_LOCAL_MACHINE
- HKEY_USERS
- HKEY_CURRENT_CONFIG
- HKEY_DYN_DATA (Windows 9*x* only)

These hives store all the keys (subfolders) that make up the registry. These keys store all the values (entries), which specify all the individual system settings.

HKEY_LOCAL_MACHINE

HKEY_LOCAL_MACHINE (HKLM) stores all software, hardware, network, security, and Windows system information. This hive is the largest registry hive and stores two of the main registry hives.

HKEY_CLASSES_ROOT

HKEY_CLASSES_ROOT (HKCR) is actually a virtual link to HKLM\Software\Classes. This hive stores information about all file extensions, descriptions, icons, associations, shortcuts, automation, class IDs, and more.

HKEY_USERS

HKEY_USERS (HKU) stores information about all users of the system and their individual settings. These individual settings include environment variables, color schemes, fonts, icons, desktop configuration, Start menu items, network, and more. Each time a new user logs on, a new key is created based on a default key.

HKEY_CURRENT_USER

HKEY_CURRENT_USER (HKCU) is actually a link to the currently logged-in user's key stored in HKEY_USERS. This hive is named by the user's SID (Security Identifier) value and not by the user's name. This key is rebuilt each time the system reboots.

HKEY_CURRENT_CONFIG

HKEY_CURRENT_CONFIG (HKCC) is actually a link to the currently selected hardware profile stored in HKEY_LOCAL_MACHINE. Hardware profiles allow you to specify which device drivers are to be loaded for a given Windows session. Hardware profiles are commonly used with laptops to distinguish RAS, network, and local Windows sessions.

HKEY_DYN_DATA

HKEY_DYN_DATA (HKDD) is not permanently stored in the registry, but rather written dynamically when the system boots up. This hive stores information about any plug-and-play devices detected at system bootup.

Registry Data Types

Like any other database, the registry contains various data types to store different types of values. Table 5.1, from *Windows 2000 Registry Little Black Book* (**www.coriolis.com**) lists the various registry data types.

Table 5.1 Registry data types.

Data Type	Raw Type	Function
REG_NONE	Unknown	Encrypted data
REG_SZ	String	Text characters
REG_EXPAND_SZ	String	Text with variables
REG_BINARY	Binary	Binary data
REG_DWORD	Number	Numerical data
REG_DWORD_BIG_ENDIAN	Number	Non-Intel numbers
REG_LINK	String	Path to a file
REG_MULTI_SZ	Multistring	String arrays
REG_RESOURCE_LIST	String	Hardware resource list
REG_FULL_RESOURCE_DESCRIPTOR	String	Hardware resource ID
REG_RESOURCE_REQUIREMENTS_LIST	String	Hardware resource ID

REGEDIT vs. REGEDT32

Because the registry is stored in multiple binary files, it cannot be viewed with a regular text editor. Windows NT/2000 includes two registry editing tools: REGEDIT and REGEDT32. Both of these tools contain various functions, and it's best to know when to use which one.

Using REGEDIT

REGEDIT is the registry-editing tool that comes included in all of Microsoft's 32-bit operating systems. Using this tool, you can add, delete, modify, back up, and restore registry keys and values from a local or remote machine. REGEDIT displays all the registry hives, even the aliased ones (see Figure 5.1). It also has the capability to search for registry keys and values. The most important thing to remember about REGEDIT is that changes happen immediately. There is no Apply, Cancel, or OK button here. The moment you make a change, the change is implemented—so be careful.

TIP: The Windows 2000 version of REGEDIT includes additional features such as a registry Favorites menu and the capability to remember the last key viewed before closing REGEDIT.

5. Inside the Registry

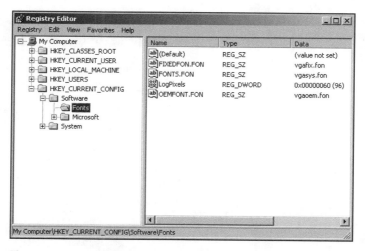

Figure 5.1   The Windows REGEDIT screen.

WARNING! *REGEDIT does not recognize all the registry data types. If you edit an unrecognized data type, it will be converted to a type that REGEDIT can recognize.*

Using REGEDT32

REGEDT32 is a registry-editing tool that comes included in Windows NT/2000 (see Figure 5.2). REGEDT32 displays each hive in a separate window, and only displays the HKEY_LOCAL_MACHINE and

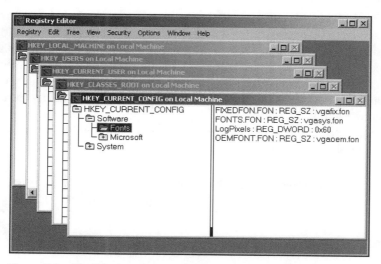

Figure 5.2   The Windows REGEDT32 screen.

HKEY_USERS hives when accessing a registry remotely. REGEDT32 includes all the editing features of REGEDIT, but has only a simple find key function. Unlike REGEDIT, REGEDT32 does not apply changes immediately. It applies changes only as you close the application. Some additional features include auto-refresh, read-only mode, and the ability to set registry permissions.

NOTE: *Although remote registry access through REGEDT32 only displays two hives, from within these two hives you can still access all the aliased hives that REGEDIT normally displays.*

Registry Editing Safety Tips

You've heard it a thousand times, but here it is again: editing the registry is dangerous. An incorrect registry setting can leave your system in shambles (trust me, I know). Here are some helpful registry editing tips:

- Back up the entire registry or key you intend to modify. If your system starts acting up, you'll be glad you did.
- Update your emergency repair disk (ERD) before you make any registry changes. This proves to be a valuable asset if your machine refuses to boot up properly.
- Do not blindly make changes to the registry. Know what your intended registry change does. Research it.
- Make one change at a time. This makes it easier to narrow down the cause of any problems you may have after editing the registry.
- Always use REGEDT32 when you can. REGEDT32 does not apply changes until you exit the application and can work in read-only mode.

Immediate Solutions

Backing Up and Restoring the Registry

Before modifying the registry, you should perform a backup that you can revert to in case of any system failures. Knowing the different methods to back up and restore the entire registry properly can save you hours of unnecessary data recovery and troubleshooting.

Backing Up the Windows 9x Registry

To back up the registry in Windows 9x, you can simply make a copy of the two registry files. Here is a simple batch file to back up the registry:

```
@Echo Off
CLS
ATTRIB -R -H %WINDIR%\USER.DAT
ATTRIB -R -H %WINDIR%\SYSTEM.DAT
COPY %WINDIR%\USER.DAT %WINDIR%\USER.BAK
COPY %WINDIR%\SYSTEM.DAT %WINDIR%\SYSTEM.BAK
ATTRIB +R +H %WINDIR%\USER.DAT
ATTRIB +R +H %WINDIR%\SYSTEM.DAT
```

Restoring the Windows 9x Registry

Here is a simple batch file to restore the registry:

```
@Echo Off
CLS
ATTRIB -R -H %WINDIR%\USER.DAT
ATTRIB -R -H %WINDIR%\SYSTEM.DAT
COPY %WINDIR%\USER.BAK %WINDIR%\USER.DAT
COPY %WINDIR%\SYSTEM.BAK %WINDIR%\SYSTEM.DAT
ATTRIB +R +H %WINDIR%\USER.DAT
ATTRIB +R +H %WINDIR%\SYSTEM.DAT
```

Understanding Windows NT/2000 Registry Backup Misconceptions

Backing up the Windows NT/2000 registry is a tricky subject. Here is a list of some common misconceptions about backing up the Windows NT/2000 registry:

- You can back up the entire registry by simply making a copy of the registry files. Unlike Windows 9*x*, Windows NT/2000 accesses many sections of the registry directly. These files are open, so you cannot back them up because they are already in use.

- You can back up the entire registry by running RDISK /S. The RDISK (Repair Disk) utility backs up important system files and parts of the registry to an ERD (Emergency Repair Disk). This disk is used in conjunction with the setup disks to restore critical parts of the operating system that may be damaged. It cannot and was never intended to be used as a registry backup utility.

- You can use REGEDIT to back up and restore the entire registry. REGEDIT for Windows NT/2000 does not support the same switches as the Windows 9*x* version. Although you may be able to back up the registry manually into one large REG file, you will not be able to restore it. The registry has special security settings on certain keys that prevent restoring or modifying.

WARNING! *The version of RDISK that shipped with Windows NT contains a security hole that allows all users open access to critical system files during the time of their use. The security hole is known as the RDISK registry enumeration file vulnerability. You should download and use the updated version of RDISK from Microsoft.*

Backing Up the Windows NT/2000 Registry

There are two methods to back up the entire Windows NT/2000 registry. The first method is to use the built-in backup utility to perform a complete backup of the registry. This will be discussed in more detail in Chapter 13. The second method is to use a resource kit utility called REGBACK. To perform a complete backup of the registry using REGBACK, proceed as follows:

1. Create a new directory to store all files included in this example.

2. Obtain the latest version of REGBACK.EXE from the resource kit and copy it to the new directory.

3. Select Start|Run and enter *"scriptfile*.bat".

Here, ***scriptfile*** is the full path and file name of a script file that contains the following:

```
@Echo Off
REGBACK C:\REGBACKUP.RBU
if errorlevel 1 echo Error during backup
if errorlevel 0 echo Successfully backed up
```

Restoring the Windows NT/2000 Registry

The resource kit utility REGREST is used to restore registry backups created by REGBACK. To restore a registry backup created by REGBACK, proceed as follows:

1. Create a new directory to store all files included in this example.

2. Obtain the latest version of REGREST.EXE from the resource kit and copy it to the new directory.

3. Select Start|Run and enter "*scriptfile*.bat".

Here, *scriptfile* is the full path and file name of a script file that contains the following:

```
@Echo Off
REGREST C:\REGBACKUP.RBU C:\REGSAVE.RBU
if errorlevel 1 echo Error during restore
if errorlevel 0 echo Successfully restored
```

Here, **C:\REGSAVE.RBU** is an arbitrary name to which your current registry is backed up before restoring your backup.

Modifying the Registry with Shell Scripting

Because shell scripting was created before the birth of the registry, it does not contain any functions to modify the registry. To manipulate the registry through shell scripting, you can use a resource kit utility called REG.EXE. REG.EXE supports the following parameters:

- **Add**—Adds keys or values
- **Backup**—Identical to the Save parameter
- **Compare**—Compares a registry key or value to another or to a string
- **Copy**—Copies a registry key or value from one machine to another
- **Delete**—Deletes keys and values
- **Export**—Saves keys and values to a REG file
- **Find**—Finds and replaces keys or values
- **Import**—Loads registry keys and values from a REG file
- **Load**—Loads hive files to the registry

- **Query**—Displays the contents of keys and values
- **Restore**—Restores registry keys from hive files
- **Save**—Stores registry keys to hive files
- **Unload**—Removes hive files from the registry
- **Update**—Replaces information in a key or value

NOTE: *There is a known bug updating DWORD values using the Windows NT Resource Kit version of REG.EXE. You should obtain the updated version from Microsoft or use the version included in the Windows 2000 Resource Kit. REG.EXE is a registry management tool for Windows NT/2000. This tool will not work properly with Windows 9x.*

Backing Up a Registry Key

To back up a registry key using REG.EXE, start a command prompt and enter the following:

```
REG SAVE key file
```

Here, **key** is the registry key to back up, and **file** is the hive file to back up the registry key.

Restoring a Registry Key

To restore a registry key using REG.EXE, start a command prompt and enter the following:

```
REG LOAD file key
```

Here, **file** is the hive file to restore; and **key** is the registry key to which to restore the hive.

Querying the Registry

To display registry keys or values from the command line using REG.EXE, start a command prompt and enter the following:

```
REG QUERY keyval
```

Here, **keyval** is the registry key or value you want to display. For example, to display the current cursor blink rate, start a command prompt and enter the following:

```
REG QUERY "HKCU\Control Panel\Desktop\CursorBlinkRate"
```

NOTE: *If a registry entry contains a space, you must surround it with quotation marks.*

Searching the Registry

Sometimes the registry stores information you wish it didn't, such as usernames and passwords. You can use the resource kit utility SCANREG.EXE to search the registry for these values. To search the registry for a key containing a specific phrase, proceed as follows:

```
SCANREG string start -k
```

Here, ***string*** is the phrase to search for, and ***start*** is where to start searching in the registry.

Modifying Windows 2000

With the introduction of a new operating system come new features, and with new features come new annoyances. To remove these annoyances, you simply need to make a few registry changes.

Disabling Start Menu Scrolling

When the Windows NT Start menu grows larger than one column, it creates a new column to fit the additional Start menu items. Although Windows 2000 has the capability of organizing the Start menu this way, the default is to not create a new column and simply scroll the original column. This can become quite annoying when you have a large Start menu. To disable the Start menu scrolling using REG.EXE, start a command prompt and enter the following:

```
REG UPDATE HKCU\Software\Microsoft\Windows\CurrentVersion\
Explorer\Advanced\StartMenuScrollPrograms=NO
```

NOTE: *The code above must be placed on one line.*

Disabling Pop-up Descriptions

A new feature in Windows 2000 is the pop-up descriptions that appear when the mouse pointer remains above certain objects for a short period of time. Although initially helpful, these pop-ups quickly become annoying. To disable the pop-up descriptions using REG.EXE, start a command prompt and enter the following:

```
REG UPDATE HKCU\Software\Microsoft\Windows\CurrentVersion\
Explorer\Advanced\ShowInfoTip=0
```

NOTE: *The code above must be placed on one line.*

Modifying Windows NT

Just because Microsoft wants you to jump aboard the Windows 2000 express doesn't mean that you're going to do so. For reasons of compatibility, familiarity, or simply politics, you might have to remain with Windows NT for a while. You can configure Windows NT to give you some of Windows 2000's features, simply by making a few registry changes.

Making Windows NT Power Down at Shutdown

Unlike Windows 2000, Windows NT does not power down the machine when you choose to shut down. If you have an ATX-compliant motherboard and Service Pack 4 or higher, you can configure your NT machine to actually power down at shutdown. To make Windows NT power off at shutdown using REG.EXE, start a command prompt and enter the following:

```
REG ADD HKLM\SOFTWARE\Microsoft\Windows NT\CurrentVersion\
Winlogon\PowerDownAfterShutdown=1
```

NOTE: *The code above must be placed on one line. If your system does not support the power down option, your machine may simply reboot at shutdown.*

Disabling Shortcut Link Tracking

When a shortcut is created in Windows NT, it secretly embeds the Universal Naming Convention (UNC) path within the shortcut (for example, \\computer\c$). When a user activates a shortcut, it attempts to connect through the UNC method first. This is called file link embedding. Most of the time this is not a problem; however, if you copy a shortcut from one computer to another or change the computer name, the other machine may be prompted for a user name and password for the UNC share of the first machine. To disable file link embedding using REG.EXE, start a command prompt and enter the following:

```
REG ADD HKLM\Software\Microsoft\Windows\CurrentVersion\
Policies\Explorer\LinkResolveIgnoreLinkInfo=1
```

NOTE: *The code above must be placed on one line.*

Related solution:	Found on page:
Removing Embedded File Links from Shortcuts	152

Enabling Automatic File Name Completion

Windows NT has the capability to complete file names as you type within a command prompt, if you simply press a key. (This capability is already enabled by default in Windows 2000.) To enable automatic file name completion using REG.EXE, start a command prompt and enter the following:

```
REG ADD HKCU\Software\Microsoft\CommandProcessor\
CompletionChar=9
```

NOTE: *The code above must be placed on one line. The CompletionChar 9 is the tab key.*

Removing Explorer's View/Options Selection

If you have NT Service Pack 4 or higher, you can prevent users from changing Explorer view settings by removing the View|Options selection. To remove the View|Options selection using REG.EXE, start a command prompt and enter the following:

```
REG ADD HKCU\Software\Microsoft\Windows\CurrentVersion\
Policies\Explorer\NoOptions=1 REG_DWORD
```

NOTE: *The code above must be placed on one line.*

Deleting Registry Keys Using REGEDIT

Although you can use REG.EXE to delete registry keys, you can also use REGEDIT. To delete registry keys using REGEDIT, select Start|Run and enter "regedit *regfile*". Here, *regfile* is a registry file that contains the following:

```
REGEDIT4
[-COMPLETEKEY]
```

Here, **COMPLETEKEY** is the complete registry key to delete, such as HKEY_LOCAL_MACHINE\SOFTWARE\APPLE.

NOTE: *The minus sign in front of **COMPLETEKEY** causes the key to be deleted.*

Clearing the Run Dialog List

Every time you run a command through the Start|Run dialog box, that command is stored in a Most Recently Used (MRU) list within the registry. To delete this list from the registry, select Start|Run and enter "regedit *regfile*". Here, **regfile** is a registry file that contains the following:

```
REGEDIT4
[-HKEY_CURRENT_USER\Software\Microsoft\Windows\
CurrentVersion\Explorer\RunMRU]
```

> **NOTE:** The highlighted code above must be placed on one line.

Deleting Persistent Drive Mappings

Whenever you map a drive to "reconnect at logon" or map it persistent through the NET USE command, the settings for this drive mapping are stored within the registry. To remove persistent drive mappings for the current user, select Start|Run and enter "regedit *regfile*". Here, **regfile** is a registry file that contains the following:

```
REGEDIT4
[-HKEY_CURRENT_USER\Software\Microsoft\Windows NT\
CurrentVersion\Network\Persistent Connections]
```

> **NOTE:** The highlighted code above must be placed on one line.

Modifying the Registry with REGINI.EXE

REGINI.EXE is a powerful resource kit utility designed to manipulate the registry through a batch file. It can add or update registry values as well as set registry key permissions. REGINI.EXE interprets registry hives differently because it only works with kernel mode. See Table 5.2.

Table 5.2   Regular mode versus kernel mode.

Regular Mode	Kernel Mode
HKEY_LOCAL_MACHINE	\Registry\Machine
HKEY_USERS	\Registry\User

5. Inside the Registry

Disabling Dr. Watson

Dr. Watson is an annoying debugging utility that appears every so often during application or system crashes. To disable Dr. Watson, proceed as follows:

1. Create a new directory to store all files included in this example.

2. Obtain the latest version of REGINI.EXE from the Resource Kit and copy it to the new directory.

3. Select Start|Run and enter "REGINI *scriptfile*".

Here, **scriptfile** is the full path of the new directory from step 1 and file name of a script file that contains the following:

```
\Registry\Machine
        SOFTWARE
                Microsoft
                        Windows NT
                                CurrentVersion
                                        AeDebug
                                                AUTO = REG_SZ 0
```

TIP: *To re-enable Dr. Watson, run **DRWTSN32 -I** from the command prompt.*

Securing Recycle Bin Properties

To restrict users from modifying the Recycle Bin properties, proceed as follows:

1. Create a new directory to store all files included in this example.

2. Obtain the latest version of REGINI.EXE from the Resource Kit and copy it to the new directory.

3. Select Start|Run and enter "REGINI *scriptfile*".

Here, **scriptfile** is the full path of the new directory from step 1 and file name of a script file that contains the following:

```
\Registry\Machine
        SOFTWARE
                Microsoft
                        Windows
                                CurrentVersion
                                        Explorer
                                                BitBucket [1 17 8]
```

Modifying the Registry with KiXtart

KiXtart provides many functions to manipulate the registry:

- **AddKey**—Adds a subkey to the regsitry
- **DelKey**—Deletes a subkey from the registry
- **Deltree**—Deletes a key and all its subkeys
- **DelValue**—Deletes a value from the registry
- **EnumKey**—Lists the keys within a key or subkey
- **EnumValue**—Lists the values within a key or subkey
- **ExistKey**—Checks for the existence of a subkey
- **LoadHive**—Loads HKEY_LOCAL_MACHINE or HKEY_USER hive information from a REG file
- **LoadKey**—Loads a registry key from a hive file
- **ReadType**—Determines the value type
- **ReadValue**—Reads the data within a registry value
- **SaveKey**—Saves a key to a hive file
- **WriteValue**—Writes data to or creates a registry value

NOTE: *For complete usage details, see the KiXtart manual.*

Backing Up a Registry Key

To back up a registry key to a hive file using KiXtart, proceed as follows:

1. Create a new directory to store all files included in this example.
2. Download and extract the latest version of KiXtart, from **www.microsoft.com**, to the new directory.
3. Select Start|Run and enter "kix32 *scriptfile*".

Here, *scriptfile* is the full path of the new directory from step 1 and file name of a script file that contains the following:

```
$RegKey = "key"
$RegFile = "file"
SaveKey($RegKey, $RegFile)
```

Here, *key* is the registry key to back up, and *file* is the hive file to back up the registry key.

Restoring a Registry Key

To restore a registry key from a hive file using KiXtart, proceed as follows:

1. Create a new directory to store all files included in this example.

2. Download and extract the latest version of KiXtart, from **www.microsoft.com**, to the new directory.

3. Select Start|Run and enter "kix32 *scriptfile*".

Here, ***scriptfile*** is the full path of the new directory from step 1 and file name of a script file that contains the following:

```
$RegKey = "key"
$RegFile = "file"
LoadKey($RegKey, $RegFile)
```

Here, ***key*** is the registry key to restore, and ***file*** is the hive file to restore from.

Disabling Welcome Screens

Microsoft has made it a habit to greet every new user to a machine running its operating system. Under Windows NT, this is performed through the Welcome screen, and under Windows 2000, this is performed by the Getting Started screen. Although this greeting seems like a good idea, it can quickly become annoying to users as they travel from machine to machine.

Disabling the Windows NT Welcome Screen

To disable the Windows NT Welcome screen, proceed as follows:

1. Create a new directory to store all files included in this example.

2. Download and extract the latest version of KiXtart, from **www.microsoft.com**, to the new directory.

3. Select Start|Run and enter "kix32 *scriptfile*".

Here, ***scriptfile*** is the full path of the new directory from step 1 and file name of a script file that contains the following:

```
$RegKey = "HKEY_USERS\.DEFAULT\Software\Microsoft\Windows\
CurrentVersion\Explorer"
WriteValue($RegKey, "Show", "0", "REG_DWORD")
```

NOTE: *The highlighted code above must be placed on one line.*

Disabling the Windows 2000 Getting Started Screen

To disable the Windows 2000 Getting Started screen, proceed as follows:

1. Create a new directory to store all files included in this example.

2. Download and extract the latest version of KiXtart, from **www.microsoft.com**, to the new directory.

3. Select Start|Run and enter "kix32 *scriptfile*".

Here, ***scriptfile*** is the full path of the new directory from step 1 and file name of a script file that contains the following:

```
$RegKey = "HKEY_LOCAL_MACHINE\SOFTWARE\Microsoft\Windows\
CurrentVersion\Policies\Explorer"
WriteValue($RegKey, "NoWelcomeScreen", "1", "REG_DWORD")
```

NOTE: *The highlighted code above must be placed on one line.*

Working with Icons

Microsoft Windows includes many default icons on the desktop for your convenience. You can easily delete or hide these icons or modify their properties by manipulating the registry.

Removing the My Computer Icon from the Desktop

To remove the My Computer icon from the desktop, proceed as follows:

1. Create a new directory to store all files included in this example.

2. Download and extract the latest version of KiXtart, from **www.microsoft.com**, to the new directory.

3. Select Start|Run and enter "kix32 *scriptfile*".

Here, ***scriptfile*** is the full path of the new directory from step 1 and file name of a script file that contains the following:

```
$RegKey = "HKEY_CLASSES_ROOT\CLSID\
{20D04FE0-3AEA-1069-A2D8-08002B30309D}"
Deltree($RegKey)
```

NOTE: *The highlighted code above must be placed on one line.*

Removing the Dial-Up Networking Icon from My Computer

To remove the Dial-Up Networking icon from My Computer, proceed as follows:

1. Create a new directory to store all files included in this example.

2. Download and extract the latest version of KiXtart, from **www.microsoft.com**, to the new directory.

3. Select Start|Run and enter "kix32 *scriptfile*".

Here, ***scriptfile*** is the full path of the new directory from step 1 and file name of a script file that contains the following:

```
$RegKey = "HKEY_LOCAL_MACHINE\SOFTWARE\Microsoft\Windows\
CurrentVersion\ Explorer\MyComputer\NameSpace\
{a4d92740-67cd-11cf-96f2-00aa00a11dd9}"
Deltree($RegKey)
```

NOTE: *The highlighted code above must be placed on one line.*

Removing the Scheduled Tasks Icon from My Computer

To remove the Scheduled Tasks icon from My Computer, proceed as follows:

1. Create a new directory to store all files included in this example.

2. Download and extract the latest version of KiXtart, from **www.microsoft.com**, to the new directory.

3. Select Start|Run and enter "kix32 *scriptfile*".

Here, ***scriptfile*** is the full path of the new directory from step 1 and file name of a script file that contains the following:

```
$RegKey = "HKEY_LOCAL_MACHINE\SOFTWARE\Microsoft\Windows\
CurrentVersion\ Explorer\MyComputer\NameSpace\
{D6277990-4C6A-11CF-8D87-00AA0060F5BF}"
Deltree($RegKey)
```

NOTE: *The highlighted code above must be placed on one line.*

Hiding the Network Neighborhood Icon

To hide the Network Neighborhood icon from the desktop for the current user, proceed as follows:

1. Create a new directory to store all files included in this example.

2. Download and extract the latest version of KiXtart, from **www.microsoft.com**, to the new directory.

3. Select Start|Run and enter "kix32 *scriptfile*".

Here, *scriptfile* is the full path of the new directory from step 1 and file name of a script file that contains the following:

```
$RegKey = "SOFTWARE\Microsoft\Windows\CurrentVersion\
Policies\Explorer"
WriteValue($RegKey, "NoNetHood", "1", "REG_DWORD")
```

NOTE: *The highlighted code above must be placed on one line.*

Hiding All Desktop Icons

To hide the desktop icons for the current user, proceed as follows:

1. Create a new directory to store all files included in this example.

2. Download and extract the latest version of KiXtart, from **www.microsoft.com**, to the new directory.

3. Select Start|Run and enter "kix32 *scriptfile*".

Here, *scriptfile* is the full path of the new directory from step 1 and file name of a script file that contains the following:

```
$RegKey = "SOFTWARE\Microsoft\Windows\CurrentVersion\
Policies\Explorer"
WriteValue($RegKey, "NoDesktop", "1", "REG_DWORD")
```

NOTE: *The highlighted code above must be placed on one line.*

Modifying the Registry with Windows Script Host

Windows Script Host provides the easiest way to manipulate the registry. You can modify the registry using the WScript object. This object contains three simple registry methods:

- **RegDelete**—Deletes registry keys and values
- **RegRead**—Reads registry keys or values
- **RegWrite**—Writes registry keys or values

NOTE: *Windows Script Host does not include any methods to back up or restore registry keys or values.*

Disabling Windows Security Menu Options

Once Windows NT is up and running, you can press Ctrl+Alt+Del to call up the Windows security menu to perform common tasks. Although this is convenient for users, you may want to selectively disable these options for guest or kiosk stations.

Disabling the Lock Workstation Button

To disable the Lock Workstation button, proceed as follows:

1. Create a new directory to store all files included in this example.

2. Download and install the latest version of Windows Script Host, from **www.microsoft.com**, to the new directory.

3. Select Start|Run and enter "cscript *scriptfile*.vbs".

Here, ***scriptfile*** is the full path and file name of a script file that contains the following:

```
On Error Resume Next
Set SHELL = CreateObject("WScript.Shell")
RegValue = "HKCU\Software\Microsoft\Windows\" & _
"CurrentVersion\Policies\System\DisableLockWorkstation"
SHELL.RegWrite RegValue, 1, "REG_DWORD"
```

Disabling the Change Password Button

To disable the Change Password button, proceed as follows:

1. Create a new directory to store all files included in this example.

2. Download and install the latest version of Windows Script Host, from **www.microsoft.com**, to the new directory.

3. Select Start|Run and enter "cscript *scriptfile*.vbs".

Here, ***scriptfile*** is the full path and file name of a script file that contains the following:

```
On Error Resume Next
Set SHELL = CreateObject("WScript.Shell")
RegValue = "HKCU\Software\Microsoft\Windows\" & _
"CurrentVersion\Policies\System\DisableChangePassword"
SHELL.RegWrite RegValue, 1, "REG_DWORD"
```

Disabling the Logoff Button

To disable the Logoff button, proceed as follows:

1. Create a new directory to store all files included in this example.

2. Download and install the latest version of Windows Script Host, from **www.microsoft.com**, to the new directory.

3. Select Start|Run and enter "cscript *scriptfile*.vbs".

Here, *scriptfile* is the full path and file name of a script file that contains the following:

```
On Error Resume Next
Set SHELL = CreateObject("WScript.Shell")
RegValue = "HKCU\Software\Microsoft\Windows\" & _
"CurrentVersion\Policies\System\NoLogOff"
SHELL.RegWrite RegValue, 1, "REG_DWORD"
```

Modifying NTFS Properties

NTFS includes many benefits over the regular FAT file system. The price of these benefits is the extra overhead and access time of the file system. You can modify the registry to disable some of these features.

Disabling 8.3 File Naming

When a file is created, it retains both long and short (DOS 8.3) file names. If you do not use DOS programs, you can disable 8.3 file naming to increase performance. To disable 8.3 file naming, proceed as follows:

1. Create a new directory to store all files included in this example.

2. Download and install the latest version of Windows Script Host, from **www.microsoft.com**, to the new directory.

3. Select Start|Run and enter "cscript *scriptfile*.vbs".

Here, *scriptfile* is the full path and file name of a script file that contains the following:

```
On Error Resume Next
Set SHELL = CreateObject("WScript.Shell")
RegValue = "HKLM\System\CurrentControlSet\Control\FileSystem\" & _
"NTFSDisable8dot3NameCreation"
SHELL.RegWrite RegValue, 1, "REG_DWORD"
```

5. Inside the Registry

Related solution:	Found on page:
Renaming Files with Short File Names	77

Disabling the Last Access Time Stamp

When a file is accessed, a time stamp is placed on that file. If you do not need this information, you can disable the last access time stamp to increase performance. To disable the last access time stamp, proceed as follows:

1. Create a new directory to store all files included in this example.

2. Download and install the latest version of Windows Script Host, from **www.microsoft.com**, to the new directory.

3. Select Start|Run and enter "cscript *scriptfile*.vbs".

Here, ***scriptfile*** is the full path and file name of a script file that contains the following:

```
On Error Resume Next
Set SHELL = CreateObject("WScript.Shell")
RegValue = "HKLM\System\CurrentControlSet\Control\FileSystem\" & _
"NTFSDisableLastAccessUpdate"
SHELL.RegWrite RegValue, 1, "REG_DWORD"
```

Chapter 6

Local System Management

In Brief

It's such a shame. You spend months creating the perfect drive image for your company, only to have users and fellow administrators destroy it little by little through installing new applications, deleting files, and disorganizing the file system. Almost brings a tear to your eye. In this chapter, you will learn how to reorganize the disorganized, secure your systems, and perform updates to keep your imaged systems and servers healthy and clean.

Common Locations

Microsoft uses a common organized structure to store user data. If you know the locations of these directories and the quickest way to access them, you can easily modify their contents within your scripts. Tables 6.1 through 6.3 list the common locations for the various versions of Windows.

Table 6.1 Common data storage paths in Windows 9*x*.

Data Type	Path
Desktop	%*WINDIR*%\Desktop
Favorites	%*WINDIR*%\Favorites
NetHood	%*WINDIR*%\NetHood
PrintHood	%*WINDIR*%\PrintHood
Quick Launch	%*WINDIR*%\Application Data\Microsoft\Internet Explorer\Quick Launch
SendTo	%*WINDIR*%\SendTo
Start Menu	%*WINDIR*%\Start Menu

Table 6.2 Common data storage paths in Windows NT.

Data Type	Path
All Users Desktop	%*WINDIR*%\Profiles\All Users\Desktop
All Users Start Menu	%*WINDIR*%\Profiles\All Users\Start Menu
Desktop	%*USERPROFILE*%\Desktop
Favorites	%*USERPROFILE*%\Favorites

(continued)

Table 6.2   Common data storage paths in Windows NT *(continued)*.

Data Type	Path
NetHood	%*USERPROFILE*%\NetHood
PrintHood	%*USERPROFILE*%\PrintHood
Quick Launch	%*USERPROFILE*%\Application Data\Microsoft\Internet Explorer\Quick Launch
SendTo	%*USERPROFILE*%\SendTo
Start Menu	%*USERPROFILE*%\Start Menu

Table 6.3   Common data storage paths in Windows 2000.

Data Type	Path
All Users Desktop	%*ALLUSERSPROFILE*%
All Users Start Menu	%ALLUSERSPROFILE%
Desktop	%*USERPROFILE*%\Desktop
Favorites	%*USERPROFILE*%\Favorites
NetHood	%*USERPROFILE*%\NetHood
PrintHood	%*USERPROFILE*%\PrintHood
Quick Launch	%USERPROFILE%\Application Data\Microsoft\Internet Explorer\Quick Launch
SendTo	%*USERPROFILE*%\SendTo
Start Menu	%*USERPROFILE*%\Start Menu

Accessing SpecialFolders with Windows Script Host

The WshShell object contains a property called SpecialFolders used to access these common locations. To access the SpecialFolders property, proceed as follows:

```
Set SHELL = CreateObject("WScript.Shell")
Set SF = SHELL.SpecialFolders
```

Here is a list of the folders available to the SpecialFolder property:

- AllUsersDesktop
- AllUsersStartMenu
- AllUsersPrograms
- AllUsersStartup
- AppData

- Desktop
- Favorites
- Fonts
- MyDocuments
- NetHood
- PrintHood
- Programs
- Recent
- SendTo
- StartMenu
- Startup
- Templates

Here is an example of how to access these special folders in Windows Script Host:

```
Set SHELL = CreateObject("WScript.Shell")
Set SF = SHELL.SpecialFolders
Wscript.Echo "Desktop: " & SF("Desktop")
```

NOTE: *Access to these folders is dependent on your version of Windows. For example, there is no AllUsersDesktop folder for Windows 9x.*

Sharing

Sharing is the basic principle to networking: making resources easily available to multiple users. Windows allows you to share files, folders, and even devices to allow others to access your resources over the network.

NOTE: *Because Windows NT Workstation allows only 10 concurrent network connections, this is the maximum number of simultaneous users that can access a share. The limit for a Windows server is dependent on the number of concurrent licenses you have for each server.*

To share a resource, right-click the resource and choose Sharing. Select Share This Folder and specify a share name. Resources are shared by their share names. Share names do not need to be the same name as the actual resource. For example, a folder called FILES can have a share name called MYFILES. To remain compatible with the DOS naming convention, your share names should not exceed eight characters.

6. Local System Management

Once a resource is shared, you can control access to it by modifying its share permissions. When a resource is shared, the default settings are to share that object with everyone. You can set varying access levels for your shared resources, and the process is identical to modifying NTFS permissions. Although NTFS is not required to set share permissions, you can increase security and functionality by using it.

NTFS Overview

NTFS (NT File System) is a file system designed solely for Windows NT/2000. This file system contains significant improvements over the previous Windows file systems. Some of these improvements include:

- Maximum size: 16 exabytes
- Long file name support
- File, folder, and volume security
- Compression
- Bad cluster recovery

Converting to NTFS

If you are currently using the FAT (File Allocation Table) file system, you can gain the benefits of NTFS by safely converting to it using CONVERT.EXE. To convert from FAT to NTFS, start a command prompt and enter the following:

```
CONVERT drive /FS:NTFS
```

Here, *drive* is the drive to convert to NTFS (for example, C:).

WARNING! *This is a one-way conversion process. Microsoft does not provide any method to convert an NTFS volume to FAT or FAT32. Remember, NTFS drives are only accessible to Windows NT/2000.*

NTFS Security

NTFS stores extra information such as file ownership and uses access control lists (ACLs) to secure its files and folders from users and groups. The ACL contains access control entries (ACEs) that determine which type of access will be given. NTFS provides different ACEs for files and folders. To view the different ACEs you can set, open Windows Explorer and select Properties|Security|Permissions for a specific file or folder (see Figure 6.1).

In addition to the default NTFS permissions, you can specifically set individual permissions through the Type of Access|Special Access selection, as shown in Figure 6.2.

WARNING! *Setting "No Access" to the group Everyone will prevent even administrators from accessing the affected resources.*

Windows 2000 NTFS

Windows 2000 uses an updated version of NTFS containing many additional features. Some of these improvements include:

- *Disk quotas*—Disk usage limits you can set on a per-user basis
- *Encryption*—A method to make data unreadable for unauthorized viewers using the 56 Bit DES (Data Encryption Standard)

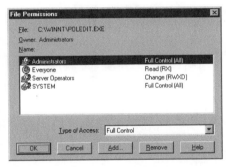

Figure 6.1   Editing NTFS general permissions.

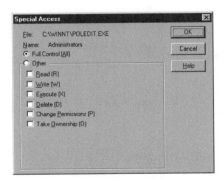

Figure 6.2   Editing NTFS special access permissions.

6. Local System Management

- *Reparse points*—An enhancement to file objects that allows developers to extend file system functionality

- *Sparse files*—Files that can be created at any size, but which grow only as needed

- *Change Journal*—Originally called the Update Sequence Number (USN) journal, a hidden journal that records changes to the file system

---

TIP: *If you are using Windows NT Service Pack 4 or later, you can read and write to Windows 2000 NTFS volumes.*

Immediate Solutions

Interacting with the User

When scripting, you might often need the ability to prompt or ask the user for input. This is useful when you need to inform the user that the script has ended, display error messages, ask for the location of a directory, and more.

Using Dialog Boxes with Shell Scripting

Shell scripting does not contain any built-in method to create dialog boxes from the command line. Msgbox.exe is a freeware utility from Dave G. Thomas that you can use to create dialog boxes from the command line. The basic syntax of msgbox is as follows:

```
Msgbox /commands "title" text
```

Here, *title* is the dialog box window title. Any characters after *title* will display *text* in the body of the dialog box. Multiple quoted phrases of *text* will result in multiple body lines of text. The available *commands* are as follows:

- **/BARI**—Displays Abort, Retry, and Ignore buttons
- **/BO**—Displays the OK button
- **/BOC**—Displays the OK and Cancel buttons
- **/BRC**—Displays the Retry and Cancel buttons
- **/BYN**—Displays the Yes and No buttons
- **/BYNC**—Displays the Yes, No, and Cancel buttons
- **/D***x*—Selects a default button where x is the button number, from left to right
- **/F1**—Sets the dialog box to the foreground before input
- **/F2**—Sets the dialog box to the foreground after input
- **/H**—Hides the console window during the prompt
- **/I!**—Displays the exclamation icon
- **/II**—Displays the information icon
- **/IQ**—Displays the question icon
- **/IS**—Displays the stop icon

145

- **/MA**—Normal display (Application Modal)
- **/MS**—On top display (System Modal)
- **/MT**—Normal display, includes title icon (Task Modal)
- **/T.x**—Times out after *x* seconds

To create a batch file example to illustrate the use of msgbox.exe, proceed as follows:

1. Create a new directory to store all files included in this example.

2. Download msgbox.exe from **www.mindspring.com/~dgthomas/** to the new directory.

3. Start a command prompt and enter "*scriptfile*.bat".

Here, **scriptfile** is the full path of the new directory from step 1 and file name of a script file that contains the following:

```
@Echo Off
:Start

MSGBOX /H /MT /BO /I! "MSGBOX Example"
"This example illustrates how to make"
"dialog boxes from the command line."

MSGBOX /H /MT /BARI /IS "Fake Error"
"Non critical program error."
"Pressing a button will continue the example."

MSGBOX /H /MT /BYN /D2 /IQ "Repeat Example?"
"Would you like to repeat this example?"

If errorlevel 5 goto End
If errorlevel 2 goto Start

:End
```

NOTE: *The highlighted code above must be placed on one line.*

Using Dialog Boxes with KiXtart

The KiXtart command **MessageBox** allows you to display a dialog box to the user. To display a dialog box using KiXtart, proceed as follows:

1. Create a new directory to store all files included in this example.

2. Download and extract the latest version of KiXtart, from **www.microsoft.com**, to the new directory.

3. Select Start|Run and enter "kix32 *scriptfile*".

Here, **scriptfile** is the full path of the new directory from step 1 and file name of a script file that contains the following:

```
MessageBox("This is a dialog box.", "DIALOG BOX", 0)
```

NOTE: The **MessageBox** command supports many functions, such as allowing for different buttons and icons. See the KiXtart manual for all the included features.

Using Dialog Boxes with Windows Script Host

Windows Script Host provides several methods to display dialog boxes. In the previous chapters, you have seen the Wscript.Echo used to display command prompt lines of text to the user when invoked using CSCRIPT.EXE, the command-line Windows Script Host. If you start your scripts with WSCRIPT.EXE, the line of text will be displayed in a message box:

```
WScript.Echo "This is a dialog box."
```

Another method of displaying dialog boxes is using WshShell's **PopUp**:

```
Set SHELL = CreateObject("WScript.Shell")
SHELL.PopUp "Window Text", 0, "Window Title", 0
```

NOTE: PopUp is very similar to KiXtart's **MessageBox**. See the WSH documentation for all the included features.

Accepting User Input with Shell Scripting

Shell scripting does not include any method to accept user input, aside from creating temporary files and then parsing the files. Included in the resource kit is a utility called CHOICE.EXE that allows you to accept user choices (one key press) from the command line:

```
CHOICE /C:ABC
IF ERRORLEVEL 1 ECHO You pressed A
IF ERRORLEVEL 2 ECHO You pressed B
IF ERRORLEVEL 3 ECHO You pressed C
```

Here, the **/C** switch states which keys are allowed for input (for example, **/C:ABC**). You can determine which key has been pressed by checking the appropriate errorlevel. The first key allowed, in this example A, is associated with the first errorlevel (errorlevel 1), and so on.

Accepting User Input with KiXtart

The KiXtart command **GETS** allows you to store a line of user input to a variable. To accept user input using KiXtart, proceed as follows:

1. Create a new directory to store all files included in this example.

2. Download and extract the latest version of KiXtart, from **www.microsoft.com**, to the new directory.

3. Select Start|Run and enter "kix32 *scriptfile*".

Here, *scriptfile* is the full path of the new directory from step 1 and file name of a script file that contains the following:

```
GETS $variable
FLUSHKB
```

Here, *variable* is the variable to store the user input. The **FLUSHKB** command clears the keyboard buffer.

*TIP: You can use the KiXtart command **Get** to accept a single key of input.*

Accepting User Input with Windows Script Host

The Windows Script Host command **InputBox** allows you to store a line of user input to a variable. To accept user input using Windows Script Host, proceed as follows:

1. Create a new directory to store all files included in this example.

2. Download and install the latest version of Windows Script Host, from **www.microsoft.com**, to the new directory.

3. Select Start|Run and enter "cscript *scriptfile*.vbs".

Here, *scriptfile* is the full path and file name of a script file that contains the following:

```
Name = InputBox("Please type enter your name:",
"YOUR NAME REQUIRED", "JOHN BREYAN")
Wscript.Echo "Hello " + Name
```

NOTE: The highlighted code above must be placed on one line.

Changing the Desktop Wallpaper

KiXtart includes a command called **SETWALLPAPER** to change the desktop wallpaper for the current user. To change the desktop wallpaper using KiXtart, proceed as follows:

1. Create a new directory to store all files included in this example.

2. Download and extract the latest version of KiXtart, from **www.microsoft.com**, to the new directory.

3. Select Start|Run and enter "kix32 *scriptfile*".

Here, *scriptfile* is the full path of the new directory from step 1 and file name of a script file that contains the following:

```
SETWALLPAPER("wallpaper")
```

Here, *wallpaper* is the complete path and file name of the bitmap to use.

Working with Shortcuts

Shortcuts are merely pointers to the files and folders you use most often. Shortcuts are easily identified by their .lnk extension and are the building blocks of the Start menu. Most users live and breathe shortcuts, and would be lost without them. Through shell scripting and Windows Script Host, you can easily modify or create shortcuts anywhere on a system.

Creating Shortcuts Using Shell Scripting

SHORTCUT.EXE is a resource kit utility you can use to create shortcuts from the command line. To create a shortcut using SHORTCUT.EXE, start a command prompt and enter the following:

```
SHORTCUT -F -T "target" -N "name" -D "directory"
```

Here, **-F** overwrites existing shortcuts; *target* is the full path and name of the item to create a shortcut to; *name* is the full path and name of the shortcut; and *directory* is the full directory path to start the target in.

TIP: *SHORTCUT.EXE supports many command-line parameters. Type "shortcut.exe -?" for more information.*

Creating Shortcuts Using KiXtart

KiXtart does not have the ability to create shortcuts, other than within the Start menu. If you want to create a shortcut somewhere else, you can create a Start menu shortcut, copy the shortcut to the desired location, and then delete the original shortcut. To create a shortcut using KiXtart, proceed as follows:

1. Create a new directory to store all files included in this example.

2. Download and extract the latest version of KiXtart, from **www.microsoft.com**, to the new directory.

3. Select Start|Run and enter "kix32 *scriptfile*".

Here, ***scriptfile*** is the full path of the new directory from step 1 and file name of a script file that contains the following:

```
$SName = "name"
$STarget = "target"
$SDir = "directory"
$SDest = "destination"

$RCODE = AddProgramItem($STarget,$SName,"",0,$SDir,0,0)
Copy "SMPDIR\$SName.lnk" $SDest
$RCODE = DelProgramItem($SName)
```

Here, ***name*** is the name of the shortcut without the extension or path; ***target*** is the full path and name of the item to create a shortcut to; ***directory*** is the full directory path to start the target in; ***smpdir*** is the full path of the Start Menu\Programs directory; and ***destination*** is where to store the shortcut.

TIP: *If you just want to create a shortcut in the Start menu, simply use the* **AddProgramItem** *command.*

Creating Shortcuts Using Windows Script Host

To create a shortcut using Windows Script Host, proceed as follows:

1. Create a new directory to store all files included in this example.

2. Download and install the latest version of Windows Script Host, from **www.microsoft.com**, to the new directory.

3. Select Start|Run and enter "cscript *scriptfile*.vbs".

Here, ***scriptfile*** is the full path and file name of a script file that contains the following:

```
Set Shell = CreateObject("WScript.Shell")
sNAME = "name"
sTARGET = "target"
sDIR = "directory"
sICON = "icon"
sHKEY = "hotkey"

Set Scut = Shell.CreateShortcut(sNAME)
Scut.TargetPath = Shell.ExpandEnvironmentStrings(sTARGET)
Scut.WorkingDirectory = Shell.ExpandEnvironmentStrings(sDIR)
Scut.WindowStyle = 4
Scut.IconLocation = Shell.ExpandEnvironmentStrings(sICON)
Scut.HotKey = sHKEY
Scut.Save
```

Here, **name** is the complete path and name of the shortcut; **target** is the item to place a shortcut to; **directory** is the item's working directory; **icon** is the shortcut icon to use; and **hotkey** is the quick key combination to activate the shortcut (for example, ALT+SHIFT+Q).

Deleting Broken Shortcuts

Shortcuts are merely pointers to a file or folder on your system, and when those target items get moved or deleted, those shortcuts are useless. To delete a broken shortcut using Windows Script Host, proceed as follows:

1. Create a new directory to store all files included in this example.

2. Download and install the latest version of Windows Script Host, from **www.microsoft.com**, to the new directory.

3. Select Start|Run and enter "cscript *scriptfile*.vbs".

Here, **scriptfile** is the full path and file name of a script file that contains the following:

```
Set FSO = CreateObject("Scripting.FileSystemObject")
Set Shell = CreateObject("Wscript.Shell")
sDIR = directory

Set objDIR = GetFolder(sDIR)
GoSubFolders objDIR

Sub MainSub (objDIR)
  For Each efile in objDIR.Files
    fEXT = FSO.GetExtensionName(efile.Path)
    If LCase(fEXT) = LCase("lnk") Then
```

```
          Set Shortcut = Shell.CreateShortcut(efile)
          If NOT FSO.FileExists(Shortcut.TargetPath) Then
              If NOT FSO.FolderExists(Shortcut.TargetPath) Then
                  DelFile efile
              End If
          End If
        End If
      Next
    End Sub
```

Here, **directory** is the location to start searching for broken shortcuts.

NOTE: *You need to append the **GoSubFolders**, **DelFile**, and **GetFolder** routines, listed in Chapter 3, to this script in order for it to run.*

TIP: *You can use the resource kit utility CHKLNKS.EXE to perform the same task manually.*

Removing Embedded File Links from Shortcuts

In Chapter 5, you learned about file link tracking within shortcuts and how to prevent it. To remove existing embedded file links within shortcuts using Windows Script Host, proceed as follows:

1. Create a new directory to store all files included in this example.

2. Download and install the latest version of Windows Script Host, from **www.microsoft.com**, to the new directory.

3. Select Start|Run and enter "cscript *scriptfile*.vbs".

Here, **scriptfile** is the full path and file name of a script file that contains the following:

```
Set FSO = CreateObject("Scripting.FileSystemObject")
Set Shell = CreateObject("Wscript.Shell")
sDIR = directory
sLOG = logfile
sSCUT = shortcutexe

Set objDIR = GetFolder(sDIR)
GoSubFolders objDIR

Sub MainSub (objDIR)
  For Each efile in objDIR.Files
    fEXT = FSO.GetExtensionName(efile.Path)
```

```
   If LCase(fEXT) = LCase("lnk") Then
     SHELL.Run sSCUT & " -S """ & objDIR & "\" & _
       efile.Name & """ -1 " & sLOG,0,true
   End If
 Next
End Sub
```

Here, ***directory*** is the location to start removing embedded file links from shortcuts; ***logfile*** is the file to record any errors to while fixing the shortcuts; and ***shortcutexe*** is the name and path to the SHORTCUT.EXE resource kit utility.

NOTE: *You need to append the **GoSubFolders** and **GetFolder** routines, listed in Chapter 3, to this script in order for it to run.*

Related solution:	Found on page:
Disabling Shortcut Link Tracking	125

Controlling the Start Menu

The Start menu is the central point for organizing application and system shortcuts. For every new application installed, more than likely an associated shortcut or two is installed in the Start menu. Users can spend a good portion of their day navigating through this menu to get to the application or data they want, so it is important to organize this data effectively.

Adding a Program Group with KiXtart

As you learned in the previous section, you can create Start menu shortcuts using the command **AddProgramItem**. KiXtart also includes a function called **AddProgramGroup** to create folders in the Start menu:

```
AddProgramGroup("Folder", Location)
```

Here, ***folder*** is the name of the group to create, and ***location*** specifies whether to place the group in the common or user Start menu. A value of 0 specifies the user Start menu, whereas a value of 1 specifies the common Start menu.

Moving All Uninstall Shortcuts to a Central Directory

When an application installer places its shortcuts in the Start menu, an uninstall icon is normally included to uninstall this product quickly and easily. Unfortunately, a user quickly browsing through the Start menu might click on an uninstall icon and accidentally remove or damage application or system files. To move the uninstall shortcuts from the Start menu to a central directory, proceed as follows:

1. Create a new directory to store all files included in this example.

2. Download and install the latest version of Windows Script Host, from **www.microsoft.com**, to the new directory.

3. Select Start|Run and enter "cscript *scriptfile*.vbs".

Here, ***scriptfile*** is the full path and file name of a script file that contains the following:

```
Set FSO = CreateObject("Scripting.FileSystemObject")
Set Shell = CreateObject("Wscript.Shell")
sMENU = Shell.SpecialFolders("Programs")
sDIR = "C:\UNINSTALL"
  If Not FSO.FolderExists(sDIR) Then
    FSO.CreateFolder sDIR
  End If


Set objDIR = GetFolder(sMENU)
GoSubFolders objDIR


Sub MainSub (objDIR)
  For Each efile in objDIR.Files
    fEXT = FSO.GetExtensionName(efile.Path)
    fNAME = LCase(FSO.GetBaseName(efile.Path))
    Folder = FSO.GetBaseName(objDIR)
    If LCase(fEXT) = LCase("lnk") Then
      If InStr(fNAME, "uninstall") <> 0 Then
        If fNAME = "uninstall" Then
          efile.Name = fNAME & " " & Folder & "." & fEXT
        End If
       MoveFile efile, sDIR
      End If
    End If
  Next
End Sub
```

NOTE: You need to append the **GoSubFolders**, **MoveFile**, and **GetFolder** routines, listed in Chapter 3, to this script in order for it to run.

Deleting Old User Profiles

Whenever a new user logs on, a user profile is created. User profiles consist of the user's own personal Start menu, shortcuts, and user registry. As time progresses, profiles can take up a good portion of hard drive space. DELPROF.EXE is a resource kit utility that allows you to delete old profiles that haven't been used for a while. To delete old user profiles, proceed as follows:

```
DELPROF /Q /I /D:days
```

Here, **/Q** disables prompting during profile deletion; **/I** instructs DELPROF to ignore errors and continue deletion; and **/D** indicates to delete profiles inactive more than the specified number of *days*.

NOTE: *DELPROF does not work on Windows 9x. If a specific user profile cannot be deleted by DELPROF, it might be in use. This includes the current user profile and profiles belonging to accounts associated with running services. You will need administrative privileges to delete other user's profiles.*

Managing Services from the Command Line

Services are processes that run in the background, independent of a user logon. Normally, these services are managed manually through the Control Panel|Services applet, but in this section you will learn how to manage services from the command line.

Installing a Service

INSTSRV.EXE is a resource kit utility to install a service from the command line. To install a service, start a command prompt and enter the following:

```
INSTSRV name exe -a account -p password
```

Here, ***name*** is the name to give the service; ***exe*** is the path and name of the executable to run; ***account*** is the name of the account to run the service under; and ***password*** is the password of the account.

NOTE: *After you install a service with INSTRV.EXE, the service is not automatically started. See the following section on starting services from the command line.*

Uninstalling a Service

To uninstall a service, start a command prompt and enter the following:

```
INSTSRV name Remove
```

Here, *name* is the name of the service to uninstall. The keyword **remove** instructs INSTSRV to uninstall the service.

Related solution:	Found on page:
Deleting a Service	184

Starting a Service

You can use NET.EXE, built into Windows NT/2000, to control services from the command line. To start a service from the command line, start a command prompt and enter the following:

```
NET START "service"
```

Here, *service* is the name of the service to start.

Related solution:	Found on page:
Starting Services	181

Pausing a Service

To pause a started service from the command line, start a command prompt and enter the following:

```
NET PAUSE "service"
```

Here, *service* is the name of the started service to pause.

Related solution:	Found on page:
Pausing Services	182

Resuming a Service

To resume a paused service from the command line, start a command prompt and enter the following:

```
NET CONTINUE "service"
```

Here, *service* is the name of the paused service to resume.

6. Local System Management

Related solution:	*Found on page:*
Resuming Services	183

Stopping a Service

To stop a started service from the command line, start a command prompt and enter the following:

```
NET STOP "service"
```

Here, **service** is the name of the started service to stop.

Related solution:	*Found on page:*
Stopping Services	181

Locking the Floppy Disk

The resource kit utility FLOPLOCK.EXE allows you to control access to the floppy drive. Once FlopLock is installed as a service, only members of specific groups have access to the floppy drive. This service is best used when you are working in a highly secure environment or on systems with confidential data. To install the FlopLock service, start a command prompt and enter the following:

```
INSTSRV name flopexe -a account -p password
NET start "service"
```

Here, **name** is the name to give the FlopLock service; **flopexe** is the path and name of FLOPLOCK.EXE; **account** is the name of the administrative account to run the service under; and **password** is the password of the account.

Managing NTFS from the Command Line

In Chapter 3, you learned how to modify file and folder properties. NTFS adds additional properties that you can modify through scripting.

Modifying NTFS Permissions

The resource kit utility XCACLS.EXE allows you to change NTFS permissions from the command line. Most administrators use this utility in a batch file to lock down their desktops and servers. To secure

the *%WINDIR%*\Repair directory access to just administrators, start
a command prompt and enter the following:

```
XCACLS C:\%WINDIR%\REPAIR\*.* /G administrators:F
```

TIP: *XCACLS contains many command-line parameters. Enter "XCACLS /?" for more information.*

Changing a File Owner

The resource kit utility SUBINACL.EXE allows you to view or modify
file, registry, and service security properties. You can use this utility
to change the NTFS owner of a file. To set a new owner using
SUBINACL.EXE, start a command prompt and enter the following:

```
SUBINACL /FILE/filename/SETOWNER=ownername
```

Here, *filename* is the full path and name of the file whose ownership
is to be changed.

Managing Encryption in Windows 2000

Although NTFS permissions allow you to secure your files and folders from other users, several methods are available to bypass this
security (for example, NTFSDOS). Windows 2000 uses an encrypting
file system (EFS) to secure your files.

Encrypting Files from the Command Line

CIPHER.EXE is a utility that allows you to encrypt/decrypt your files
from the command line. This utility supports the following parameters:

- **/A**—Specifies to act on files and folders
- **/D**—Decrypts files and folders
- **/E**—Encrypts files and folders
- **/F**—Forces encryption, even on files already encrypted
- **/H**—Includes system and hidden files
- **/I**—Ignores errors
- **/K**—Creates a new encryption key for the current user
- **/Q**—Runs in silent mode
- **/S**—Performs action on the current folder and all subfolders

WARNING! *Encrypted files cannot be read during the boot process. Encrypting files that the system needs to access while booting will cause your system not to boot.*

To silently encrypt all the files and folders within a directory, start a command prompt and enter the following:

```
CIPHER /E /A /S /F /Q /H "directory"
```

Here, *directory* is the folder to encrypt.

Decrypting Files from the Command Line

To decrypt all the files within a directory, start a command prompt and enter the following:

```
CIPHER /D /A /S /Q "directory"
```

Here, *directory* is the folder to encrypt.

Managing Shares from the Command Line

Shares allow users to access resources from one common source on the network. As more and more systems and devices are added and shared on your network, managing shares can become an intensive chore.

Listing Shares

You can list shares from the command line using the built-in **NET** command. To list all shares from the command line, start a command prompt and enter the following:

```
NET SHARE
```

Adding Shares

Sharing a resource makes that object available on the network. To share a resource from the command line, start a command prompt and enter the following:

```
NET SHARE name=path /USERS:maxnum /REMARK:"comment"
```

Here, *name* is the name of the share; *path* is the path to create the share to; *maxnum* is the maximum number of users allowed to simultaneously access the share; and *comment* is the comment to give the share.

TIP: *If you want to allow an unlimited number of users to access the share simultaneously, replace the /users:maxnum switch with the /unlimited switch.*

Related solution:	Found on page:
Creating a Share	175

Removing Shares

To delete a share from the command line, start a command prompt and enter the following:

```
NET name /DELETE
```

Here, **name** is the name of the share.

TIP: */D is the abbreviated form of the /DELETE switch. When you delete a share, you are only disabling sharing for that resource, not deleting that resource.*

Related solution:	Found on page:
Deleting a Share	177

Copying Share Permissions

Currently, there is no Microsoft method to set share permissions from the command line. However, you can use the resource kit utility PERMCOPY.EXE to copy permissions from one share to another. To use PERMCOPY.EXE to copy permissions from one share to another, start a command prompt and enter the following:

```
PERMCOPY \\source sname \\destination dname
```

Here, **source** is the computer containing the share (**sname**) with proper permissions; and **destination** is the computer containing the share (**dname**) to copy permissions to.

TIP: *Supplying both the source and destination with the local computer name will copy permissions from one local share to another.*

WARNING! *Do not use PERMCOPY.EXE to copy permissions on administrative shares (for example, C$). This will cause SERVICES.EXE to crash.*

Creating Shares with Permissions

Currently, there is no Microsoft method to create shares with permissions from the command line. RMTSHARE.EXE is a resource kit utility to create shares with permissions on remote stations. You can provide this utility with the local computer name to create shares with permissions on the local station. To use RMTSHARE.EXE to create shares with permissions, start a command prompt and enter the following:

```
RMTSHARE \\computer\name=path /GRANT guser:permission
/REMOVE ruser
```

NOTE: *The code above must be placed on one line.*

Here, **computer** is the computer name to create the share on; **name** is the name of the share; **path** is the path to create the share to; **guser** is the username to grant **permissions** to; and **ruser** is the username to deny share access to.

TIP: *RMTSHARE.EXE also supports the same switches as the **NET SHARE** command.*

Calling System Events

In Chapter 4, you learned how to call system events (for example, shutdown, restart) using DLL calls. In this section, you will learn how to call these events without using DLL calls.

Shutting Down/Restarting the Computer

The resource kit utility SHUTDOWN.EXE allows you to shut down or restart Windows. The basic syntax of the SHUTDOWN command is:

```
SHUTDOWN parameters
```

The available parameters for SHUTDOWN.EXE are as follows:

- **"message"** —Displays a message prior to shutdown
- **/A**—Used to abort a shutdown performed with the **/T** switch

- /C—Force-closes all running applications
- /L—Specifies to work with the local computer
- /R—Restarts the computer after shutdown
- /T:*seconds*—Performs a shutdown after the number of seconds specified
- /Y—Answers YES to any dialog box prompts

WARNING! Using the /C switch will close all applications without saving and might result in losing data. Use this switch only when you are certain that the local machine does not have any open unsaved files.

Related solution:	Found on page:
Shutting Down a System	185

Logging Off a User

The resource kit utility LOGOFF.EXE allows you to log off a user from a current Windows session. The basic syntax of the LOGOFF command is:

```
LOGOFF /F /N
```

Here, **/F** force-closes all running applications and **/N** removes any user prompts.

WARNING! Using the /F switch will close all applications without saving and may result in losing data. Use this switch only when you are certain that the local machine does not have any open unsaved files.

Chapter 7

Remote System Management

In Brief

Remote management is essential to becoming a good administrator. When you're working at a site with 300 or more systems, visiting and updating every single system becomes an impossible task. In this chapter, you will learn how to manage remote systems from the command line and through Windows Management Instrumentation.

Administrative Shares

By default, Windows NT/2000 creates special shares so that administrators can perform various tasks remotely. These special shares are called *administrative shares* and are automatically created when you install the operating system and whenever you add a nonremovable drive or partition. Administrative shares are hidden shares that only administrators can access. The permissions, names, and settings for these shares cannot be modified, and these shares can only be removed by making special registry entries. The most common administrative shares are:

- ADMIN$—Shares the directory Windows was installed in (for example, C:\WINNT)
- *DRIVE*$—Shares all available drives, where *drive* is the specific drive letter
- IPC$—Share that represents the named pipes communication mechanism
- PRINT$—Share for shared printer drivers
- REPL$—Shares replication directory on a server

Attaching to Shares

Many remote administrative tasks can be performed through network share access. Once you attach to a share, you can perform tasks on these shares as if they were local resources. The process of attaching to a network share and assigning that connection a drive letter is called *mapping*. Mapping a drive requires that you specify the complete Universal Naming Convention (UNC) path of the share and the available drive letter to which you want to map it.

Once you map a drive to a share, you will be able to perform many of the tasks you perform on your drives locally. To map a drive from

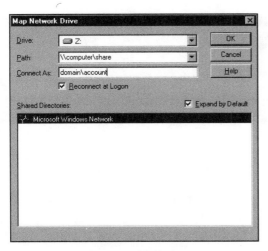

Figure 7.1   Mapping a network drive.

within Windows, right-click Network Neighborhood and select Map Drive. The Map Network Drive dialog box will appear (see Figure 7.1).

To map a drive from the command line, start a command prompt and enter the following:

```
NET USE DRIVE: \\COMPUTER\SHARE
```

Here, **DRIVE** is the drive letter you want to map the **SHARE** name to, and **COMPUTER** is the system holding the shared resource.

Performing Tasks through a Share

Once a remote share has been mapped, you can perform command-line tasks on it as if it were a local drive. Here is an example to delete all the files within a directory on a remote system:

```
NET USE DRIVE: \\COMPUTER\SHARE
DEL DRIVE:\*.*
```

Once a drive is successfully mapped, you can utilize any of the file management methods that were detailed in Chapter 4.

Disconnecting Mapped Shares

When you no longer need to access the resources of a mapped share, you can disconnect it to free up available drives. To disconnect a mapped drive from within Windows, right-click Network Neighborhood

7. Remote System Management

Figure 7.2   Disconnecting a mapped drive.

and select Disconnect Drive. When the Disconnect Network Drive dialog box appears (see Figure 7.2), select the drive and click OK.

To disconnect a mapped share from the command line, start a command prompt and enter the following:

```
NET USE DRIVE: /DELETE
```

Here, **DRIVE** is the drive letter mapped to the share that you want to disconnect.

TIP: /D is the abbreviated form of the /DELETE switch.

Windows Management Instrumentation

As enterprises grow larger, they become more difficult to manage. Web-Based Enterprise Management (WBEM) is an initiative to provide an environment-independent solution to manage data and devices. WBEM was developed by the Desktop Management Task Force (DMTF), a collective organization consisting of Microsoft, Compaq, and other large corporations. Windows Management Instrumentation (WMI) is Microsoft's Windows implementation of the WBEM initiative.

What Is WMI?

WMI, formerly called WBEM, provides scripters and developers with a standardized method to monitor and manage local and remote resources. It comes included in Windows 98 and Windows 2000, and is available as a download for Windows 95 and Windows NT (Service Pack 5 or higher). WMI provides a standard, scriptable interface to various resources. The devices and applications controlled by WMI are known as *managed objects*. Managed objects can be anything from hardware, such as a hub or motherboard, to software, such as the operating system or an application.

The WMI Process

The executable that provides all the functionality of WMI is called WINMGMT.EXE. WINMGMT.EXE runs as a standard executable on Windows 9x (because Windows 9x does not support services) and as a service on Windows NT/2000 systems. When a script or application (known as a consumer) issues calls to the WMI namespace, the executable awakes and passes these calls to the CIM Object Manager (CIMOM). The CIMOM is the entrance to the WMI infrastructure. It allows for the initial object creation and provides a uniform method to access managed objects. When CIMOM receives a request to control a managed object, it first checks the CIMOM object repository.

The CIMOM object repository is a storage area for the Common Information Model (CIM). The CIM contains the WMI object models and a description of all the available managed objects, called the *management schema*. This repository is full of all the different access methods and properties of manageable objects, known as static management data. If the information requested cannot be found in the repository, the repository passes the request down to the object provider.

A *provider* is the interface between the device to be managed and the CIMOM. The provider collects the information from a device and makes it available to the CIMOM. This information is known as dynamic management data. Developers create providers when the CIM does not contain methods to access a managed resource. Several providers come packaged with WMI:

- Active Directory provider
- Event Log provider
- Performance Counter provider
- Registry provider
- SNMP provider
- View provider
- WDM provider
- Win32 provider
- Windows Installer provider

Once the provider has completed processing the request, it sends all results back to the originating script or application.

7. Remote System Management

Scripting WMI

In Chapter 3, you learned how to connect to a WSH object. The process of connecting to the WMI object model is similar to connecting to the WSH object model. To gain access to an object, you use the **GetObject** function and set it to a variable. This is called *instantiating* an object, as in the following example:

```
Set variable = GetObject("winmgmts:{impersonationLevel=
impersonate}!\\computer\root\namespace").ExecQuery
(WQL)
```

NOTE: *The code above must be placed on one line.*

Here, ***variable*** is the variable used throughout your script to access all the properties and methods within the object. The **winmgmts** namespace specifies a call to the WMI service.

Impersonation

{Impersonationlevel=impersonate}! instructs WMI to execute the script with the credentials of the caller (person who executed the script) and not the credentials of the currently logged-on user of the targeted system. This instruction is extremely useful when administrators are running remote scripts on Windows NT/2000 systems, and the users do not have sufficient privileges to perform all the specified requests.

TIP: *{Impersonationlevel=impersonate}! is the default impersonation level on Windows 2000, and therefore can be omitted from your scripts if you are running Windows 2000. It is included in the scripts in this book only for Windows NT compatibility. Impersonations are not supported by Windows 9x because the operating system does not support user privileges.*

Namespaces

Computer is the name of the target system to run the script on, and **\ROOT*namespace*** specifies which namespace to connect to within the CIMOM object repository. Namespaces are organized containers of information within a schema. Namespace hierarchy runs from left to right and is separated with backslashes. ROOT is the parent namespace for WMI and contains all the child namespaces. WMI includes three child namespaces:

- *Cimv2*—Stores Win32 system classes
- *Default*—Stores system classes
- *Security*—Stores WMI security classes

Most of your WMI scripting will include the Cimv2 namespace, because it holds many classes and instances for a Win32 system.

WMI Query Language

WMI uses a rich query language called the WMI Query Language (WQL). This language, similar to SQL (Structured Query Language), allows you to query WMI information. The basic syntax for a WQL statement is as follows:

```
.ExecQuery("select propmeth from class")
```

TIP: *In addition to the **select** and **from** statements above, you can use many statements and keywords based on SQL.*

ExecQuery runs the WQL statement, which is stored in quotes and surrounded by parentheses. **Propmeth** specifies the property or method to retrieve from the specified **class**. Classes are organized containers for properties and methods of a manageable device. For example, the **Win32_TapeDrive** class contains all the properties and methods to manage tape drives.

In addition to the **ExecQuery**, you can also use the **ExecNotification-Query** to perform WQL queries. The **ExecNotificationQuery** method is used to detect when instances of a class are modified. In plain English, this method allows you to poll for events. Combined with WQL, you can use this method to monitor the event log, CPU, memory, and more based on a specified interval.

The WMI SDK: Worth Its Weight in Gold

Microsoft creates software developer kits (SDKs) to assist third-party application developers in creating Windows applications. The WMI SDK includes the core WMI installation, documentation, utilities, and examples. You can obtain the WMI SDK free from **msdn.microsoft.com**.

WMI Object Browser

The WMI Object Browser (see Figure 7.3) is a Web application to explore WMI namespaces. Through it, you can view and manipulate all the classes and their properties and methods. The application runs within a Web browser and allows you to connect to any namespace on a local or remote system.

7. Remote System Management

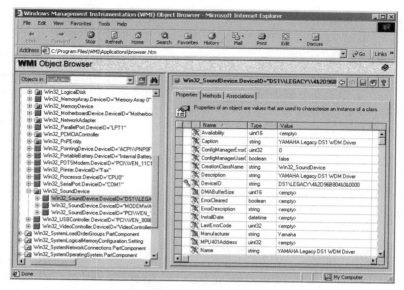

Figure 7.3   The WMI Object Browser.

NOTE: *The WMI Object Browser is an intensive Web application. If it seems to be frozen when navigating through the various classes, it may actually be loading the properties, methods, and subclasses into memory.*

Immediate Solutions

Remote Management from the Command Line

Most local system management is performed from the Control Panel or from administrative tools on Windows NT/2000 systems. Although most of these tools include some remote management capability, you can use command-line utilities to create scripts for remote management.

Installing the Remote Console

Remote Console is a resource kit utility that allows you to run a client/server command-prompt session between two systems, similar to a telnet session. To install the Remote Console, start a command prompt and enter the following:

```
RSETUP \\computer
```

WARNING! *The resource kit version of Remote Console has a memory leak. You should obtain the updated version from www.microsoft.com.*

Installing the Remote Command

Remote Command is a resource kit utility that allows you to run a program and a command prompt session on a remote computer from your local station. In essence, you call up a command prompt window on your machine that will run commands on the remote machine. To install the remote command service, start a command prompt and enter the following:

```
RCMDSVC -INSTALL
NET START "Remote Command Service"
```

Executing Commands on a Remote System

You can start commands on a remote system using either the remote command (RCMD) or Remote Console utilities. The remote command utility allows you to start either a batch file or a program on a remote system. To start a command on a remote system using the remote command, start a command prompt and enter the following:

```
RCMD \\computer program
```

The Remote Console utility allows you to start a batch file on a remote system. To start a batch file on a remote system using Remote Console, start a command prompt and enter the following:

```
RCLIENT \\computer /RUNBATCH program
```

Here, **computer** is the remote system to run the *program* on.

Listing Shares and Permissions

SRVCHECK.EXE is a resource kit utility to list shares and permissions on a remote system. To view the shares and permission on a remote system, start a command prompt and enter the following:

```
SRVCHECK \\computer
```

Here, **computer** is the name of the remote system.

Related solution:	Found on page:
Listing Shares	159

Creating Shares with Permissions

RMTSHARE.EXE is a resource kit utility to create shares with permissions on remote stations. To use RMTSHARE.EXE to create shares with permissions, start a command prompt and enter the following:

```
RMTSHARE \\computer\name=path /GRANT guser:permission
/REMOVE ruser
```

NOTE: *The code above must be placed on one line.*

Here, **computer** is the computer name to create the share on; **name** is the name of the share; **path** is the path to create the share to; **guser** is the username to grant **permissions** to; and **ruser** is the username to deny share access to.

TIP: *RMTSHARE.EXE also supports the same switches as the **NET SHARE** command.*

Related solution:	Found on page:
Creating Shares with Permissions	161

Listing Processes

PULIST.EXE is a resource kit utility that allows you to list running processes and their associated IDs on a remote system. To display remote processes, start a command prompt and enter the following:

```
PULIST \\COMPUTER
```

Terminating Processes

The resource kit provides a service called RKILLSRV.EXE that allows you to view and terminate processes on a remote PC. Unfortunately, not all of us are lucky enough to have the time or authority to install any services we like. PSKILL.EXE is a free utility from Sysinternals (**www.sysinternals.com**) that allows you to terminate a process or a remote station without having to add any additional services or configuration. To terminate a process on a remote system, start a command prompt and enter the following:

```
PSKILL \\computer -U username -P password process
```

Here, ***computer*** is the name of the remote system, ***username*** and ***password*** are the administrative credentials for the remote system, and ***process*** is the name or process ID to terminate. Here is a quick example to terminate a user running Notepad:

```
PSKILL \\computer -U username -P password notepad
```

Listing Services

SCLIST.EXE is a resource kit utility that allows you to list running services on a remote system. To display remote services, start a command prompt and enter the following:

```
SCLIST \\computer parameters
```

7. Remote System Management

Here, *computer* is the name of the remote system to display services. The available *parameters* for SCLIST are as follows:

- */M*—Displays all services
- */R*—Displays running services
- */S*—Displays stopped services

Alternatively, you can use the resource kit utility NETSVC to list services:

```
NETSVC /LIST
```

Managing Services

NETSVC is a resource kit utility that allows you to manage services on remote systems. The basic syntax for NETSVC is:

```
NETSVC parameter service \\computer
```

Here, *parameter* is the action to perform; *service* is the specific service to work with; and *computer* is the remote system to manage. Here is a list of available NETSVC parameters:

- */CONTINUE*—Restarts a service
- */LIST*—Lists services, do not specify a service name
- */PAUSE*—Pauses a service
- */QUERY*—Displays the status of a service
- */START*—Starts a service
- */STOP*—Stops a service

Related solution:	Found on page:
Managing Services from the Command Line	155

Remote Management through WMI

WMI provides a standard scriptable interface to your local and network resources. Using WMI, you can monitor and manipulate many settings on any resource on your network.

Listing Shares

The **Win32_Share** class manages all shared resources on a system. These devices include directories, drives, printers, removable media, or any other shareable resource. To list all shares on a system using WMI, proceed as follows:

1. Create a new directory to store all files included in this example.
2. Download and install the latest version of WMI and Windows Script Host, from **www.microsoft.com**, to the new directory.
3. Select Start|Run and enter "cscript *scriptfile*.vbs".

Here, *scriptfile* is the full path and file name of a script file that contains the following:

```
On Error Resume Next
Computer = InputBox("Enter the computer name",
"List Shares", "localhost")

Set Shares = GetObject("winmgmts:{impersonationLevel=
impersonate}!\\" & Computer & "\root\cimv2").ExecQuery
("select * from Win32_Share")

For each Share in Shares
   SList = SList & Share.Caption & " = " & Share.Path & VBlf
Next

WScript.Echo "Shares:" & VBlf & VBlf & SList
```

NOTE: *The highlighted code above must be placed on one line.*

Related solution:	Found on page:
Listing Shares	159

Creating a Share

The **Create** method for **Win32_Share** allows you to share a resource. To create a share using WMI, proceed as follows:

1. Create a new directory to store all files included in this example.
2. Download and install the latest version of WMI and Windows Script Host, from **www.microsoft.com**, to the new directory.
3. Select Start|Run and enter "cscript *scriptfile*.vbs".

Here, *scriptfile* is the full path and file name of a script file that contains the code shown on the next page.

```
On Error Resume Next
Computer = InputBox("Enter the computer name", "Create Share",
"localhost")

SName = InputBox("Enter the name of the share", "Share Name",
"Temp")

SPath = InputBox("Enter the path of the share", "Share Path",
"C:\Temp")

TypeMenu = "Choose a share type:" & VBlf & VBlf & _
   "0 - Disk Drive" & VBlf & _
   "1 - Print Queue" & VBlf & _
   "2 - Device" & VBlf & _
   "3 - IPC" & VBlf & _
   "2147483648 - Disk Drive Admin" & VBlf & _
   "2147483649 - Print Queue Admin" & VBlf & _
   "2147483650 - Device Admin" & VBlf & _
   "2147483651 - IPC Admin"

SType = InputBox(TypeMenu, "Share Type", 0)
SMax = InputBox("Enter the maximum number of users",
"Maximum Users", 10)

SDescribe = InputBox("Enter the description of the share",
"Share Description", "Temp Share")

SPass = InputBox("Enter the password to access the share",
"Share Password", "Temp Password")

Set Security = GetObject("winmgmts:{impersonationLevel=
impersonate,(Security)}!\\" & Computer & "\root\cimv2")

Set Share = Security.Get("Win32_Share")
Set Methods = Share.Methods_("Create").
InParameters.SpawnInstance_()
   Methods.Properties_.Item("Description") = SDescribe
   Methods.Properties_.Item("MaximumAllowed") = SMax
   Methods.Properties_.Item("Name") = SName
   Methods.Properties_.Item("Password") = SPass
   Methods.Properties_.Item("Path") = SPath
   Methods.Properties_.Item("Type") = SType
Set Complete = Share.ExecMethod_("Create", Methods)
```

NOTE: *The highlighted code above must be placed on one line. The* **(Security)** *statement is necessary because this script modifies share access.*

Related solution:	Found on page:
Adding Shares	159

Deleting a Share

The **Delete** method for **Win32_Share** allows you to delete a share from a manageable system. To delete a share using WMI, proceed as follows:

1. Create a new directory to store all files included in this example.

2. Download and install the latest version of WMI and Windows Script Host, from **www.microsoft.com**, to the new directory.

3. Select Start|Run and enter "cscript *scriptfile*.vbs".

Here, *scriptfile* is the full path and file name of a script file that contains the following:

```
On Error Resume Next
Computer = InputBox("Enter the computer name",
"Delete Share", "localhost")

SName = InputBox("Enter the name of the share",
"Delete Share")

Set Shares = GetObject("winmgmts:{impersonationLevel=
impersonate}!\\" & Computer & "\root\cimv2").ExecQuery
("select * from Win32_Share where Name = '" & SName & "'")

For each Share in Shares
  Share.Delete()
Next
```

NOTE: *The highlighted code above must be placed on one line.*

Related solution:	Found on page:
Removing Shares	160

Listing Processes

The **Win32_Process** class manages all running processes on a system. These processes include all running applications, background tasks, and hidden system processes. To list all running processes using WMI, proceed as follows:

1. Create a new directory to store all files included in this example.

2. Download and install the latest version of WMI and Windows Script Host, from **www.microsoft.com**, to the new directory.

3. Select Start|Run and enter "cscript *scriptfile*.vbs".

Here, ***scriptfile*** is the full path and file name of a script file that contains the following:

```
On Error Resume Next
Computer = InputBox("Enter the computer name",
"List Processes", "localhost")

Set Processes = GetObject("winmgmts:{impersonationLevel=
impersonate}!\\" & Computer & "\root\cimv2").ExecQuery
("select * from Win32_Process")

For each Process in Processes
   PList = PList & Process.Description & VBlf
Next

WScript.Echo "Processes:" & VBlf & VBlf & UCase(PList)
```

NOTE: *The highlighted code above must be placed on one line.*

Creating a Process

The **Create** method for **Win32_Process** allows you to create a new process. The key benefit of this method is the ability to launch an application, such as a virus scanner or an application update, on a remote system. To create a process using WMI, proceed as follows:

1. Create a new directory to store all files included in this example.

2. Download and install the latest version of WMI and Windows Script Host, from **www.microsoft.com**, to the new directory.

3. Select Start|Run and enter "cscript *scriptfile*.vbs".

Here, ***scriptfile*** is the full path and file name of a script file that contains the following:

```
On Error Resume Next
Computer = InputBox("Enter the computer name", _
"Start Process", "localhost")


AName = InputBox("Enter the executable to run",
"Start Process", "explorer")


Set Process = GetObject("winmgmts:{impersonationLevel=
impersonate}!\\" & Computer & "\root\cimv2:Win32_Process")


Process.Create AName,null,null,null
```

NOTE: *The highlighted code above must be placed on one line.*

Terminating a Process

The **Terminate** method for **Win32_Process** allows you to end a process and all its threads. The key benefit of this method is the ability to forcibly close a running application, such as an unauthorized port scanner or a corrupted program, on a remote system. To terminate a process using WMI, proceed as follows:

1. Create a new directory to store all files included in this example.

2. Download and install the latest version of WMI and Windows Script Host, from **www.microsoft.com**, to the new directory.

3. Select Start|Run and enter "cscript *scriptfile*.vbs".

Here, *scriptfile* is the full path and file name of a script file that contains the following:

```
On Error Resume Next
Computer = InputBox("Enter the computer name",
"Terminate Process", "localhost")


PName = InputBox("Enter the name of the process",
"Terminate Process")


Set Processes = GetObject("winmgmts:{impersonationLevel=
impersonate}!\\" & Computer & "\root\cimv2").ExecQuery
("select * from Win32_Process where Name = '" & PName & "'")
```

```
For each Process in Processes
   Process.Terminate
Next
```

NOTE: *The highlighted code above must be placed on one line.*

Listing Services

The **Win32_Service** class manages all services installed on a system. This class does not apply to Windows 9*x*, because Windows 9*x* does not support services. To list all installed services using WMI, proceed as follows:

1. Create a new directory to store all files included in this example.

2. Download and install the latest version of WMI and Windows Script Host, from **www.microsoft.com**, to the new directory.

3. Select Start|Run and enter "cscript *scriptfile*.vbs".

Here, ***scriptfile*** is the full path and file name of a script file that contains the following:

```
On Error Resume Next
Computer = InputBox("Enter the computer name",
"List Services", "localhost")

Set Services = GetObject("winmgmts:{impersonationLevel=
impersonate}!\\" & Computer & "\root\cimv2").ExecQuery
("select * from Win32_Service")

For each Service in Services
   If Service.State = "Paused" Then
     PList = PList & Service.Description & VBlf
   End If
   If Service.State = "Running" Then
     RList = RList & Service.Description & VBlf
   End If
   If Service.State = "Stopped" Then
     SList = SList & Service.Description & VBlf
   End If
Next

WScript.Echo "Paused Services: " & VBlf & VBlf & PList
WScript.Echo "Running Services: " & VBlf & VBlf & RList
WScript.Echo "Stopped Services: " & VBlf & VBlf & SList
```

Starting Services

The **StartService** method for **Win32_Service** allows you to start a stopped service. This method applies only to stopped services; paused services have their own method for resumption. To start a stopped service using WMI, proceed as follows:

1. Create a new directory to store all files included in this example.

2. Download and install the latest version of WMI and Windows Script Host, from **www.microsoft.com**, to the new directory.

3. Select Start|Run and enter "cscript *scriptfile*.vbs".

Here, *scriptfile* is the full path and file name of a script file that contains the following:

```
On Error Resume Next
Computer = InputBox("Enter the computer name",
"Start Service", "localhost")

SName = InputBox("Enter the name of the service",
"Start Service")

Set Services = GetObject("winmgmts:{impersonationLevel=
impersonate}!\\" & Computer & "\root\cimv2").ExecQuery
("select * from Win32_Service where Name = '" & SName & "'")

For each Service in Services
    Service.StartService()
Next
```

Related solution:	Found on page:
Starting a Service	156

Stopping Services

The **StopService** method for **Win32_Service** allows you to stop a service. Through this method, you can stop a running or paused service. To stop a service using WMI, proceed as follows:

1. Create a new directory to store all files included in this example.

7. Remote System Management

2. Download and install the latest version of WMI and Windows Script Host, from **www.microsoft.com**, to the new directory.

3. Select Start|Run and enter "cscript *scriptfile*.vbs".

Here, ***scriptfile*** is the full path and file name of a script file that contains the following:

```
On Error Resume Next
Computer = InputBox("Enter the computer name",
"Stop Service", "localhost")

SName = InputBox("Enter the name of the service",
"Stop Service")

Set Services = GetObject("winmgmts:{impersonationLevel=
impersonate}!\\" & Computer & "\root\cimv2").ExecQuery
("select * from Win32_Service where Name = '" & SName & "'")

For each Service in Services
   Service.StopService()
Next
```

NOTE: *The highlighted code above must be placed on one line.*

Related solution:	Found on page:
Stopping a Service	157

Pausing Services

The **PauseService** method for **Win32_Service** allows you to pause a running service. This method will not place a stopped service into paused mode. To pause a running service using WMI, proceed as follows:

1. Create a new directory to store all files included in this example.

2. Download and install the latest version of WMI and Windows Script Host, from **www.microsoft.com**, to the new directory.

3. Select Start|Run and enter "cscript *scriptfile*.vbs".

Here, *scriptfile* is the full path and file name of a script file that contains the following:

```
On Error Resume Next
Computer = InputBox("Enter the computer name",
"Pause Service", "localhost")

SName = InputBox("Enter the name of the service",
"Pause Service")

Set Services = GetObject("winmgmts:{impersonationLevel=
impersonate}!\\" & Computer & "\root\cimv2").ExecQuery
("select * from Win32_Service where Name = '" & SName & "'")

For each Service in Services
  Service.PauseService()
Next
```

NOTE: *The highlighted code above must be placed on one line.*

Resuming Services

The **ResumeService** method for **Win32_Service** allows you to resume a paused service. This method will not start a stopped service. To create a process using WMI, proceed as follows:

1. Create a new directory to store all files included in this example.

2. Download and install the latest version of WMI and Windows Script Host, from **www.microsoft.com**, to the new directory.

3. Select Start|Run and enter "cscript *scriptfile*.vbs".

Here, *scriptfile* is the full path and file name of a script file that contains the following:

```
On Error Resume Next
Computer = InputBox("Enter the computer name",
"Resume Service", "localhost")

SName = InputBox("Enter the name of the service",
"Resume Service")
```

7. Remote System Management

```
Set Services = GetObject("winmgmts:{impersonationLevel=
impersonate}!\\" & Computer & "\root\cimv2").ExecQuery
("select * from Win32_Service where Name = '" & SName & "'")

For each Service in Services
   Service.ResumeService()
Next
```

NOTE: *The highlighted code above must be placed on one line.*

Deleting a Service

The **Delete** method for **Win32_Services** allows you to remove a service from your system. This method will happen immediately, regardless of whether a service is running. To delete a service using WMI, proceed as follows:

1. Create a new directory to store all files included in this example.

2. Download and install the latest version of WMI and Windows Script Host, from **www.microsoft.com**, to the new directory.

3. Select Start|Run and enter "cscript *scriptfile*.vbs".

Here, *scriptfile* is the full path and file name of a script file that contains the following:

```
On Error Resume Next
Computer = InputBox("Enter the computer name",
"Delete Service", "localhost")

SName = InputBox("Enter the name of the service",
"Delete Service")

Set Services = GetObject("winmgmts:{impersonationLevel=
impersonate}!\\" & Computer & "\root\cimv2").ExecQuery
("select * from Win32_Service where Name = '" & SName & "'")

For each Service in Services
   Service.Delete()
Next
```

NOTE: *The highlighted code above must be placed on one line.*

Related solution:	*Found on page:*
Uninstalling a Service	156

Rebooting a System

The **Win32_OperatingSystem** class manages many aspects of the Windows operating system, from the serial number to the service pack. The **Reboot** method for **Win32_OperatingSystem** allows you to shut down and restart a manageable system. To reboot a system using WMI, proceed as follows:

1. Create a new directory to store all files included in this example.

2. Download and install the latest version of WMI and Windows Script Host, from **www.microsoft.com**, to the new directory.

3. Select Start|Run and enter "cscript *scriptfile*.vbs".

Here, *scriptfile* is the full path and file name of a script file that contains the following:

```
On Error Resume Next
Computer = InputBox("Enter the computer name",
"Reboot System", "localhost")

Set OS = GetObject("winmgmts:{impersonationLevel=
impersonate}!\\" & Computer & "\root\cimv2").ExecQuery
("select * from Win32_ OperatingSystem where Primary=true")

For each System in OS
  System.Reboot()
Next
```

Here, **Primary=True** is a check to ensure that Windows is the primary operating system currently running.

NOTE: *The highlighted code above must be placed on one line.*

Related solution:	*Found on page:*
Shutting Down/Restarting the Computer	161

Shutting Down a System

The **ShutDown** method for **Win32_OperatingSystem** allows you to shut down a computer to the prompt "It is now safe to turn off your computer." To shut down a system using WMI, proceed as follows:

1. Create a new directory to store all files included in this example.

2. Download and install the latest version of WMI and Windows Script Host, from **www.microsoft.com**, to the new directory.

3. Select Start|Run and enter "cscript *scriptfile*.vbs".

Here, ***scriptfile*** is the full path and file name of a script file that contains the following:

```
On Error Resume Next
Computer = InputBox("Enter the computer name",
"Reboot System", "localhost")

Set OS = GetObject("winmgmts:{impersonationLevel=
impersonate}!\\" & Computer & "\root\cimv2").ExecQuery
("select * from Win32_ OperatingSystem where Primary=true")

For each System in OS
   System.Shutdown()
Next
```

NOTE: *The highlighted code above must be placed on one line.*

Related solution:	Found on page:
Shutting Down/Restarting the Computer	161

Monitoring CPU Utilization

To monitor CPU utilization using the WMI ExecNotificationQuery method, proceed as follows:

1. Create a new directory to store all files included in this example.
2. Download and install the latest version of WMI and Windows Script Host, from **www.microsoft.com**, to the new directory.
3. Select Start|Run and enter "cscript *scriptfile*.vbs".

Here, ***scriptfile*** is the full path and file name of a script file that contains the following:

```
On Error Resume Next
Computer = InputBox("Enter the computer name",
"CPU Monitor", "localhost")

CPULoad = InputBox("Enter the CPU overload threshold",
"CPU Threshold", "75")

Poll = InputBox("Enter the polling interval",
"Poll Interval", "5")
If Computer = "" Then Computer = "Localhost"
```

```
If CPULoad = "" Then CPULoad = 75
If Poll = "" Then Poll = 5
Set ProLoad = GetObject("winmgmts:{impersonationLevel=
impersonate}!\\" & Computer & "\root\cimv2").
ExecNotificationQuery("SELECT * FROM __
InstanceModificationEvent WITHIN " & Poll & " WHERE
TargetInstance ISA 'Win32_Processor' and
TargetInstance .LoadPercentage > " & CPULoad)
If Err.Number <> 0 then
  WScript.Echo Err.Description, Err.Number, Err.Source
End If

Do
  Set ILoad = ProLoad.nextevent
  If Err.Number <> 0 then
    WScript.Echo Err.Number, Err.Description, Err.Source
    Exit Do
  Else
    AMessage = ILoad.TargetInstance.DeviceID & _
    " is overloaded at " & _
    & ILoad.TargetInstance.LoadPercentage & "%!"
    Wscript.Echo "Event Alert: " & AMessage
  End If
Loop
```

NOTE: *The highlighted code above must be placed on one line.*

Here, ***computer*** is the name of the system to monitor; ***CPULoad*** is the CPU utilization threshold to monitor for (1–100); and ***poll*** is the amount of seconds to check for events.

Related solution:	Found on page:
Scripting Microsoft Agent Using Windows Script Host	365

7. Remote System Management

Chapter 8

Enterprise Management

In Brief

Corporations spend millions of dollars a year on packaged applications and manpower to keep their computing environments running like finely tuned engines. Although most third-party solutions provide the tools to assist in enterprise management, they often come overloaded with fancy reporting features and are limited in actual functionality. And when you finally find a package that is really helpful in your administrative tasks, you'd be lucky to get the budget approval passed in this lifetime.

In this chapter, you will learn about all the important aspects of managing an enterprise environment, and how to maintain it without expensive third-party solutions. You will also learn how to accomplish most of your administrative tasks with simple scripts.

Understanding Windows NT Networks

An NT domain is a collection of computers that share a common security accounts database (SAM). The SAM (Security Account Manager) is a central repository to store user accounts and groups, as opposed to storing them individually on each computer. The SAM is stored on a server called a primary domain controller (PDC). In an NT domain, there can be only one PDC (sort of like Duncan MacCleod). The PDC replicates a read-only copy of the SAM to servers called backup domain controllers (BDCs). BDCs help reduce PDC overload by processing authentication requests and receiving SAM modification requests. Any requests to modify the SAM on a BDC are sent to and processed by the PDC (because the BDC has only a read-only copy of the SAM).

User Accounts and Groups

Within the SAM are user accounts and groups. A user account is basically an entry in a database that stores various types of information, such as the user name, password, and group membership. User accounts are used to limit resource access to anyone with the user name and password of the account. A group is basically an organized list of computer accounts. You can use groups to collectively assign privileges or organize membership. For example, placing users in the Administrators group would grant them administrative privileges (and make them very dangerous).

NT uses two types of users and groups: local and global. If an account or group is local, its information is stored in the SAM of a local computer and cannot be used outside the current domain. If an account or group is global, its information is stored on the PDC, is available throughout the entire domain, and may be used outside the domain. For example, if you are the local administrator of a computer, you have administrative privileges on that computer only and not on every computer in the domain, as a domain administrator would.

Domain Trust

To share resources across domains, NT uses a concept called "trust." You can think of a trust as a key to your office. When you give others your office key, they can unlock and access your office. You will not be able to unlock and access their offices until they give you their keys. When a domain trusts another domain, it allows the other domain to enter and access its resources as if it were part of the domain. Trusts are established through the User Manager For Domains utility and are one-way relationships. In order for two domains to share each other's resources, each domain must set up a trust for the other (a two-way trust).

Understanding Windows 2000 Networks

The biggest advantage of a Windows 2000 network as opposed to Windows NT is its restructuring and use of directory services. Windows 2000 gives you several new ways to organize and centrally manage your network.

Trees and Forests

Windows 2000 allows you to organize your domains into hierarchical groups called trees. Trees share a common schema, global catalog, replication information, and DNS namespace (for example, **www.jesseweb.com**). Once trees are established, you can organize your trees into hierarchical groups called forests. Forests also share a common schema, global catalog, and replication information, but do not share a common DNS namespace. This allows you to combine the resources of two completely separate Internet domains (for example, **www.mydomain.com** and **www.yourdomain.com**). Through trees and forests, Windows 2000 automatically establishes two-way trusts between all domains.

Objects

Windows 2000 treats all resources as objects. These objects can consist of any of the various resources on a network, such as users, computers, printers, and shares. Each object contains its own set of attributes, functions, and properties as set by the schema. Whenever you access a resource, the schema sets which properties and features are presentable. For example, a user account has a lockout property but a share does not, as instructed by the schema.

Organizational Units

Windows 2000 allows you to organize network objects into logical containers called Organizational Units (OUs). OUs can contain any network resource, such as accounts, groups, queues, shares, and even other OUs. Through OUs, you can delegate administration and assign permissions to the OU or the individual objects within. The most common use of organizational units is to organize company resources by department.

Global Catalog

Windows 2000 stores information about the objects in a tree or forest in a common database, called a global catalog. Global catalog servers reduce network searches and object query time by processing these requests directly. The first domain controller within a forest stores the global catalog, and is called a global catalog server. You can assign additional global catalog servers to help network queries.

WARNING! Global catalog servers synchronize their information through replication. A large quantity of catalog servers can cripple a network with replication traffic.

ADSI

Active Directory Services Interfaces (ADSI), previously OLE Directory Services, is Microsoft's implementation of a directory service that organizes an enterprise into a tree-like structure. A directory service provides a standard consistent method to manage and locate network resources. Directory services are actually databases that store information about all the resources on your network. Whenever a request for a network resource is made, the directory service interprets and processes the request. ADSI comes packaged with Windows 2000 Server and is available as a free, separate download from Microsoft for Windows 9*x*/NT.

The ADSI Process

When a script or application issues a call to ADSI, the call is first sent to the ADSI client, as shown in Figure 8.1. The ADSI client is included in all versions of Windows 2000 and is available as a download for Windows 9*x*/NT systems. Do not confuse the ADSI client with the Active Directory Services Interface. The client is used to access a directory service, whereas the Active Directory Services Interface is the directory service itself.

NOTE: *Windows 2000 Server contains both the Active Directory Services Interfaces and the ADSI client.*

Once the client receives the call, it passes it to the object model, called a router. The router interprets the request and passes it to the appropriate

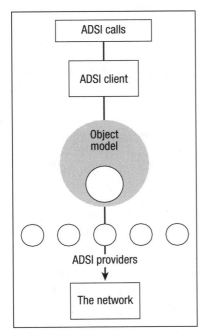

Figure 8.1   The ADSI process.

provider. The provider is then responsible to take the appropriate action based on the request.

Providers

ADSI provides a common interface to manage the network, regardless of directory service type. ADSI uses components called providers to communicate with other directory services. These providers are stored in DLL files and are loaded when ADSI is installed. The various providers included with ADSI are as follows:

- IIS (Adsiis.dll)—Provider for Internet Information Server
- LDAP (Adsldp.dll, Adsldpc.dll, and Adsmext.dll)—Provider for Windows 2000 Server and other LDAP-compliant applications
- NWCompat (Adsnw.dll)—Provider to Netware Bindery servers
- NDS (Adsnds.dll)—Provider for Novell NDS servers
- WinNT (Adsnt.dll)—Provider for Windows NT domains and Windows 2000 local resources

---

NOTE: *The provider names, specified in parentheses above, are case-sensitive.*

The next section will give you a brief overview of the two main Windows providers: LDAP and WinNT.

The LDAP Provider

Lightweight Directory Access Protocol (LDAP) was developed in 1990 as a simple alternative to the complex X.500 directory standard. The LDAP provider is used to manage Windows 2000 Active Directory servers, Exchange 5.5 or higher servers, Lotus Notes servers, Netscape directory servers, and other LDAP-compliant applications or servers. The basic syntax to bind to the LDAP provider is:

```
Set variable = GetObject("LDAP:OU=orgunit, DC=Domain")
```

Here, *variable* is an arbitrary variable that you can use to access the LDAP provider; *orgunit* is the name of the organizational unit; and *domain* is the name of the domain you want to connect to.

Windows 2000 uses Internet domain names, such as **marketing. jesseweb.com**. Each of the domain levels must be separated by commas and in descending hierarchy, as follows:

```
Set variable = GetObject("LDAP:OU=orgunit, DC=marketing,
DC=jesseweb, DC=com")
```

NOTE: *The code above must be placed on one line.*

With LDAP, you can avoid specifying domain names by binding to the directory tree directly:

```
Set Variable = GetObject("LDAP://rootDSE")
```

The WinNT Provider

The WinNT provider is used to manage Windows NT domain resources and Windows 2000 local resources. This provider is provided for backward compatibility with Windows NT domains and cannot access Windows 2000 Internet domain names. Through this provider, you can manage your NT domain without having to upgrade to Windows 2000. The basic syntax to bind to the WinNT provider is:

```
Set variable = GetObject("WinNT://Domain/Computer/
Object,Class")
```

NOTE: *The code above must be placed on one line.*

Here, *variable* is an arbitrary variable that you can use to access the WinNT provider; *domain* is the name of the domain you want to connect to; *computer* is the name of the system to connect to; *object* is the object that you want to connect to; and *class* is the class type you want to connect to (for example, user, group, computer). Any parameters specified after the provider name, in this case **WinNT:**, are optional.

If you are working outside your domain or need to use a different account to access the domain, you must use the **OpenDSObject** function:

```
Set NTObj = GetObject("WinNT:")
Set variable = NTObj.OpenDSObject("WinNT://Domain/Server/
Object, username, password, ADS_SECURE_CREDENTIALS")
```

NOTE: *The highlighted code above must be placed on one line.*

Here, *password* is the password of the *username* to connect with.

Immediate Solutions

Managing Computer Accounts from the Command Line

Computer accounts, like user accounts, allow the system to be part of the domain and access its resources. When a computer joins a domain, a computer account is created on the PDC SAM establishing a one-way trust and allowing the computer to access the domain. Although computer account management is usually done through the administrative tools of the operating system, computer account management can be scripted from the command line.

Managing Computer Accounts with the NET Command

The built-in NET.EXE command allows you to manage computer accounts from the command line on any domain controller. The basic syntax of the NET command to add computer accounts is:

```
NET COMPUTER \\compname/commands
```

Here, ***compname*** is the computer account to manage, and the available ***commands*** are:

- **/ADD**—Adds a computer account to the domain
- **/DELETE**—Removes a computer account from the domain

TIP: You can use one of the remote management methods discussed in Chapter 7 to run this command on a remote domain controller.

Managing Computer Accounts with the NETDOM Utility

NETDOM is an NT resource kit utility to manage computer accounts from the command line. The basic syntax of NETDOM is:

```
NETDOM MEMBER \\computer /D:domain /U:domain\user
/P:password /commands
```

NOTE: The code above must be placed on one line.

Here, ***computer*** is the computer account to manage; ***password*** is the password of the ***domain\user*** account with privileges to manage computer accounts on the specified ***domain***; and the available ***commands*** are as follows:

- **/ADD**—Adds a computer account to the domain
- **/DELETE**—Removes a computer account from the domain
- **/JOINDOMAIN**—Joins the computer to the domain
- **/QUERY**—Retrieves information on an existing computer account

To connect to the domain and add a computer account, you would enter:

```
NETDOM MEMBER \\computer /D:domain /U:domain\user
/P:password /JOINDOMAIN

NETDOM MEMBER \\computer /D:domain /U:domain\user
/P:password /ADD
```

NOTE: *The code above must be placed on one line.*

To connect to the domain and remove a computer account, you would enter:

```
NETDOM MEMBER \\computer /D:domain /U:domain\user
/P:password /JOINDOMAIN

NETDOM MEMBER \\computer /D:domain /U:domain\user
/P:password /DELETE
```

NOTE: *The code above must be placed on one line.*

Managing User Accounts from the Command Line

User accounts allow users to access domain and local system resources with a valid username and password. Although user management is mostly done through the administrative tools of the operating system, scripting user account management from the command line is significantly faster when dealing with remote systems and multiple modifications.

Managing Computer Accounts with the NET Command

One of the most unused command-line utilities to manage user accounts is the NET command. The basic syntax of the NET command to manage user accounts is:

```
NET USER USERNAME PASSWORD /commands
```

Here, **username** is the user account to manage; **password** is either the password of the account or an asterisk (*) to be prompted for a password; and the available **commands** are as follows:

- **/ACTIVE:X**—Controls the activation of an account where X is YES or NO.

- **/ADD**—Adds a user account.

- **/DELETE**—Removes a user account.

- **/DOMAIN**—Creates the account in the currently active domain.

- **/COMMENT**: "X"—Sets the account description where X is the comment.

- **/COUNTRYCODE:X**—Sets the account's country code.

- **/USERCOMMENT**: "X"—Sets the user comment where X is the comment.

- **/EXPIRES:X**—Sets the expiration date of the account where X is either **NEVER** or a date in the format of MM/DD/YY. This format may differ depending on your country code.

- **/FULLNAME**: "X"—Sets the full account name where X is the name.

- **/HOMEDIR:X**—Sets the home directory where X is the path.

- **/PASSWORDCHG:X**—Controls the user's ability to change the password where X is **YES** or **NO**.

- **/PASSWORDREQ:X**—Sets whether a password is required where X is **YES** or **NO**.

- **/PROFILEPATH:X**—Sets the profile directory where X is the path.

- **/SCRIPTPATH:X**—Sets the logon script directory where X is the path.

- **/TIMES:X**—Sets the hours a user may log on where X is either **ALL** or days and times separated by commas.

Here is an example showing how to add an account using the NET command:

```
NET USER "Tyler" TEMPPASSWORD /ADD /COMMENT:"Project Account"
/ACTIVE:NO /EXPIRES:12/31/03 /FULLNAME:"Tyler Durden"
/HOMEDIR:C:\ /PASSWORDCHG:NO /PASSWORDREQ:YES
/PROFILEPATH:C:\PROFILES\TD /USERCOMMENT:"Corporate Sponsor"
/WORKSTATIONS:STATION1 /SCRIPTPATH:SOMEWHERE\OUTTHERE
/TIMES:MONDAY-THURSDAY,8AM-5PM
```

NOTE: *The code above must be placed on one line.*

Managing Computer Accounts with the ADDUSERS Utility

ADDUSERS.EXE is a resource kit utility to manage user accounts from the command line. This utility reads command-delimited text files and can create or delete user accounts. The basic syntax of ADDUSERS to manage user accounts is:

```
ADDUSERS \\computer commands file
```

Here, *computer* is the computer account to manage; *file* is the name of the comma-delimited text file to use; and the available *commands* are as follows:

- /C—Creates user accounts or groups specified in the *file*
- /D—Dumps the user account or group information to the *file*
- /E—Deletes user account specified in the *file*
- /P:X—If combined with /C, specifies the creating parameters where X is:
  - C—User cannot change password
  - D—Account disabled
  - E—Password never expires
  - L—Do not change password at next logon

TIP: *To add a user account to the local computer, omit the computer name from the command line.*

8. Enterprise Management

The basic syntax of the comma-delimited *file* is:

```
[User]
UserName,FullName,Password,Comment,Home,Profile,Script,
```

Here, *Comment* is the account description; *Home* is the path to the user home directory; *Profile* is the path to the user's profile; *Script* is the name of the logon script to use; and *UserNames* are the user names (separated by commas) to add to the groups.

The following example adds a user called JFROST to the computer BOB:

```
ADDUSERS \\BOB/C file
```

Here, *file* is the full path and file name of a text file that contains the following:

```
[User]
JFROST,Jack E. Frost,Password,Project Manager,\\SERVER\HOME\
JFROST,\\SERVER\PROFILE\JFROST,LOGON.KIX,
```

NOTE: *The highlighted code above must be placed on one line.*

Managing User Accounts with the CURSMGR Utility

CURSMGR.EXE is a resource kit utility to modify current account or group properties. This utility supports many switches, all of which are case-sensitive. The basic syntax of CURSMGR is:

```
CURSMGR -u username -m \\computer commands
```

Here, *username* is the user account to manage; *computer* is the computer name on which to perform management; and the available *commands* are as follows:

- **-C**—Sets user comment
- **-D**—Deletes a user account
- **-F**—Sets user full name
- **-h**—Sets the path to the user's home directory
- **-H**—Sets the drive letter to map the user's home directory
- **-n**—Sets the path to the logon script's directory
- **-p**—Sets a random password
- **-P**—Sets the password to Password

- **+-S**—Use the **+S** or **-S** to set or reset the following properties

  - **AccountLockout**—Locks/unlocks a user account

  - **MustChangePassword**—Sets/resets the User Must Change Password At Next Logon option

  - **CanNotChangePassword**—Sets/resets the User Cannot Change Password option

  - **PasswordNeverExpires** —Sets/resets the Password Never Expires option

  - **AccountDisabled**—Disables/enables an account

  - **RASUser**—Enables/disables remote access dial-in

- **-U**—Sets the path to the user's profile directory

Here is an example of how to modify a user account:

```
CUSRMGR -u name -m \\computer -h \\server\homeshare -f
"fullname" -c "description" -H Q
```

NOTE: *The code above must be placed on one line.*

Here, *name* is the user name; *computer* is the system that holds the account; *\\server\homeshare* is where the user's home directory resides; *fullname* is the user's fullname; and *description* is the account description.

Managing Groups from the Command Line

Groups allow administrators a method of organizing and assigning user account privileges. Groups are also helpful when attempting to identify a collection of users with a common trait (for example, temporary employees). You can script group management from the command line to automate your daily tasks.

Managing Groups with the NET Command

The built-in NET.EXE command allows you to manage local and global groups from the command line. The basic syntax of the NET command to manage global groups is:

```
NET type name commands
```

Here, **type** is the keyword **GROUP** for global or **LOCALGROUP** for local group management; **name** is the group to manage, and the available **commands** are as follows:

- **/ADD**—Adds user accounts to the specified group where multiple user accounts are separated by spaces

- **/COMMENT:"X"**—Sets the group comment

- **/DELETE**—Deletes a group or removes the user account from the specified group

- **/DOMAIN**—Performs the operation on the primary domain controller

- **username**—Specifies a user account to add or remove from the group

Managing Groups with the ADDUSERS Utility

Earlier in this chapter, you learned how to use the resource kit utility ADDUSERS.EXE to manage user accounts from the command line. This utility can also be used to add groups and group members from the command line. The basic syntax of ADDUSERS to add groups is:

```
ADDUSERS \\computer /C file
```

Here, **computer** is the computer account to manage, and **file** is the name of the comma-delimited text file to use. The basic syntax of the comma-delimited **file** is:

```
[Global]
Name,Comment,UserNames,
[Local]
Name,Comment,UserNames,
```

Here, the **[GLOBAL]** sections add global groups; **name** is the name of the group to add; **comment** is the group description; and **usernames** are the users, separated by commas, to add to the group.

Managing Groups with the USRTOGRP Utility

USRTOGRP.EXE is a resource kit utility to add user accounts to groups from the command line. The basic syntax of the USRTOGRP utility is:

```
USRTOGRP file
```

Here, *file* is a text file with the following format:

```
DOMAIN: computer grouptype: group users
```

Here, **computer** is the name of the system or domain that contains the specified group; **grouptype** specifies the group type as either **LOCALGROUP** or **GLOBALGROUP**; **group** is the name of the group; and **users** are the usernames, separated by spaces, to add to the group.

Here is a quick example to add two users to the Domain Admins group in the PROJECT domain:

```
USRTOGRP file
```

Here, *file* is the full path and file name of a text file that contains the following:

```
DOMAIN: PROJECT GLOBALGROUP: Domain Admins JACK TYLER
```

Managing the Enterprise with ADSI

Prior to ADSI, your only alternatives to manage network resources were command-line utilities and administrative tools. Through ADSI, you can create simple scripts to control all the resources of your network.

Listing a Share

To list shares using ADSI, proceed as follows:

1. Create a new directory to store all files included in this example.

2. Download and install the latest version of ADSI and Windows Script Host, from **www.microsoft.com**, to the new directory.

3. Select Start|Run and enter "cscript *scriptfile*.vbs".

Here, **scriptfile** is the full path and file name of a script file that contains the following:

```
On Error Resume Next
Set DomObj = GetObject("WinNT://Domain/Computer/lanmanserver,
FileService")
```

```
For each Share in DomObj
  List = List + Share.Name & VB1F
Next
Wscript.echo List
```

NOTE: *The highlighted code above must be placed on one line.*

Here, **domain** is the name of the domain, and **computer** is the computer name containing the shares to list.

Related solution:	Found on page:
Listing Shares	159

Creating a Share

To create a share using ADSI, proceed as follows:

1. Create a new directory to store all files included in this example.

2. Download and install the latest version of ADSI and Windows Script Host, from **www.microsoft.com**, to the new directory.

3. Select Start|Run and enter "cscript *scriptfile*.vbs".

Here, **scriptfile** is the full path and file name of a script file that contains the following:

```
On Error Resume Next
Set DomObj = GetObject("WinNT://Domain/Computer/
lanmanserver")
Set Share = DomObj.Create("fileshare", "ShareName")
Share.Path = "SharePath"
Share.Description = "ShareDescribe"
Share.MaxUserCount = maxnum
Share.SetInfo
```

NOTE: *The highlighted code above must be placed on one line.*

Here, **domain** is the name of the domain; **computer** is the computer name on which you want to create shares; **sharename** is the name of the share to create; **sharepath** is the path to the new share; **sharedescribe** is the share comment; and **maxnum** is the maximum number of simultaneous connections to the share.

Related solution:	Found on page:
Listing Shares	159

Deleting a Share

To delete a share using ADSI, proceed as follows:

1. Create a new directory to store all files included in this example.

2. Download and install the latest version of ADSI and Windows Script Host, from **www.microsoft.com**, to the new directory.

3. Select Start|Run and enter "cscript *scriptfile*.vbs".

Here, *scriptfile* is the full path and file name of a script file that contains the following:

```
On Error Resume Next
Set DomObj = GetObject("WinNT://Domain/Computer/lanmanserver")
DomObj.Delete "fileshare", "ShareName"
```

Here, *domain* is the name of the domain; *computer* is the computer name on which you want to create shares; and *sharename* is the name of the share to delete.

Related solution:	Found on page:
Removing Shares	160

Creating a Computer Account

To create a computer account using ADSI, proceed as follows:

1. Create a new directory to store all files included in this example.

2. Download and install the latest version of ADSI and Windows Script Host, from **www.microsoft.com**, to the new directory.

3. Select Start|Run and enter "cscript *scriptfile*.vbs".

Here, *scriptfile* is the full path and file name of a script file that contains the following:

```
On Error Resume Next
Set DomObj = GetObject("WinNT://Domain")
Set Computer = DomObj.Create("Computer", "name")
Computer.SetInfo
```

Here, *domain* is the name of the domain, and *name* is the computer name to assign to the computer account.

Deleting a Computer Account

To delete a computer account, proceed as follows:

1. Create a new directory to store all files included in this example.

2. Download and install the latest version of ADSI and Windows Script Host, from **www.microsoft.com**, to the new directory.

3. Select Start|Run and enter "cscript *scriptfile*.vbs".

Here, ***scriptfile*** is the full path and file name of a script file that contains the following:

```
On Error Resume Next
Set DomObj = GetObject("WinNT://Domain")
DomObj.Delete "Computer", "name"
```

Here, ***domain*** is the name of the domain, and ***name*** is the name of the computer account to delete.

Setting a User's Domain Password

To set a user's domain password using ADSI, proceed as follows:

1. Create a new directory to store all files included in this example.

2. Download and install the latest version of ADSI and Windows Script Host, from **www.microsoft.com**, to the new directory.

3. Select Start|Run and enter "cscript *scriptfile*.vbs".

Here, ***scriptfile*** is the full path and file name of a script file that contains the following:

```
On Error Resume Next
Set DomObj = GetObject("WinNT://Domain/Name,user")
DomObj.SetPassword "pswd"
```

Here, ***domain*** is the name of the domain; ***name*** is the user account to modify; and ***pswd*** is the new password to assign.

Changing the Local Administrator Password

A common administrative task is to change the local administrator password on a system. To change the local administrator password using ADSI, proceed as follows:

1. Create a new directory to store all files included in this example.

2. Download and install the latest version of ADSI and Windows Script Host, from **www.microsoft.com**, to the new directory.

3. Select Start|Run and enter "cscript *scriptfile*.vbs".

Here, **scriptfile** is the full path and file name of a script file that contains the following:

```
On Error Resume Next
Set DomObj - GetObject("WinNT://Domain/Computer/
Administrator,user")
DomObj.SetPassword "pswd"
```

NOTE: *The highlighted code above must be placed on one line.*

Here, **domain** is the name of the domain; **computer** is the computer containing the local administrator account; **Administrator** is the name of the local administrator account; and **pswd** is the new password to assign.

Creating a User Account

To create a user account using ADSI, proceed as follows:

1. Create a new directory to store all files included in this example.
2. Download and install the latest version of ADSI and Windows Script Host, from **www.microsoft.com**, to the new directory.
3. Select Start|Run and enter "cscript *scriptfile*.vbs".

Here, **scriptfile** is the full path and file name of a script file that contains the following:

```
On Error Resume Next
Set DomObj - GetObject("WinNT://Domain")
Set User = DomObj.Create("User", "Name")
User.SetPassword("pswd")
User.FullName - "fullname"
User.HomeDirectory - "homedir"
User.Profile - "profiledir"
User.LoginScript - "script"
User.Description - "describe"
User.SetInfo
```

Here, **domain** is the name of the domain; **name** is the name of the user account to create; **pswd** is the password to assign to the new account; **fullname** is the user's full name; **homedir** is the path of the user's home directory; **profiledir** is the path of the user's profile; **script** is the name of the logon script; and **describe** is the user description.

8. Enterprise Management

TIP: *You can create new users with initial blank passwords by omitting the highlighted line in the script above.*

Deleting a User Account

To delete a user account using ADSI, proceed as follows:

1. Create a new directory to store all files included in this example.
2. Download and install the latest version of ADSI and Windows Script Host, from **www.microsoft.com**, to the new directory.
3. Select Start|Run and enter "cscript *scriptfile*.vbs".

Here, *scriptfile* is the full path and file name of a script file that contains the following:

```
On Error Resume Next
Set DomObj = GetObject("WinNT://Domain")
DomObj.Delete "User", "name"
```

Here, *domain* is the name of the domain, and *name* is the name of the user account to delete.

Unlocking a User Account

To unlock a user account using ADSI, proceed as follows:

1. Create a new directory to store all files included in this example.
2. Download and install the latest version of ADSI and Windows Script Host, from **www.microsoft.com**, to the new directory.
3. Select Start|Run and enter "cscript *scriptfile*.vbs".

Here, *scriptfile* is the full path and file name of a script file that contains the following:

```
On Error Resume Next
Set User = GetObject("WinNT://Domain/Name,User")
User.Put "UserFlags", User.Get("UserFlags") - 16
User.SetInfo
```

Here, *domain* is the name of the domain, and *name* is the name of the user account to unlock.

NOTE: *Although ADSI can unlock a user account, it cannot lock an account.*

Disabling a User Account

To disable an active user account using ADSI, proceed as follows:

1. Create a new directory to store all files included in this example.

2. Download and install the latest version of ADSI and Windows Script Host, from **www.microsoft.com**, to the new directory.

3. Select Start|Run and enter "cscript *scriptfile*.vbs".

Here, ***scriptfile*** is the full path and file name of a script file that contains the following:

```
On Error Resume Next
Set User = GetObject("WinNT://Domain/Name,User")
If User.AccountDisabled = "False" Then
  User.Put "UserFlags", User.Get("UserFlags") + 2
  User.SetInfo
End If
```

Here, ***domain*** is the name of the domain, and ***name*** is the name of the user account to unlock.

TIP: *To enable a disabled account, change the False to True and the + 2 to -2 in the above script.*

Creating Groups

To create a global group using ADSI, proceed as follows:

1. Create a new directory to store all files included in this example.

2. Download and install the latest version of ADSI and Windows Script Host, from **www.microsoft.com**, to the new directory.

3. Select Start|Run and enter "cscript *scriptfile*.vbs".

Here, ***scriptfile*** is the full path and file name of a script file that contains the following:

```
On Error Resume Next
Set DomObj = GetObject("WinNT://Domain")
Set Group = DomObj.Create("group", "name")
Group.GroupType = 4
Group.Description = "describe"
Group.SetInfo
```

8. Enterprise Management

Here, **domain** is the name of the domain; **name** is the name of the group to create; and **describe** is the group description.

TIP: To create a local group, omit the highlighted line in the script above.

Deleting Groups

To delete a group using ADSI, proceed as follows:

1. Create a new directory to store all files included in this example.

2. Download and install the latest version of ADSI and Windows Script Host, from **www.microsoft.com**, to the new directory.

3. Select Start|Run and enter "cscript *scriptfile*.vbs".

Here, *scriptfile* is the full path and file name of a script file that contains the following:

```
On Error Resume Next
Set DomObj = GetObject("WinNT://Domain")
DomObj.Delete "group", "name"
```

Here, **domain** is the name of the domain, and **name** is the name of the group to delete.

Adding a User Account to a Group

To add a user account to a group using ADSI, proceed as follows:

1. Create a new directory to store all files included in this example.

2. Download and install the latest version of ADSI and Windows Script Host, from **www.microsoft.com**, to the new directory.

3. Select Start|Run and enter "cscript *scriptfile*.vbs".

Here, **scriptfile** is the full path and file name of a script file that contains the following:

```
On Error Resume Next
Set Group = GetObject("WinNT://Gdomain/groupname,group")
Group.Add "WinNT://UDomain/useraccount,User"
```

Here, **gdomain** is the name of the domain containing the specified **groupname**, and **udomain** is the domain containing the **useraccount** to add to the specified group.

Removing a User Account from a Group

To remove a user account from a group using ADSI, proceed as follows:

1. Create a new directory to store all files included in this example.

2. Download and install the latest version of ADSI and Windows Script Host, from **www.microsoft.com**, to the new directory.

3. Select Start|Run and enter "cscript *scriptfile*.vbs".

Here, ***scriptfile*** is the full path and file name of a script file that contains the following:

```
On Error Resume Next
Set Group = GetObject("WinNT://gdomain/groupname,group")
Group.Remove "WinNT://udomain/useraccount,User"
```

Here, ***gdomain*** is the name of the domain containing the specified ***groupname***, and ***udomain*** is the domain containing the ***useraccount*** to remove from the specified group.

Managing Windows 2000 through LDAP

Most of the previous ADSI examples merely need the binding statement changed in order to convert a WinNT provider script to an LDAP provider script. This section will illustrate a few of the changes you need to make to use these scripts in a Windows 2000 domain.

Creating OUs under Windows 2000

To create an organizational unit under Windows 2000, proceed as follows:

1. Create a new directory to store all files included in this example.

2. Download and install the latest version of ADSI and Windows Script Host, from **www.microsoft.com**, to the new directory.

3. Select Start|Run and enter "cscript *scriptfile*.vbs".

Here, ***scriptfile*** is the full path and file name of a script file that contains the following:

```
On Error Resume Next
Set Root = GetObject("LDAP://RootDSE")
Set DomObj = GetObject( "LDAP://" & Root.Get
("defaultNamingContext"))
Set OU = DomObj.Create("organizationalUnit", "OU=name")
OU.Description = "describe"
OU.SetInfo
```

Here, *name* is the name of the organizational unit to create, and *describe* is the OU description.

Deleting OUs under Windows 2000

To delete an organizational unit under Windows 2000, proceed as follows:

1. Create a new directory to store all files included in this example.
2. Download and install the latest version of ADSI and Windows Script Host, from **www.microsoft.com**, to the new directory.
3. Select Start|Run and enter "cscript *scriptfile*.vbs".

Here, *scriptfile* is the full path and file name of a script file that contains the following:

```
On Error Resume Next
Set Root = GetObject("LDAP://RootDSE")
Set DomObj = GetObject( "LDAP://" &
Root.Get("defaultNamingContext"))
DomObj.Delete "organizationalUnit", "OU=name"
```

NOTE: *The highlighted code above must be placed on one line.*

Here, *name* is the name of the organizational unit to delete.

Creating Computer Accounts under Windows 2000

To create a computer account using LDAP, proceed as follows:

1. Create a new directory to store all files included in this example.
2. Download and install the latest version of ADSI and Windows Script Host, from **www.microsoft.com**, to the new directory.
3. Select Start|Run and enter "cscript *scriptfile*.vbs".

Here, *scriptfile* is the full path and file name of a script file that contains the following:

```
On Error Resume Next
Set Root = GetObject("LDAP://RootDSE")
Set DomObj = GetObject( "LDAP://" & Root.Get
("defaultNamingContext"))
Set Computer = DomObj.Create("computer", "CN=name")
Computer.samAccountName = "name"
Computer.SetInfo
```

Here, *name* is the name of the computer account to create.

Deleting Computer Accounts under Windows 2000

To delete a computer account using LDAP, proceed as follows:

1. Create a new directory to store all files included in this example.

2. Download and install the latest version of ADSI and Windows Script Host, from **www.microsoft.com**, to the new directory.

3. Select Start|Run and enter "cscript *scriptfile*.vbs".

Here, ***scriptfile*** is the full path and file name of a script file that contains the following:

```
On Error Resume Next
Set Root = GetObject("LDAP://RootDSE")
Set DomObj = GetObject( "LDAP://" & Root.Get
("defaultNamingContext"))
Set Computer = DomObj.Create("computer", "CN=name")
Computer.samAccountName = "name"
Computer.SetInfo
```

NOTE: *The highlighted code above must be placed on one line.*

Here, ***name*** is the name of the computer account to delete.

Creating User Accounts under Windows 2000

To create a user account using LDAP, proceed as follows:

1. Create a new directory to store all files included in this example.

2. Download and install the latest version of ADSI and Windows Script Host, from **www.microsoft.com**, to the new directory.

3. Select Start|Run and enter "cscript *scriptfile*.vbs".

Here, ***scriptfile*** is the full path and file name of a script file that contains the following:

```
On Error Resume Next
Set Root = GetObject("LDAP://RootDSE")
Set DomObj = GetObject( "LDAP://" & Root.Get
("defaultNamingContext"))
Set User = DomObj.Create("user", "CN=fullname")
User.samAccountName = "name"
User.SetInfo
```

Here, ***name*** is the name of the user account to create, and ***fullname*** is the user's full name.

Deleting User Accounts under Windows 2000

To delete a user account using LDAP, proceed as follows:

1. Create a new directory to store all files included in this example.

2. Download and install the latest version of ADSI and Windows Script Host, from **www.microsoft.com**, to the new directory.

3. Select Start|Run and enter "cscript *scriptfile*.vbs".

Here, **scriptfile** is the full path and file name of a script file that contains the following:

```
On Error Resume Next
Set Root = GetObject("LDAP://RootDSE")
Set DomObj = GetObject( "LDAP://" & Root.Get
("defaultNamingContext"))
DomObj.Delete "user", "CN=name"
```

NOTE: *The highlighted code above must be placed on one line.*

Here, **name** is the name of the user account to delete.

Chapter 9

Managing Inventory

In Brief

Managing inventory in an enterprise is an extremely involved task. Although several expensive inventory management packages are available, many companies cannot afford to purchase these systems and train employees to implement them. In this chapter, you will learn how to inventory your enterprise with simple, customizable scripts. In the previous chapters, you learned how to collect information about various items such as files, folders, shares, and services. In this chapter, you will learn how to collect information from various system and device components, such as a battery, mouse, monitor, sound card, printer, and more.

Windows System Tools

Microsoft Windows contains many tools you can use to view and modify system resource information. Each tool provides a central location to easily identify resources and conflicts, and modify device settings and drivers.

Microsoft System Diagnostics

Microsoft System Diagnostics (MSD) is a command-line utility included with MS-DOS 6.*x* or higher to display system resources and settings of a local system. MSD is also available in the Other\MSD directory on the Windows 95 retail CD or can be freely downloaded from **www.microsoft.com**. MSD provides a central location to view system information, print reports, locate system errors, and more. MSD is an invaluable utility to have on a Windows 95 boot disk because it can help you troubleshoot and locate hardware and software errors, such as IRQ (Interrupt ReQuest) conflicts.

NOTE: *This program is a DOS utility and might not function correctly if run under Windows.*

MSD accepts command-line parameters to control MSD behavior and report system information. The basic syntax of the MSD command is:

```
MSD /commands
```

Here, the available ***commands*** are:

- **/B**—Runs MSD in black and white
- **/F** *file*—Prompts for various information and then sends a complete report output to a file
- **/I**—Does not attempt hardware detection
- **/P** *file*—Sends a complete report output to a file
- **/S**—Sends a summary report output to the default printer

Windows NT Diagnostics

Windows NT includes a utility called Windows Microsoft System Diagnostics (WINMSD), which is the 32-bit graphical version of MSD. WINMSD is commonly known as Windows NT Diagnostics and can be started by running Start|Programs|Administrative Tools (Common)|NT Diagnostics. This tool provides an easy way to view network information, determine service pack versions, view system resources, and more. Some advanced features include remote system connectivity and report generation. You can find WINMSD.EXE in your WINNT\SYSTEM32 directory.

WINMSD can also be run from the command line to connect to remote system or report system information. The basic syntax of the WINMSD command is:

```
WINMSD /commands
```

Here, the available *commands* are:

- *****computer*—Specifies the remote computer to connect to
- **/A**—Creates a complete system report
- **/F** *file*—Sends report output to a file
- **/P**—Sends report output to the default printer
- **/S**—Creates a summary report

Microsoft System Information

Windows 98 includes a replacement utility for MSD called Microsoft System Information (MSI). MSI was first introduced with Microsoft Office 97 and can be started by clicking Start|Run and entering **MSINFO32**. This utility includes quick links to other diagnostic tools (Dr. Watson and ScanDisk) under the Tools menu. One of the most valuable features of this tool is the History page. Under this page you will find a history of system changes that you can use to diagnose system malfunctions.

9. Managing Inventory

Windows 2000 follows Windows 98 and uses an updated version of Microsoft System Information. MSI is an invaluable system tool that uses WMI to provide an easy method to locate drivers, resources, components, and sources of system errors, to print reports, and more. Some advanced features include remote system connectivity and report generation. You can start this utility by clicking Start|Run and entering MSINFO32 or by entering WINMSD. MSI is actually a Microsoft Management Console (MMC) snap-in, stored as C:\Program Files\Common Files\Microsoft\Shared\MSInfo\MSInfo32.msc.

TIP: To use the original NT version of WINMSD, copy WINMSD.EXE from an NT system to overwrite the WINMSD.EXE located in the C:\WINNT\SYSTEM32 directory.

Within the same directory is a file called MSINFO32.EXE, used to run MSI from the command line. You can use MSINFO32 to connect to a remote computer or store system information to an NFO (Information) file. The basic syntax of the MSINFO32 command is:

```
MSINFO32 /commands
```

Here, the available *commands* are:

- **/CATEGORIES +/- name**—Displays (+) or does not display (-) the category name specified. Supplying the name ALL will display all categories.
- **/CATEGORY name**—Specifies the category to open at launch.
- **/COMPUTER name**—Connects to the specified computer name.
- **/MSINFO_FILE=file**—Opens an NFO or CAB file.
- **/NFO file**—Sends output to an NFO file.
- **/REPORT file**—Generates a report to the specified file.

WARNING! MSInfo32 is a memory-intensive application and might use up valuable system resources.

Device Manager

Windows 9x/2000 includes a graphical utility called Device Manager (see Figure 9.1) to manipulate the various devices on your system. From within this utility, you can view or modify system settings, device properties, device drivers, and more. Device Manager displays its items in a tree-like structure, allowing you to easily view dependencies. This utility is most commonly used among administrators to

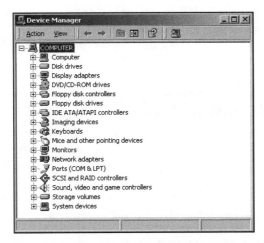

Figure 9.1   The Windows 2000 Device Manager.

determine resource conflicts (noted by yellow exclamation points) and update device drivers.

Microsoft Systems Management Server

Microsoft Systems Management Server (SMS) is a complete enterprise inventory and management package. Some of the advanced features include remote control, software licensing, and electronic software distribution (ESD). Although this product is extremely helpful, many companies cannot afford to pay for the training or licensing of SMS (about $1800 for 25 users). As related to this chapter, SMS performs system inventory using Windows Management Instrumentation. In this chapter, you will learn how to perform similar WMI queries to gather the system information you need—for free.

Immediate Solutions

Gathering Information with Shell Scripting

Shell scripting is very limited when it comes to gathering system resource information. Most new devices are designed specifically to work with Windows, not DOS, and most resource configuration tools are GUI-controlled and not command-line controllable. However, there are still several tools and methods you can utilize to collect and report resource information through shell scripting.

Collecting Information Using WINMSDP

WINMSDP is an NT resource kit utility to create Windows NT/2000 system information reports from the command line. The basic syntax of the WINMSDP command is:

```
WINMSDP /commands
```

Here, the available **commands** are:

- **/A**—Reports all system information
- **/D**—Reports drive information
- **/E**—Reports environment information
- **/I**—Reports IRQ information
- **/N**—Reports network information
- **/P**—Reports port information
- **/S**—Reports service information
- **/R**—Reports driver information
- **/W**—Reports hardware information
- **/Y**—Reports memory resource information

When WINMSDP is executed, it will output all information to a file called MSDRPT*.txt. Here is an example to display disk information using WINMSDP:

```
@ECHO OFF
ECHO Gathering Disk Information, Please Wait...
DEL MSDRPT.TXT > NUL
```

```
WINMSDP.EXE /D > NUL
TYPE MSDRPT.TXT
DEL MSDRPT.TXT > NUL
PAUSE
```

Collecting Information Using SRVINFO

SRVINFO is a resource kit utility to display various system information from the command line. The basic syntax of the SRVINFO command is:

```
SRVINFO /commands \\computer
```

Here, **computer** is the name of the computer to collect information from, and the available **commands** are:

- **-D**—Displays service drivers
- **-NS**—Does not display service information
- **-S**—Displays shares
- **-V**—Displays Exchange and SQL version information

Here is an example to display all the information SRVINFO can report:

```
SRVINFO -S -V -D
```

Collecting BIOS Information

To collect BIOS (Basic Input/Output System) information from the command line, you can use REG.EXE from the resource kit to extract the appropriate information. To display processor information using shell scripting, proceed as follows:

1. Create a new directory to store all files included in this example.

2. Obtain REG.EXE from the Resource Kit and copy it to the new directory.

3. Start a command prompt and enter "*scriptfile*.bat".

Here, **scriptfile** is the full path of the new directory from step 1 and file name of a script file that contains the following:

```
@ECHO OFF
Reg Query HKLM\HARDWARE\DESCRIPTION\System\
SystemBiosVersion > BIOS.TXT
Set Count=3
:Count
```

```
For /f "tokens=%Count%" %%I in ('TYPE BIOS.TXT'
) Do Set Version=%Version% %%I
Set /A Count+=1
If %Count% LSS 10 Goto Count
Echo BIOS Version: %Version%


Reg Query HKLM\HARDWARE\DESCRIPTION\System\
SystemBiosDate > BIOS.TXT


For /f "tokens=3" %%I in ('TYPE BIOS.TXT'
) Do Echo BIOS Date: %%I
Del BIOS.txt > Nul
Set Count=
Set Version=
```

NOTE: *The highlighted code above must be placed on one line.*

Related solution:	Found on page:
Modifying the Registry with Shell Scripting	122

Collecting Memory Information

PSTAT is a resource kit utility to display running threads from the command line. You can use this tool to display memory information. To display memory information using shell scripting, proceed as follows:

1. Create a new directory to store all files included in this example.

2. Obtain PSTAT.EXE from the Resource Kit and copy it to the new directory.

3. Start a command prompt and enter "*scriptfile*.bat".

Here, ***scriptfile*** is the full path of the new directory from step 1 and file name of a script file that contains the following:

```
PSTAT | Find " Memory: " > MEM.TXT
For /F "tokens=2" %%M In ('Type MEM.txt') Do Echo Memory: %%M
Del MEM.txt > Nul
```

WARNING! *The version of PSTAT that shipped with the NT Resource Kit might cause system errors when run on Windows 2000. You should obtain the latest version from Microsoft.*

Collecting Processor Information

To collect processor information from the command line, you can use REG.EXE from the resource kit to extract the appropriate information. To display processor information using shell scripting, proceed as follows:

1. Create a new directory to store all files included in this example.
2. Obtain REG.EXE from the Resource Kit and copy it to the new directory.
3. Start a command prompt and enter "*scriptfile*.bat".

Here, **scriptfile** is the full path of the new directory from step 1 and file name of a script file that contains the following:

```
@ECHO OFF
Reg Query HKLM\HARDWARE\DESCRIPTION\System\CentralProcessor\
0\VendorIdentifier > PROCESSOR.TXT

For /f "tokens=3" %%I in ('TYPE PROCESSOR.TXT'
) Do Echo Processor Vendor: %%I

Reg Query HKLM\HARDWARE\DESCRIPTION\System\CentralProcessor\
0\Identifier > PROCESSOR.TXT

For /f "tokens=5" %%I in ('TYPE PROCESSOR.TXT') Do Set FAMILY
=%%I

For /f "tokens=7" %%I in ('TYPE PROCESSOR.TXT') Do Set MODEL
=%%I

For /f "tokens=9" %%I in ('TYPE PROCESSOR.TXT') Do Set STEP
=%%I

If %Family%==6 (
   If %Model%==1 Set  PTYPE=Pentium Pro
   If %Model%==3 Set  PTYPE=Pentium II
   If %Model%==5 (
      If %Step%==0 Set PTYPE=Pentium II or Celeron
      If %Step%==1 Set PTYPE=Pentium II or Celeron
      If %Step%==2 Set PTYPE=Pentium II or Pentium II Xeon
      If %Step%==3 Set PTYPE=Pentium II or Pentium II Xeon
   )
   If %Model%==6 Set  PTYPE=Pentium Celeron
   If %Model%==7 Set  PTYPE=Pentium III or Pentium III Xeon
```

```
       If %Model%==8 Set PTYPE=Pentium III or Pentium III Xeon
       If %Model%==A Set PTYPE=Pentium III Xeon
)
If %Family%==5 Set PTYPE=Pentium

Echo Processor Type: %PTYPE%

Reg Query HKLM\HARDWARE\DESCRIPTION\System\CentralProcessor\
0\~MHZ > PROCESSOR.TXT

For /f "tokens=3" %%I in ('TYPE PROCESSOR.TXT'
) Do Echo Processor Speed: %%I
Del PROCESSOR.txt > Nul

Set PCount=0
:Count
Reg Query HKLM\HARDWARE\DESCRIPTION\System\CentralProcessor\
%PCount% > Nul

If errorlevel 2 Echo Processor Count: %PCount% & Goto CleanUp
Set /A PCount+=1
Goto Count

:CleanUp
Set Family=
Set Model=
Set Step=
Set Ptype=
Set PCount=
```

NOTE: *The highlighted code above must be placed on one line. The routine to determine the processor type was derived from various Intel processor spec sheets.*

Gathering Information with KiXtart

KiXtart provides many macros to retrieve user information, but only a few of these macros can be used to retrieve resource information. By combining KiXtart macros and registry commands, you can collect and report various resource information through simple scripts.

Collecting BIOS Information

KiXtart does not provide any direct method to collect BIOS information. Alternatively, you can query the registry and extract the BIOS information you want using KiXtart. To collect printer information using KiXtart, proceed as follows:

1. Create a new directory to store all files included in this example.

2. Download and extract the latest version of KiXtart, from **www.microsoft.com**, to the new directory.

3. Select Start|Run and enter "kix32 *scriptfile*".

Here, ***scriptfile*** is the full path of the new directory from step 1 and file name of a script file that contains the following:

```
; Get the system BIOS type
$SBiosType = READVALUE("HKEY_LOCAL_MACHINE\HARDWARE\
DESCRIPTION\System","SystemBiosVersion")

; Get the system BIOS date
$SBiosDate = READVALUE("HKEY_LOCAL_MACHINE\HARDWARE\
DESCRIPTION\System","SystemBiosDate")

? "BIOS Type:        $SBiosType"
? "BIOS Date:        $SBiosDate"
SLEEP 10
```

NOTE: *The highlighted code above must be placed on one line.*

Related solution:	Found on page:
Modifying the Registry with KiXtart	129

Collecting Drive Information

Although KiXtart provides no built-in method to determine all system drives and their total size, you can perform checks for available drives and free disk space. An available drive is considered to be any drive with media present. For example, a drive without a floppy or CD-ROM is an unavailable drive. To collect information on available drives using KiXtart, proceed as follows.

1. Create a new directory to store all files included in this example.

2. Download and extract the latest version of KiXtart, from **www.microsoft.com**, to the new directory.

3. Select Start|Run and enter "kix32 *scriptfile*".

9. Managing Inventory

Here, *scriptfile* is the full path of the new directory from step 1 and file name of a script file that contains the following:

```
$DLetter = 67
While $DLetter < 91
  $Drive = CHR($DLetter) + ":"
  If Exist ($Drive)
    $DiskSpace = GETDISKSPACE($Drive)
    SELECT
      CASE $DiskSpace = 0
        $DiskSpace = "0 Bytes"
      CASE $DiskSpace < 1024
        $DiskSpace = $DiskSpace * 100
        $DiskSpace = "$DiskSpace KB"
      CASE $DiskSpace => 1024 and $DiskSpace < 1048576
        $DiskSpace = ($DiskSpace * 100) / 1024
        $DiskSpace = "$DiskSpace MB"
      CASE $DiskSpace => 1048576
        $DiskSpace = $DiskSpace / 10486
        $DiskSpace = "$DiskSpace GB"
    ENDSELECT
    $DiskSpace = SUBSTR($DiskSpace, 1, LEN($DiskSpace) - 5)
     + "." + SUBSTR($DiskSpace,LEN($DiskSpace)- 4, 5)
    ?"Drive $Drive Free Space: $DiskSpace"
  EndIf
  $DLetter = $DLetter + 1
Loop
Sleep 5
```

NOTE: *The highlighted code above must be placed on one line.*

Notice that the drive letter count (*$Dletter*) starts at 67 and runs until 91. These numbers represent ASCII characters C to Z. If you start *$Dletter* with 65 (A), your script might pause and you might be prompted for a floppy disk if none is present.

Collecting Operating System Information

KiXtart does not provide any direct method to collect information about the currently running operating system (OS). Alternatively, you can use various KiXtart macros and query the registry and extract the OS information you want using KiXtart. To collect OS information using KiXtart, proceed as follows:

1. Create a new directory to store all files included in this example.

2. Download and extract the latest version of KiXtart, from **www.microsoft.com**, to the new directory.

3. Select Start|Run and enter "kix32 *scriptfile*".

Here, ***scriptfile*** is the full path of the new directory from step 1 and file name of a script file that contains the following:

```
; Initialize variables
$OS = ""
$WinDir = %windir%

; The following variables are for Windows NT/2000
$NTProdType = ReadValue("HKEY_LOCAL_MACHINE\SYSTEM\
CurrentControlSet\Control\ProductOptions","ProductType")

$NTBuildVer = ReadValue("HKEY_LOCAL_MACHINE\Software\
Microsoft\Windows NT\CurrentVersion","CurrentBuildNumber")

$NTProdID = ReadValue("HKEY_LOCAL_MACHINE\Software\Microsoft\
Windows NT\CurrentVersion","ProductID")

; The following variables are for Windows 9x
$WinVersion = ReadValue("HKEY_LOCAL_MACHINE\Software\
Microsoft\Windows\CurrentVersion","Version")

$WinSubVer = ReadValue("HKEY_LOCAL_MACHINE\Software\
Microsoft\Windows\CurrentVersion","SubVersionNumber")

$WinVerNum = ReadValue("HKEY_LOCAL_MACHINE\Software\
Microsoft\Windows\CurrentVersion","VersionNumber")

IF EXIST ("$WinDir\SYSTEM\SOFTBOOT.EXE")
  $OS = "Soft Windows:"
ENDIF

SELECT ; What OS are we running?
  CASE @inwin = 1 and $NTProdType <> "WinNT" and @dos = 5.0
    $OS = $OS + "Windows 2000 Server"
  CASE @inwin = 1 and $NTProdType = "WinNT" and @dos = 5.0
    $OS = $OS + "Windows 2000 Professional"
  CASE @inwin = 1 and $NTProdType = "LANMANNT"
    $OS = $OS + "Windows NT 4.0 Domain Controller"
  CASE @inwin = 1 and $NTProdType = "ServerNT"
    $OS = $OS + "Windows NT 4.0 Member Server"
```

```
    CASE @inwin = 1 and $NTProdType = "WinNT"
      $OS = $OS + "Windows NT Workstation"
    CASE ((@INWIN = 2) AND (@DOS >= 4.10))
      $OS = $OS + "Windows 98 $WinSubVer"
    CASE ((@INWIN = 2) AND (@DOS = 4.0))
      $OS = $OS + "Windows 95 $WinSubVer"
    CASE 1
      $OS = $OS + "UNDETERMINED"
ENDSELECT


? "Operating System: $OS" ; Display OS type
? "Build:            $NTBuildVer" ; Display the build number
? "ProdID:           $NTProdID" ; Display the product ID
? "Service Pack:     $SPack" ; Display the service pack
SLEEP 10
```

NOTE: *The highlighted code above must be placed on one line.*

Collecting Printer Information

KiXtart does not provide any direct method to collect information about all the printers installed on a system. Alternatively, you can query the registry and extract the printer information you want using KiXtart. To collect printer information using KiXtart, proceed as follows:

1. Create a new directory to store all files included in this example.

2. Download and extract the latest version of KiXtart, from **www.microsoft.com**, to the new directory.

3. Select Start|Run and enter "kix32 *scriptfile*".

Here, ***scriptfile*** is the full path of the new directory from step 1 and file name of a script file that contains the following:

```
$Printers="HKEY_LOCAL_MACHINE\SYSTEM\CurrentControlSet\
Control\Print\Printers\"
$Index=0

:GatherInfo
$Printer=enumkey("$Printers",$Index)
If @Error=0
  $Desc = Readvalue("$Printers\$Printer","Description")
  $Loc = Readvalue("$Printers\$Printer","Location")
  $Port = Readvalue("$Printers\$Printer","Port")
  $Share = Readvalue("$Printers\$Printer","Share Name")
  ? "Printer: $Printer"
```

```
? "Description: $Desc"
? "Location: $Loc"
? "Port: $Port"
? "Share: $Share"
?
$Index = $Index + 1
Goto GatherInfo
EndIf
Sleep 10
```

NOTE: *The highlighted code above must be placed on one line.*

Collecting Processor Information

KiXtart does not provide any direct method to collect information about all the processors installed on a system. Alternatively, you can query the registry and extract the processor information you want using KiXtart. To collect processor information using KiXtart, proceed as follows:

1. Create a new directory to store all files included in this example.

2. Download and extract the latest version of KiXtart, from **www.microsoft.com**, to the new directory.

3. Select Start|Run and enter "kix32 *scriptfile*".

Here, ***scriptfile*** is the full path of the new directory from step 1 and file name of a script file that contains the following:

```
;  Get the processor vendor
$ProVendor = READVALUE("HKEY_LOCAL_MACHINE\HARDWARE\
DESCRIPTION\System\CentralProcessor\0","VendorIdentifier")
IF $ProVendor = "GenuineIntel"
  $ProVendor = "Intel"
ENDIF

;  Get the processor type
$ProType = READVALUE("HKEY_LOCAL_MACHINE\HARDWARE\
DESCRIPTION\System\CentralProcessor\0","Identifier")
IF (SUBSTR($ProType, 1, 3) = "x86") AND $ProVendor = "Intel"
  $Family = SUBSTR($ProType, 12, 1)
  $Model = SUBSTR($ProType, 20, 1)
  $Step = SUBSTR($ProType, 31, 1)
  SELECT
    CASE $Family = "5"
      $ProType = "Pentium"
```

```
          CASE $Family = "6" AND $Model = "1"
            $ProType = "Pentium Pro"
          CASE $Family = "6" AND $Model = "6"
            $ProType = "Celeron"
          CASE $Family = "6" AND $Model = "5" AND (($Step = "0") OR
          ($Step = "1"))
            $ProType = "Pentium II or Celeron"
          CASE $Family = "6" AND $Model = "3"
            $ProType = "Pentium II"
          CASE $Family = "6" AND $Model = "5" AND (($Step = "2") OR
          ($Step = "3"))
            $ProType = "Pentium II or Pentium II Xeon"
          CASE $Family = "6" AND $Model = "7"
            $ProType = "Pentium III or Pentium III Xeon"
          CASE $Family = "6" AND $Model = "A"
            $ProType = "Pentium III Xeon"
          CASE $Family = "6" AND $Model = "8"
            $ProType = "Celeron, Pentium III, or Pentium III Xeon"
          CASE 1
            $ProType = "Processor"
          ENDSELECT
      ENDIF


      ;  Get the processor speed
      $ProSpeed = READVALUE("HKEY_LOCAL_MACHINE\HARDWARE\
      DESCRIPTION\System\CentralProcessor\0","~MHZ")
      $Length = LEN($ProSpeed)
      $ProTemp = (VAL(SUBSTR($ProSpeed, 1, 1)) + 1)
      IF SUBSTR($ProSpeed, 2, 1) = 9 ; (e.g. 89, 197, 496, 794)
        WHILE $Length > 1
          $ProTemp = $ProTemp * 10
          $Length = $Length - 1
        LOOP
        $ProSpeed = $ProTemp
      ENDIF


      ;  Get the number of processors
      $ProCount = 0
      $Count = 0
      WHILE $Count < 65
        $ProTemp = EXISTKEY("HKEY_LOCAL_MACHINE\HARDWARE\
        DESCRIPTION\System\CentralProcessor\$ProCount")
        IF $ProTemp = 0
          $ProCount = $ProCount + 1
        ENDIF
        $Count = $Count + 1
      LOOP
```

```
; The code below is to simply display the final results
? "Processor Count:   $ProCount"
? "Processor Vendor: $ProVendor"
? "Processor Type:    $ProType"
? "Processor Speed:  $ProSpeed MHZ"
SLEEP 10
```

NOTE: *The highlighted code above must be placed on one line. The routine to determine the processor type was derived from various Intel processor spec sheets.*

Gathering Information with WMI

Windows Management Instrumentation provides centralized management system for almost all the resources on your system. Through various WMI classes and Windows Script Host, you can collect and report various resource information through simple scripts.

TIP: *The examples in the following sections illustrate only a few of the classes and class properties that WMI has to offer. Consult the WMI SDK documentation for a complete list of classes and their properties.*

Collecting Battery Information

The **Win32_Battery** class allows you to query laptop battery and Uninterruptible Power Supply (UPS) information through WMI. To collect battery information on a system using WMI, proceed as follows:

1. Create a new directory to store all files included in this example.

2. Download and install the latest version of Windows Script Host, from **www.microsoft.com**, to the new directory.

3. Select Start|Run and enter "cscript *scriptfile*.vbs".

Here, *scriptfile* is the full path and file name of a script file that contains the following:

```
Set BatterySet = GetObject("winmgmts:").InstancesOf
("Win32_Battery")
For each Battery in BatterySet
  Select Case Battery.Chemistry
    Case 1
      BType = "Other"
```

```
        Case 2
          BType = "Unknown"
        Case 3
          BType = "Lead Acid"
        Case 4
          BType = "Nickel Cadmium"
        Case 5
          BType = "Nickel Metal Hydride"
        Case 6
          BType = "Lithium-ion"
        Case 7
          BType = "Zinc air"
        Case 8
          BType = "Lithium Polymer"
    End Select
    Select Case Battery.BatteryStatus
        Case 1
          BStatus = "Other"
        Case 2
          BStatus = "Unknown"
        Case 3
          BStatus = "Fully Charged"
        Case 4
          BStatus = "Low"
        Case 5
          BStatus = "Critical"
        Case 6
          BStatus = "Charging"
        Case 7
          BStatus = "Charging and High"
        Case 8
          BStatus = "Charging and Low"
        Case 9
          BStatus = "Charging and Critical"
        Case 10
          BStatus = "Undefined"
        Case 11
          BStatus = "Partially Charged"
    End Select
  WScript.Echo "Name: " & Battery.Description & VBlf & _
    "Type: " & BType & VBlf & _
    "% Left: " & Battery.EstimatedChargeRemaining & VBlf & _
    "Minutes Left: " & Battery.ExpectedLife & VBlf & _
    "Status: " & BStatus
  Next
```

NOTE: *The highlighted code above must be placed on one line.*

Collecting BIOS Information

The **Win32_BIOS** class allows you to query BIOS information through WMI. To collect BIOS information on a system using WMI, proceed as follows:

1. Create a new directory to store all files included in this example.

2. Download and install the latest version of Windows Script Host, from **www.microsoft.com**, to the new directory.

3. Select Start|Run and enter "cscript *scriptfile*.vbs".

Here, ***scriptfile*** is the full path and file name of a script file that contains the following:

```
Set BIOSSet = GetObject("winmgmts:").InstancesOf
("Win32_BIOS")
For each BIOS in BIOSSet
  BDate = Left(BIOS.ReleaseDate,8)
  BDate = Mid(BDate,5,2) & "/" & Mid(BDate,7,2) & "/" & _
  Mid(BDate,1,4)
  WScript.Echo "Name: " & BIOS.Name & VBlf & _
  "Manufacturer: " & BIOS.Manufacturer & VBlf & _
  "Date: " & BDate & VBlf & _
  "Version: " & BIOS.Version & VBlf & _
  "Status: " & BIOS.Status
Next
```

NOTE: *The highlighted code above must be placed on one line.*

Collecting CD-ROM Information

The **Win32_CDROMDrive** class allows you to query CD-ROM information through WMI. To collect CD-ROM information on a system using WMI, proceed as follows:

1. Create a new directory to store all files included in this example.

2. Download and install the latest version of Windows Script Host, from **www.microsoft.com**, to the new directory.

3. Select Start|Run and enter "cscript *scriptfile*.vbs".

Here, ***scriptfile*** is the full path and file name of a script file that contains the following:

```
Set CDSet = GetObject("winmgmts:").InstancesOf
("Win32_CDROMDrive")
```

9. Managing Inventory

```
For each CD in CDSet
  WScript.Echo "Name: " & CD.Name & VBlf & _
  "Drive: " & CD.Drive & VBlf & _
  "Status: " & CD.Status
Next
```

NOTE: *The highlighted code above must be placed on one line.*

Collecting Drive Information

The **Win32_LogicalDisk** class allows you to query disk information through WMI. To inventory disks on a system using WMI, proceed as follows:

1. Create a new directory to store all files included in this example.

2. Download and install the latest version of Windows Script Host, from **www.microsoft.com**, to the new directory.

3. Select Start\Run and enter "cscript *scriptfile*.vbs".

Here, ***scriptfile*** is the full path and file name of a script file that contains the following:

```
Set DiskSet = GetObject("winmgmts:").InstancesOf
("Win32_LogicalDisk")
For each Disk in DiskSet
  Select Case Disk.DriveType
      Case 0
        DType = "Unknown"
      Case 1
        DType = "No Root Directory"
      Case 2
        DType = "Removable Disk"
      Case 3
        DType = "Local Disk"
      Case 4
        DType = "Network Drive"
      Case 5
        DType = "Compact Disc"
      Case 6
        DType = "RAM Disk"
  End Select
  WScript.Echo "Drive: " & Disk.DeviceID & VBlf & _
  "Name: " & Disk.Description & VBlf & _
  "Type: " & DType & VBlf & _
  "File System: " & Disk.FileSystem & VBlf & _
```

```
   "Size: " & Disk.Size & VB1f & _
   "Free Space: " & Disk.FreeSpace & VB1f & _
   "Compressed: " & Disk.Compressed
Next
```

NOTE: *The highlighted code above must be placed on one line.*

Collecting Memory Information

The **Win32_LogicalMemoryConfiguration** class allows you to query memory information through WMI. To collect memory information on a system using WMI, proceed as follows:

1. Create a new directory to store all files included in this example.

2. Download and install the latest version of Windows Script Host, from **www.microsoft.com**, to the new directory.

3. Select Start|Run and enter "cscript *scriptfile*.vbs".

Here, ***scriptfile*** is the full path and file name of a script file that contains the following:

```
Set MemorySet = GetObject("winmgmts:").InstancesOf
("Win32_LogicalMemoryConfiguration")

For each Memory in MemorySet
  WScript.Echo "Total: " & _
  Memory.TotalPhysicalMemory/1024 & VB1f & _
  "Virtual: " & Memory.TotalVirtualMemory/1024 & VB1f & _
  "Page: " & Memory.TotalPageFileSpace/1024
Next
```

NOTE: *The highlighted code above must be placed on one line.*

Collecting Modem Information

The **Win32_POTSModem** class allows you to query modem information through WMI. To collect modem information on a system using WMI, proceed as follows:

1. Create a new directory to store all files included in this example.

2. Download and install the latest version of Windows Script Host, from **www.microsoft.com**, to the new directory.

3. Select Start|Run and enter "cscript *scriptfile*.vbs".

9. Managing Inventory

Here, **scriptfile** is the full path and file name of a script file that contains the following:

```
Set ModemSet = GetObject("winmgmts:").InstancesOf
("Win32_POTSModem")

For each Modem in ModemSet
  WScript.Echo "Name: " & Modem.Name & VBlf & _
  "Port: " & Modem.AttachedTo & VBlf & _
  "Type: " & Modem.DeviceType & VBlf & _
  "Status: " & Modem.Status
Next
```

NOTE: *The highlighted code above must be placed on one line.*

Collecting Monitor Information

The **Win32_DesktopMonitor** class allows you to query information on computer monitors through WMI. To collect monitor information on a system using WMI, proceed as follows:

1. Create a new directory to store all files included in this example.

2. Download and install the latest version of Windows Script Host, from **www.microsoft.com**, to the new directory.

3. Select Start|Run and enter "cscript *scriptfile*.vbs".

Here, **scriptfile** is the full path and file name of a script file that contains the following:

```
Set MonitorSet = GetObject("winmgmts:").InstancesOf
("Win32_DesktopMonitor")

For each Monitor in MonitorSet
  WScript.Echo "Name: " & Monitor.Name & VBlf & _
  "Height: " & Monitor.ScreenHeight & VBlf & _
  "Width: " & Monitor.ScreenWidth & VBlf & _
  "Status: " & Monitor.Status
Next
```

NOTE: *The highlighted code above must be placed on one line.*

Collecting Mouse Information

The **Win32_PointingDevice** class allows you to query mouse, trackball, touch screen, touch pad, and other pointing device information through WMI. To collect pointing device information on a system using WMI, proceed as follows:

1. Create a new directory to store all files included in this example.

2. Download and install the latest version of Windows Script Host, from **www.microsoft.com**, to the new directory.

3. Select Start|Run and enter "cscript *scriptfile*.vbs".

Here, ***scriptfile*** is the full path and file name of a script file that contains the following:

```
Set MouseSet = GetObject("winmgmts:").InstancesOf
("Win32_PointingDevice")

For each Mouse in MouseSet
  WScript.Echo "Name: " & Mouse.Name & VB1f & _
  "Manufacturer: " & Mouse.Manufacturer & VB1f & _
  "Type: " & Mouse.HardwareType & VB1f & _
  "Buttons: " & Mouse.NumberofButtons & VB1f & _
  "Status: " & Mouse.Status
Next
```

NOTE: *The highlighted code above must be placed on one line.*

Collecting Network Adapter Information

The **Win32_NetworkAdapter** class allows you to query information on network adapters through WMI. To collect Network Interface Card (NIC) information on a system using WMI, proceed as follows:

1. Create a new directory to store all files included in this example.

2. Download and install the latest version of Windows Script Host, from **www.microsoft.com**, to the new directory.

3. Select Start|Run and enter "cscript *scriptfile*.vbs".

Here, ***scriptfile*** is the full path and file name of a script file that contains the following:

```
Set NICSet = GetObject("winmgmts:").InstancesOf
("Win32_NetworkAdapter")

For each NIC in NICSet
  WScript.Echo "Name: " & NIC.Name & VB1f & _
  "Type: " & NIC.AdapterType & VB1f & _
```

9. Managing Inventory

237

```
       "Speed: " & NIC.Speed & VB1f & _
       "MAC: " & NIC.MACAddress & VB1f & _
       "Addresses: " & NIC.NetworkAddresses
    Next
```

Collecting Operating System Information

The **Win32_OperatingSystem** class allows you to query various operating system information through WMI. To collect CD-ROM information on a system using WMI, proceed as follows:

1. Create a new directory to store all files included in this example.

2. Download and install the latest version of Windows Script Host, from **www.microsoft.com**, to the new directory.

3. Select Start|Run and enter "cscript *scriptfile*.vbs".

Here, *scriptfile* is the full path and file name of a script file that contains the following:

```
Set OSSet = GetObject("winmgmts:").InstancesOf
("Win32_OperatingSystem")

For each OS in OSSet
   WScript.Echo "OS: " & OS.Caption & VB1f & _
   "Build: " & OS.BuildNumber & VB1f & _
   "Version: " & OS.Version & VB1f & _
   "Service Pack: " & OS.CSDVersion & VB1f & _
   "ProdID: " & OS.SerialNumber & VB1f & _
   "Install Date: " & OS.InstallDate & VB1f & _
   "Last Bootup: " & OS.LastBootUpTime
Next
```

Collecting Printer Information

The **Win32_Printer** class allows you to query printer information through WMI. To collect printer information on a system using WMI, proceed as follows:

1. Create a new directory to store all files included in this example.

2. Download and install the latest version of Windows Script Host, from **www.microsoft.com**, to the new directory.

3. Select Start|Run and enter "cscript *scriptfile*.vbs".

Here, ***scriptfile*** is the full path and file name of a script file that contains the following:

```
Set PrinterSet = GetObject("winmgmts:").InstancesOf
("Win32_Printer")

For each Printer in PrinterSet
   WScript.Echo "Name: " & Printer.Name & VB1f & _
   "Location: " & Printer.Location & VB1f & _
   "Share: " & Printer.ShareName & VB1f & _
   "Status: " & Printer.Status
Next
```

NOTE: *The highlighted code above must be placed on one line.*

Collecting Processor Information

The **Win32_Processor** class allows you to query processor information through WMI. To collect processor information on a system using WMI, proceed as follows:

1. Create a new directory to store all files included in this example.

2. Download and install the latest version of Windows Script Host, from **www.microsoft.com**, to the new directory.

3. Select Start|Run and enter "cscript *scriptfile*.vbs".

Here, ***scriptfile*** is the full path and file name of a script file that contains the following:

```
Set ProSet = GetObject("winmgmts:").InstancesOf
("Win32_Processor")

For each Pro in ProSet
   WScript.Echo "Name: " & Pro.Name & VB1f & _
   "Speed: " & Pro.MaxClockSpeed & VB1f & _
   "Cache: " & Pro.L2CacheSize & " Cache" & VB1f & _
   "Processor ID: " & Pro.ProcessorId
Next
```

NOTE: *The highlighted code above must be placed on one line.*

9. Managing Inventory

Collecting Sound Card Information

The **Win32_SoundDevice** class allows you to query sound card information through WMI. To collect sound card information on a system using WMI, proceed as follows:

1. Create a new directory to store all files included in this example.

2. Download and install the latest version of Windows Script Host, from **www.microsoft.com**, to the new directory.

3. Select Start|Run and enter "cscript *scriptfile*.vbs".

Here, *scriptfile* is the full path and file name of a script file that contains the following:

```
Set SoundSet = GetObject("winmgmts:").InstancesOf
("Win32_SoundDevice")

For each Sound in SoundSet
  WScript.Echo "Card: " & Sound.ProductName & VBlf & _
  "Manufacturer: " & Sound.Manufacturer
Next
```

NOTE: *The highlighted code above must be placed on one line.*

Collecting Tape Drive Information

The **Win32_TapeDrive** class allows you to query tape drive information through WMI. To collect tape drive information on a system using WMI, proceed as follows:

1. Create a new directory to store all files included in this example.

2. Download and install the latest version of Windows Script Host, from **www.microsoft.com**, to the new directory.

3. Select Start|Run and enter "cscript *scriptfile*.vbs".

Here, *scriptfile* is the full path and file name of a script file that contains the following:

```
Set TapeSet = GetObject("winmgmts:").InstancesOf
("Win32_TapeDrive")

For each Tape in TapeSet
  WScript.Echo "Name: " & Tape.Name & VBlf & _
  "Hardware Compression: " & Tape.Compression & VBlf & _
  "Needs Cleaning: " & Tape.NeedsCleaning & VBlf & _
  "Status: " & Tape.Status
Next
```

NOTE: *The highlighted code above must be placed on one line.*

Collecting Video Card Information

The **Win32_VideoController** class allows you to query video card information through WMI. To collect video card information on a system using WMI, proceed as follows:

1. Create a new directory to store all files included in this example.

2. Download and install the latest version of Windows Script Host, from **www.microsoft.com**, to the new directory.

3. Select Start|Run and enter "cscript *scriptfile*.vbs".

Here, ***scriptfile*** is the full path and file name of a script file that contains the following:

```
Set VideoSet = GetObject("winmgmts:").InstancesOf
("Win32_VideoController")

For each Video in VideoSet
   WScript.Echo "Card: " & Video.Description & VB1f & _
   "Current: " & Video.VideoModeDescription
Next
```

NOTE: *The highlighted code above must be placed on one line.*

In Brief

As sad as I am to admit this, the attitude of most administrators is "security through obscurity." This expression means that the best way of dealing with security holes is ignoring them, hoping no one will find them, and praying they will go away. Unfortunately, this attitude never works. It seems nowadays there is a new virus or security hole being publicized daily. The days of merely running **FDISK /MBR** or deleting PWL files are over. Viruses and intruders are more sophisticated than ever. In this chapter, you will learn about the Windows security architecture and how to decrease the chances of unauthorized entry.

Hackers and Crackers

If you can think of system security as a war, then hackers and crackers are your opponents. Before you go into battle, it's always good to know a little about your opponents. Here is the truth about a common myth: Hackers never intentionally damage data. Hackers are knowledgeable computer users whose pure goal is to solve problems and continually learn about the inner workings of operating systems, applications, and transmission methods. Although their methods of obtaining information may be questionable, they tend to create tools to identify or improve upon system weaknesses. Hackers like to document and publicly share their information with all who are willing to learn. Hackers usually receive bad press because people don't understand the difference between the terms "hackers" and "crackers."

Crackers are knowledgeable computer users whose goal is to break into systems and damage or steal data. They tend to reverse-engineer programs and illegally use them for even more illicit purposes. Cracking techniques usually do not involve skillful or complicated methods, but rather crude methods such as stealing files from trash bins or tricking other users into handing them information. Examples of crackers are users who sniff the network for passwords, pirate software, write Trojan horse programs or viruses, or crash the network with broadcasts or email bombs.

TIP: *For more information about hackers and crackers, visit **www.hackers.com**.*

The Infamous Rainbow Series

In order to protect the nation's interest against the attacks of crackers, the National Computer Security Center (NCSC) was born. The NCSC was created by the National Security Agency (NSA) to aggressively evaluate computer system security. NCSC works with various cooperating computer and telecommunication companies to ensure that their services are meeting the country's security requirements.

NOTE: *The NSA is part of the Department of Defense (DOD).*

The "Rainbow Series" is a collection of publications, created by the NCSC to evaluate various aspects of computer security. The cover of each report varies in color, hence the name "Rainbow Series." Over 30 security reports are available from **www.radium.ncsc.mil**. Here is a brief overview of the three key Rainbow books that were used in Windows NT C2 compliance testing.

The Orange Book

The Orange Book is an NCSC publication called *Department of Defense Trusted Computer System Evaluation Criteria*. This is the publication that sets the standards for C2 security.

The Red Book

The Red Book is an extension of the Orange Book. Its title is *Trusted Network Interpretation of the Trusted Computer System Evaluation Criteria*, and it covers the security of networks (LANs/WANs).

The Light Blue Book

The Light Blue Book is an extension of the Orange Book. Its title is *A Guide to Understanding Identification and Authentication in Trusted Systems*, and it discusses the security of user identification and authentication.

TIP: *You can visit **www.radium.ncsc.mil/tpep/library/rainbow/index.html** to download or view all of the rainbow books.*

C2 Security

C2 is a collection of security policies defined by the NCSC publication *Trusted Computer System Evaluation Criteria* (TCSEC), known as the Orange Book. The basic guidelines of the C2 standard are:

- All users must have a unique logon easily identifiable in audits.
- Deleted files must not be readable.
- Security auditing must be included.
- The contents of memory must not be readable after a process has terminated.
- The system must be able to control resource access by granting or denying individual users or groups.
- The system must be protected from external tampering.

Using C2CONFIG

C2CONFIG (C2 Configuration) is an NT resource kit utility designed to analyze and modify system security to comply to C2 security standards. C2CONFIG is a graphical utility that analyzes your system and allows you to easily modify system settings through a file menu. Figure 10.1 shows the C2CONFIG screen.

NOTE: *C2CONFIG is an NT resource kit utility and is not meant to be run on Windows 2000.*

Windows Authentication Protocols

Authentication is the process of validating a known user account and password and is the most important aspect of system security. Authentication happens every time you log on or access a network resource. Depending on your flavor of Windows, an authentication protocol specifies how account and password validation and resource access are to be handled.

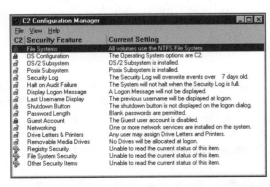

Figure 10.1   The Windows NT Resource Kit Utility C2CONFIG.

Challenge Handshake Authentication Protocol

Windows NT uses a challenge/response scheme called Challenge Handshake Authentication Protocol (CHAP) to ensure that only authenticated users can access resources. These exchanges are encrypted based on the account password to prevent unauthorized users from intercepting them. When a user logs on, the password is stored as an encrypted registry entry called the *hash*. The process of translating a password into a hash is called a one-way hash because you supposedly cannot extract the password from the hash (more on this later in the section "Using the SYSKEY Utility"). A hash encrypts its information using a predefined mathematical algorithm.

LAN Manager Authentication

Windows NT also includes the less secure LAN Manager authentication protocol that Windows 3.*x* and 9*x* use. Passwords are not case sensitive, so before the password is encrypted and stored in the hash, it is first transformed to all uppercase. This password scheme is less secure than that of Windows NT. The security risk increases when these systems are allowed to communicate on unregulated mediums, such as the Internet.

A security downfall of both the Challenge/Response and LAN Manager protocols is the lack of a random salt value when encrypting and storing passwords to the hash. A random salt value is a random number that is incorporated into the encrypted password version stored in the hash. Several other operating systems already use salt values in their encryption schemes (I'll give you a hint; one of them rhymes with Unix). Because both NT password schemes do not use random salt values, intruders can use simple passwords and analyze them against the hash to decrypt other stored passwords on a system (more on this later).

Kerberos v5

Windows 2000 uses the more secure Kerberos v5 authentication protocol, while still supporting the LAN Manager authentication protocol. Kerberos was originally created by Massachusetts Institute of Technology (MIT) and provides faster authentication access times and a more secure authentication process. As opposed to LAN Manager, which uses shared passwords, Kerberos uses a shared cryptographic key that is used to encrypt and decrypt transmitted data. This is more secure than the earlier Windows authentication protocols because the password is never transmitted over the network.

Security Configuration and Analysis Tool

Windows NT uses many utilities, such as User Manager, Server Manager, and Policy Editor, to control system security. With the birth of NT Service Pack 4, the Microsoft Security Configuration and Analysis tool (MSSCE) provides a centralized method to analyze or modify a system's security settings. Figure 10.2 shows this tool. MSSCE is a Microsoft Management Console (MMC) snap-in that allows you to create or use security templates to apply to your environment. These security settings are stored in configuration files and can be applied to all the machines in your environment.

Predefined Security Templates

The MSSCE includes several predefined templates in the %WINDIR%\Security\Templates directory. The security templates included with the MSSCE are:

- *Basicdc.inf*—Default domain controller
- *Basicsv.inf*—Default server
- *Basicwk.inf*—Default workstation

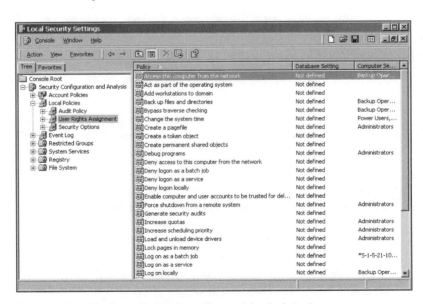

Figure 10.2   The Security Configuration and Analysis tool.

These three basic security templates contain the standard security settings for each system.

- *Compatws.inf*—Compatible workstation or server

The compatibility template contains lower security settings to allow regular users maximum control of installed applications. Applying the compatibility template will remove all users from the power users group.

- *Dedicadc.inf*—Dedicated domain controller

The dedicated template contains security settings for domain controllers that will not be running server-based applications.

- *Hisecdc.inf*—Highly secure domain controller
- *Hisecws.inf*—Highly secure workstation or server

The high security templates provide the maximum security settings for the system. Applying this template on a Windows 2000 system will restrict that system to communicating only with other Windows 2000 systems.

- *Securedc.inf*—Secure domain controller
- *Securews.inf*—Secure workstation or server

The secure templates are the recommended security settings.

Important Security Practices

Here is a list of several security practices to help protect your environment:

- Administrators should always lock their system when not in use. This should be a top priority for administrators. It takes only a few seconds of distraction for an intruder to go to work under your logged-on account.

- Do not allow other accounts to access or log on to an administrator's system. If another user can access your system (even if you are not logged on), he or she can potentially extract passwords, grab your files, and more.

- Always use the latest security patches and service pack. It seems Microsoft is always releasing security patches and service packs to combat system exploits. These patches don't do any good unless they are actually loaded onto your system.

- Use the maximum password length allowed. Microsoft Windows NT/2000 uses a maximum password length of 14 characters. To slow down brute-force password utilities, you should always use the maximum password length allowed.

- Passwords should be a mix of upper- and lowercase, letters, and numbers. The more complex your passwords are, the longer it takes for a password-cracking program to guess a password.

- Do not use dictionary-based passwords (for example, MyKids). Dictionary-based passwords are the easiest and usually the first passwords determined through password-guessing utilities.

- Use the New Technology File System (NTFS). In addition to increased reliability, NTFS provides dramatically increased security compared to the other Windows file systems.

- Set your system BIOS to boot from the hard drive only. Even if you use NTFS, a hacker can access all your protected files by booting from removable media.

Immediate Solutions

Setting the Boot Timeout

Allowing users to choose other operating systems (OS) at bootup is a security risk because the other operating systems can be used to bypass or defeat Windows security.

Setting the Boot Timeout Using KiXtart

To set the boot timeout using KiXtart, proceed as follows:

1. Create a new directory to store all files included in this example.

2. Download and extract the latest version of KiXtart, from **www.microsoft.com**, to the new directory.

3. Select Start|Run and enter "kix32 *scriptfile*".

Here, ***scriptfile*** is the full path of the new directory from step 1 and file name of a script file that contains the following:

```
$File = "C:\boot.ini"

$RCode = SetFileAttr($File,128)
WriteProfileString($File, "boot loader", "timeout", "0")
$RCode = SetFileAttr($File,1)
```

This script first clears any file attributes on BOOT.INI, modifies the boot timeout, and then marks the file as read-only.

Related solution:	*Found on page:*
Setting File or Folder Attributes	57

Setting the Boot Timeout Using WMI

To set the boot timeout to zero using WMI, proceed as follows:

1. Create a new directory to store all files included in this example.

2. Download and install the latest version of WMI and Windows Script Host, from **www.microsoft.com**, to the new directory.

3. Select Start|Run and enter "cscript *scriptfile*.vbs".

Here, ***scriptfile*** is the full path and file name of a script file that contains the following:

```
On Error Resume Next
Computer = InputBox("Enter the computer name", "Boot Timeout"
, "localhost")

Set Boot = GetObject("winmgmts:{impersonationLevel=
impersonate}!\\" & Computer & "\root\cimv2").
ExecQuery("select * from Win32_ComputerSystem")

For each Item in Boot
  Item.SystemStartupDelay = 0
  Item.Put_()
Next
```

NOTE: *The highlighted code above must be placed on one line.*

Removing POSIX and OS/2 Subsystems

By default, Windows NT/2000 includes three environment subsystems: OS/2, POSIX, and Win32 subsystems. Originally developed by Microsoft, OS/2 is IBM's operating system for the personal computer. POSIX stands for Portable Operating System Interface for Unix and is a set of interface standards used by developers to design applications and operating systems.

Win32 is the main subsystem used by Windows, whereas the others are merely present for compatibility with other operating systems and applications. When Windows NT was submitted for evaluation, the POSIX and OS/2 subsystems were disabled to reduce the size of the evaluation. You should remove these subsystems to comply to C2-level security. To remove the POSIX and OS/2 subsystems from the command line, proceed as follows:

1. Create a new directory to store all files included in this example.

2. For Windows NT, obtain RMDIR.EXE from the Resource Kit and copy it to the new directory.

3. Start a command prompt and enter "*scriptfile*.bat".

Here, **scriptfile** is the full path of the new directory from step 1 and
file name of a script file that contains the following:

```
@ECHO OFF
RMDIR /Q /S "%WINDIR%\System32\OS2"
DEL /F /Q "%WINDIR%\SYSTEM32\PSXDLL.DLL"
DEL /F /Q "%WINDIR%\SYSTEM32\PSXSS.EXE"
DEL /F /Q "%WINDIR%\SYSTEM32\POSIX.EXE"
DEL /F /Q "%WINDIR%\SYSTEM32\PSXSS.EXE"
DEL /F /Q "%WINDIR%\SYSTEM32\OS2.EXE"
DEL /F /Q "%WINDIR%\SYSTEM32\OS2SRV.EXE"
DEL /F /Q "%WINDIR%\SYSTEM32\OS2SS.EXE"

ECHO REGEDIT4 > C:\OS2.REG
ECHO [-HKEY_LOCAL_MACHINE\SOFTWARE\Microsoft\
OS/2 Subsystem for NT] >> C:\OS2.REG
REGEDIT /S C:\OS2.REG
DEL  /F /Q C:\OS2.REG
```

NOTE: *The highlighted code above must be placed on one line.*

TIP: *You can perform the same removal using the C2Config Tool, discussed earlier in this
chapter.*

Removing Administrative Shares

Administrative shares are hidden shares created by the system to
allow administrators to access files remotely. Although these shares
are hidden, they are no secret to the savvy user and should be removed for maximum security. To remove administrative shares,
proceed as follows:

1. Create a new directory to store all files included in this example.

2. Download and install the latest version of Windows Script Host,
   from **www.microsoft.com**, to the new directory.

3. Select Start|Run and enter "cscript *scriptfile*.vbs".

Here, *scriptfile* is the full path and file name of a script file that contains the following:

```
On Error Resume Next
Set SHELL = CreateObject("WScript.Shell")
Set Drives = FSO.Drives

For Each Drive in Drives
   SHELL.Run "NET SHARE " & Drive & "\ /D", 0, False
   SHELL.Run "NET SHARE " & Drive & "\WINNT /D", 0, False
Next
```

WARNING! *Certain programs use administrative shares and might not work if they are removed.*

Related solution:	Found on page:
Removing Shares	160

Locking Down Administrative Tools

Administrative tools, such as User Manager and REGEDT32, should be locked down for administrative access only. To lock down various administrative tools, proceed as follows:

1. Create a new directory to store all files included in this example.
2. Copy XCACLS.EXE from the resource kit to the new directory.
3. Start a command prompt and enter "*scriptfile*.bat".

Here, *scriptfile* is the full path of the new directory from step 1 and file name of a script file that contains the following:

```
@ECHO OFF
XCACLS "%WINDIR%\POLEDIT.EXE" /G Administrators:F;F /Y
XCACLS "%WINDIR%\REGEDIT.EXE" /G Administrators:F;F /Y
XCACLS "%WINDIR%\SYSTEM32\CACLS.EXE" /G Administrators:F;F /Y
XCACLS "%WINDIR%\SYSTEM32\CLIPBRD.EXE" /G
Administrators:F;F /Y
```

```
XCACLS "%WINDIR%\SYSTEM32\NCADMIN.EXE" /G
Administrators:F;F /Y

XCACLS "%WINDIR%\SYSTEM32\NTBACKUP.EXE" /G
Administrators:F;F /Y

XCACLS "%WINDIR%\SYSTEM32\REGEDT32.EXE" /G
Administrators:F;F /Y

XCACLS "%WINDIR%\SYSTEM32\RASADMIN.EXE" /G
Administrators:F;F /Y
XCACLS "%WINDIR%\SYSTEM32\RDISK.EXE" /G Administrators:F;F /Y
XCACLS "%WINDIR%\SYSTEM32\SYSKEY.EXE" /G
Administrators:F;F /Y

XCACLS "%WINDIR%\SYSTEM32\USRMGR.EXE" /G
Administrators:F;F /Y

XCACLS "%WINDIR%\SYSTEM32\WINDISK.EXE" /G
Administrators:F;F /Y
```

NOTE: *The highlighted code above must be placed on one line. Although this script prevents an ordinary user from accessing these tools, they could always bring them in and run them from an alternate source, such as a floppy disk.*

Related solution:	Found on page:
Modifying NTFS Permissions	157

Using the SYSKEY Utility

Not too long ago in a galaxy not too far away, a small group of rebels called LOpht Heavy Industries created a tool called LOPHTCRACK.EXE to extract passwords from an encrypted hash within the registry or an emergency repair disk (ERD). Provided with Service Pack 3, SYSKEY is a utility that allows you to encrypt the hash with 128-bit cryptography, which prevents password extraction by the Lophtcrack utility.

NOTE: *SYSKEY encryption is enabled by default on Windows 2000 systems.*

To enable SYSKEY to encrypt the hash locally, proceed as follows:

1. Download and install AutoIt, from **www.hiddensoft.com/autoit**.
2. Select Start|Run and enter "*autoit2 scriptfile*".

Here, *autoit2* is the complete path and name of the AUTOIT executable, and *scriptfile* is a text file that contains the following:

```
RUN, C:\\WINNT\\SYSTEM32\\SYSKEY.EXE
WINWAIT, Securing the Windows, ,5
SEND, !E{ENTER}
WINWAIT, Confirm, ,5
IfWinNotExist, Confirm, , Exit
SEND, {TAB}{ENTER}
WINWAIT, Account Database, ,5
SEND, {TAB}{ENTER}
WINWAIT, Success, ,5
SEND, {ENTER}
```

***WARNING!** There is a bug with the keystream used by the Windows NT version of SYSKEY. For more information and to obtain the security patch, see the Microsoft TechNet article Q248183.*

Running Commands under Different Security Contexts

Every time someone logs on to the network with an administrator account, it creates a big security risk. Malicious ActiveX components from the Web, Trojan horses, or even a hidden batch file can wipe out an entire server, database, and more when run under administrative privileges. If you think about it, you don't really need administrative privileges when you are checking your mail or surfing the Net. A common solution to this security problem is to log on with a regular user account and use a utility to run trusted applications under the security context of an administrative account.

A security context specifies all the rights and privileges granted to a user. For administrators, this security context allows them to manage users, groups, trusts, and domains. The process of switching to the security context of another user is known as impersonation. Impersonation is mostly used by system services.

Installing the SU Utility

Named after the Unix SU command, the SU (Switch User) utility is an NT resource kit utility that allows users to run applications under the security context of a different user. This utility runs as a service and is commonly used within logon script for locked-down environments. To install the SU utility, proceed as follows:

1. Create a new directory to store all files included in this example.

2. For Windows NT, obtain RMDIR.EXE from the Resource Kit and copy it to the new directory.

3. Start a command prompt and enter "*scriptfile*.bat".

Here, **scriptfile** is the full path of the new directory from step 1 and file name of a script file that contains the following:

```
@ECHO OFF
COPY SUSS.EXE %WINDIR%\SYSTEM32
%WINDIR%\SYSTEM32\SUSS -INSTALL
```

TIP: *A common mistake when installing the SU utility is not installing it from a local copy of the SUSS.EXE. Installing straight from the Resource Kit CD will set the service to always look to run the SU utility from the CD.*

Running the SU Utility with a Password Environment Variable

The SU utility can use an environment variable called SU_PASSWORD to access the account's password. Once the command has completed, the variable can be removed. To run the SU utility using an environment variable, proceed as follows:

1. Create a new directory to store all files included in this example.

2. Install the SU utility from the Windows NT resource kit and copy SU.EXE to the new directory.

3. Start a command prompt and enter "*scriptfile*.bat".

Here, **scriptfile** is the full path of the new directory from step 1 and file name of a script file that contains the following:

```
@ECHO OFF
SET SU_PASSWORD=password
SU username command domain
SET SU_PASSWORD=
```

Here, *password* is the password of the *domain\username* with rights to run the specified *command*.

Running the SU Utility with a Password Text File

Another common method is to store the password in a text file and redirect it to the SU utility. To redirect the password from a text file to the SU utility, proceed as follows:

1. Create a new directory to store all files included in this example.

2. Install the SU utility from the Windows NT resource kit.

3. Start a command prompt and enter "*scriptfile*.bat".

Here, *scriptfile* is the full path of the new directory from step 1 and file name of a script file that contains the following:

```
@ECHO OFF
SU username command domain < password.txt
```

Here, *password.txt* is the text file containing the password of the *domain\username*, with rights to run the specified *command*.

Using the Windows 2000 RunAs Command

Windows 2000 includes the utility RUNAS.EXE, which allows users to run applications under the security context of a different user. This utility is integrated into the Windows shell, which allows you to set up shortcuts to utilize the RUNAS utility. The basic syntax of the RUNAS utility is:

```
RUNAS /commands program
```

Here, *program* is the shortcut, Control Panel applet, MMC console, or application to run. The available *commands* are:

- **/ENV**—Keep the current environment.

- **/NETONLY**—Specifies for remote access only.

- **/PROFILE**—Loads the specified user's profile.

- **/USER:*username***—Specifies the *username* to run application as. Valid name formats are *domain\user* or *user@domain*.

NOTE: *Once you have entered the command, you will be prompted for the password associated with the account.*

To start an instance of User Manager using an administrator account called ADMIN@MYDOMAIN.COM, enter the following:

```
RUNAS /USERNAME:ADMIN@MYDOMAIN.COM USRMGR
```

Using the SECEDIT Utility

The SECEDIT.EXE utility is the command-line version of the Microsoft security configuration editor that allows you to run security configuration and analysis from the command line.

Running a Security Analysis

The basic syntax to run an analysis using SECEDIT is as follows:

```
secedit /analyze /commands
```

Here, the available **commands** are:

- **/DB** *filename*—Required, specifies the database to compare against

- **/CFG** *filename*—Valid with **/DB**, specifies the security template to be imported

- **/LOG** *logpath*—Specifies the log file to use

- **/VERBOSE**—Specifies to include more detail to the log or output

- **/QUIET**—Runs the analysis with no screen or log output

Here is an example to run a system analysis against the high security template for a domain controller:

```
Secedit /analyze /DB "%WINDIR%\Security\Database\hisecdc.sdb"
/CFG "%WINDIR%\Security\Templates\hisecdc.inf"
/LOG "%WINDIR%\Security\Logs\hisecdc.log" /VERBOSE
```

NOTE: *The code above must be placed on one line.*

Reapplying a Group Policy

To reapply a local or user policy, start a command prompt and enter the following:

```
SECEDIT /REFRESHPOLICY policy /ENFORCE
```

Here, **/ENFORCE** forces the policy to be reapplied, even if no security changes were found.

Applying a Security Template

The basic syntax to apply a security template using SECEDIT is as follows:

```
secedit /configure /commands
```

Here, the available *commands* are:

- **/AREAS** *name*—Specifies the specific security areas to apply, where *name* is:
  - **FILESTORE**—Local file security
  - **GROUP_MGMT**—Group settings
  - **REGKEYS**—Local registry security
  - **SECURITYPOLICY**—Local or domain policy
  - **SERVICES**—Local services security
  - **USER_RIGHTS**—User's rights and privileges
- **/CFG** *filename*—Valid with **/DB**; specifies the security template to be imported
- **/DB** *filename*—Required; specifies the database containing the template to be applied
- **/OVERWRITE**—Valid with **/CFG**; specifies to overwrite templates in the database
- **/LOG** *logpath*—Specifies the log file to use
- **/VERBOSE**—Specifies to include more detail to the log or output
- **/QUIET**—Runs the analysis with no screen or log output

Fixing Security on a Windows NT to Windows 2000 Upgrade

When you upgrade from Windows NT to Windows 2000, the security settings on the system are not modified. This means none of the intended Windows 2000 security settings are implemented. To apply the Windows 2000 basic security settings, start a command prompt and enter the following:

```
Secedit /configure
/db "%WINDIR%\Security\Database\basicwk.sdb"
```

```
/cfg "%WINDIR%\Security\Templates\basicwk.inf"
/log "%WINDIR%\Security\Logs\basicwk.log"
/verbose
```

NOTE: *The code above must be placed on one line.*

Exporting Security Settings

The basic syntax to export security settings using SECEDIT is as follows:

```
secedit /export /commands
```

Here, the available *commands* are:

- **/AREAS** *name*—Specifies the specific security areas to export, where *name* is:
  - **FILESTORE**—Local file security
  - **GROUP_MGMT**—Group settings
  - **REGKEYS**—Local registry security
  - **SECURITYPOLICY**—Local or domain policy
  - **SERVICES**—Local services security
  - **USER_RIGHTS**—User's rights and privileges
- **/DB** *filename*—Required; specifies the database containing the template to be exported
- **/CFG** *filename*—Valid with **/DB**; specifies the security template to export to
- **/MERGEDPOLICY**—Valid with **/CFG**; specifies to overwrite templates in the database
- **/LOG** *logpath*—Specifies the log file to use
- **/VERBOSE**—Specifies to include more detail to the log or output
- **/QUIET**—Runs the analysis with no screen or log output

Here is an example of how to export the local registry security area to the registry template:

```
Secedit /export /mergedpolicy
/db "%WINDIR%\Security\Database\security.sdb"
/cfg "%WINDIR%\Security\Templates\registry.inf"
/log "%WINDIR%\Security\Logs\registry.log"
/verbose
```

Using the PASSPROP Utility

PASSPROP is an NT resource kit utility that allows you to modify domain password policies from the command line. The basic syntax of the PASSPROP utility is:

```
PASSPROP /commands
```

Here, the available **commands** are:

- **/ADMINLOCKOUT**—Allows the administrator account to lock out for remote logons
- **/COMPLEX**—Forces passwords to contain numbers or symbols and upper- and lowercase letters
- **/NOADMINLOCKOUT**—Does not allow the administrator account to be locked out
- **/SIMPLE**—Allows simple passwords

For example, to implement a strong domain password policy, you would use the following command:

```
PASSPROP /ADMINLOCKOUT /COMPLEX
```

Using the NET ACCOUNTS Command

The built-in NET command has an ACCOUNTS parameter to modify the password and logon requirements for the local computer or a specified domain. The basic syntax of the NET ACCOUNTS utility is:

```
NET ACCOUNTS /commands
```

Here, the available **commands** are:

- **/DOMAIN**—If used, performs the specified operations on the primary domain controller of the current domain; otherwise, performs the operations on the local computer.
- **/FORCELOGOFF:*min***—Sets the number of minutes before a user session is terminated where ***min*** is either the number of minutes or **NO** to specify no forced logoff.
- **/MAXPWAGE:*days***—Specifies the maximum duration a password is valid where ***days*** is either the number of days (1 through 49,710) or **UNLIMITED** to set no maximum time.

- **/MINPWAGE:*days*** —Specifies the minimum duration before a user can change his or her password, where *days* is either the number of days (1 through 49,710) or **UNLIMITED** to set no time limit. This value must be less than the **MAXPWAGE**.

- **/MINPWLEN:*length*** —Specifies the minimum password length.

- **/SYNC** —Forces backup domain controllers to synchronize their password and logon requirements with those set on the primary domain controller.

- **/UNIQUEPW:*changes*** —Specifies that users cannot repeat the same password for the specified amount of password changes (0 through 24).

For example, to modify the logon and password requirements using the NET ACCOUNTS command, you would enter the following command:

```
NET ACCOUNTS /DOMAIN /MAXPWAGE:30 /MINPWAGE:UNLIMITED
/MINPWLEN:14
```

NOTE: *The code above must be placed on one line.*

TIP: *When the administrator has specified a forced logoff, the user receives a warning that a domain controller will force a logoff shortly.*

Managing Security through ADSI

Active Directory Services Interfaces provides another medium to control security. In Chapter 8, you learned how to manage shares, groups, and user accounts through ADSI. In the following section, you will learn how to manage security through ADSI.

Setting the Minimum Password Length

For maximum security, you should set your domain password minimum length to the maximum value, 14. To set the minimum password length for the domain using ADSI, proceed as follows:

1. Create a new directory to store all files included in this example.

2. Download and install the latest version of ADSI and Windows Script Host, from **www.microsoft.com**, to the new directory.

3. Select Start|Run and enter "cscript *scriptfile*.vbs".

Here, ***scriptfile*** is the full path and file name of a script file that contains the following:

```
On Error Resume Next
Set objDomain = GetObject("WinNT://Domain")
objDomain.Put "MinPasswordLength", max
objDomain.SetInfo
```

Here, ***domain*** is the name of the domain, and ***max*** is the maximum password length to set. Again, you should set ***max*** equal to 14 for maximum security.

NOTE: *The maximum password length allowed by Windows NT/2000 is 14 characters.*

Setting the Password Age

For maximum security, you should implement a policy to force users to change their password regularly. To set the password age for the domain using ADSI, proceed as follows:

1. Create a new directory to store all files included in this example.

2. Download and install the latest version of ADSI and Windows Script Host, from **www.microsoft.com**, to the new directory.

3. Select Start|Run and enter "cscript *scriptfile*.vbs".

Here, ***scriptfile*** is the full path and file name of a script file that contains the following:

```
On Error Resume Next

Set objDomain = GetObject("WinNT://Domain")
objDomain.Put "MinPasswordAge", Min * (60*60*24)
objDomain.Put "MaxPasswordAge", Max * (60*60*24)
objDomain.SetInfo
```

Here, ***domain*** is the name of the domain; ***min*** is the minimum duration in days before a user can change his or her password; and ***max*** is the maximum duration in days a password is valid. The formula 60×60×24 is the calculation from seconds to days (60 seconds × 60 minutes × 24 hours).

Setting Unique Password Changes

For maximum security, you should implement a policy to force users to select passwords different from their previous passwords. To set the unique password duration for the domain using ADSI, proceed as follows:

1. Create a new directory to store all files included in this example.

2. Download and install the latest version of ADSI and Windows Script Host, from **www.microsoft.com**, to the new directory.

3. Select Start|Run and enter "cscript *scriptfile*.vbs".

Here, ***scriptfile*** is the full path and file name of a script file that contains the following:

```
On Error Resume Next

Set objDomain = GetObject("WinNT://Domain")
objDomain.Put "PasswordHistoryLength", min
objDomain.SetInfo
```

Here, ***domain*** is the name of the domain, and ***min*** is the minimum number of passwords used before a user can repeat that previous password. The formula 60×60×24 is the calculation from seconds to days (60 seconds × 60 minutes × 24 hours).

Setting the Account Lockout Policy

For maximum security, you should implement a policy to lock out accounts after a certain number of bad attempts. To implement an account lockout policy using ADSI, proceed as follows:

1. Create a new directory to store all files included in this example.

2. Download and install the latest version of ADSI and Windows Script Host, from **www.microsoft.com**, to the new directory.

3. Select Start|Run and enter "cscript *scriptfile*.vbs".

Here, ***scriptfile*** is the full path and file name of a script file that contains the following:

```
On Error Resume Next

Set objDomain = GetObject("WinNT://Domain")
objDomain.Put "MaxBadPasswordAllowed", Max
objDomain.SetInfo
```

Here, **domain** is the name of the domain. The formula 60×60×24 is the calculation from seconds to days (60 seconds × 60 minutes × 24 hours).

Searching for Locked-Out Accounts

It's good practice to regularly search the domain for locked-out accounts. To search for locked-out accounts using ADSI, proceed as follows:

1. Create a new directory to store all files included in this example.

2. Download and install the latest version of ADSI and Windows Script Host, from **www.microsoft.com**, to the new directory.

3. Select Start|Run and enter "cscript *scriptfile*.vbs".

Here, **scriptfile** is the full path and file name of a script file that contains the following:

```
On Error Resume Next
Set objDomain = GetObject("WinNT://Domain")

For Each Item in objDomain
  If Item.Class = "User" Then
    If Item.IsAccountLocked = "True" Then
      Wscript.Echo "Name: " & Item.Name & VBlf & _
      "Bad Password Attempts: " & _
      Item.BadPasswordAttempts & VBlf & _
      "Last Login: " & Item.LastLogin
    End If
  End If
Next
```

Here, **domain** is the name of the domain.

Related solution:	Found on page:
Unlocking a User Account	208

Renaming the Administrator Account

Windows NT/2000 creates a default administrative account called "Administrator" to be the master account for that system. This account cannot be deleted, but should be renamed to foil hackers attempting to gain access through this account. To rename the administrator account using ADSI, proceed as follows:

1. Create a new directory to store all files included in this example.

2. Download and install the latest version of ADSI and Windows Script Host, from **www.microsoft.com**, to the new directory.

3. Select Start|Run and enter "cscript *scriptfile*.vbs".

Here, ***scriptfile*** is the full path and file name of a script file that contains the following:

```
On Error Resume Next

Set objDomain = GetObject("WinNT://Computer")
Set objUser = ObjDomain.GetObject("User", "Administrator")
objDomain.MoveHere objUser.AdsPath, Name
```

Here, ***computer*** is the name of the computer holding the account, and ***name*** is the new name to give the account.

TIP: *You can use this script to rename any account simply by replacing the word ADMINIS-TRATOR with the user account name desired.*

Searching for Unused Accounts

It's good practice to regularly search the domain for accounts that have either been logged on for a long duration of time or have not logged on in a long time. To search for unused accounts using ADSI, proceed as follows:

1. Create a new directory to store all files included in this example.

2. Download and install the latest version of ADSI and Windows Script Host, from **www.microsoft.com**, to the new directory.

3. Select Start|Run and enter "cscript *scriptfile*.vbs".

Here, ***scriptfile*** is the full path and file name of a script file that contains the following:

```
On Error Resume Next
Days = amount

Set objDomain = GetObject("WinNT://Domain")

For Each Item in objDomain
   If Item.Class="User" Then
      DUR = DateDiff("D", Item.LastLogin, Date)
      If DUR > Days Then
```

```
    Wscript.Echo "Name: " & Item.Name & VBlf & _
    "Account Disabled: " & Item.AccountDisabled & VBlf & _
    "Last Login: " & Item.LastLogin & VBlf & _
    "Amount of days: " & DUR
  End If
 End If
Next
```

Here, ***domain*** is the name of the domain to search, and ***amount*** is the least number of days since the last logon.

Using the Microsoft Script Encoder

The Microsoft Script Encoder allows you to protect your scripts using a simple encoding scheme. This encoding scheme is not intended to prevent advanced cracking techniques, but to merely make your scripts unreadable to the average user. The default supported file types are asa, asp, cdx, htm, html, js, sct, and vbs. The basic syntax of the script encoder is as follows:

```
SCRENC inputfile outputfile
```

Here, ***inputfile*** is the file to encode and ***outputfile*** is the encoded result. Microsoft Script Encoder supports many command-line parameters, as shown in Table 10.1.

WARNING!: Always back up your scripts before encoding them. Once a script is overwritten with an encoded version, there is no way to return it to its original state.

Table 10.1   Microsoft Script Encoder parameters.

Parameter	Description
/E *extension*	Specifies a known extension for unrecognized input file types
/F	Specifies to overwrite the input file with the encoded version
/L *language*	Specifies to use the scripting language Jscript or VBScript
/S	Specifies to work in silent mode
/X1	Specifies not to include to @language directive to ASP files

Previous Security Scripts

Some of the scripts included in previous chapters can increase your system security. These scripts are shown in Table 10.2.

Table 10.2   Security scripts.

Chapter	Script
Chapter 5	Disabling 8.3 File Naming
Chapter 5	Disabling the Lock Workstation Button
Chapter 5	Disabling the Change Password Button
Chapter 5	Disabling the Logoff Button
Chapter 5	Modifying the Registry with REGINI.EXE
Chapter 6	Locking the Floppy Disk
Chapter 6	Managing Encryption in Windows 2000
Chapter 6	Modifying NTFS Permissions
Chapter 8	Changing the Local Administrator Password

Chapter 11
Logging and Alerting

(continued)

In Brief

The purpose of logging is to record the status of an operation generated by the system or an application. Along with many scripts and applications, Windows NT/2000 has a built-in method to log events and errors. Managing event logs across an enterprise can become an involved process. Third-party utilities such as Dorian Software's Event Archiver and Key Technology's Event Log Utilities allow you to read, write, modify, and archive event logs and entries. Although these utilities are available at a modest price, this chapter will show you how to access and control the event log through simple scripts, for free.

Logs provide a good method of recording events, but they are only as good as the time and frequency with which you check them. Alerting is the method of notifying a user when an event occurs. In this chapter, you will learn the various methods to create alerts to keep you informed of the many events that occur in your environment.

The Windows NT/2000 Event Log

Windows NT/2000 includes a built-in event-logging system known as the event log. Before an interaction with the event log is performed, a request is sent to the Service Control Manager (SCM). SCM is controlled by *%WINDIR%*\System32\SERVICES.EXE. When the system first boots up, the event log service is started and the event log files are opened. Once the service receives the request, it processes it by storing or modifying an event in the proper event log.

Types of Logs

The event log is divided into three categories:

- *Application Log (AppEvent.Evt)*—Stores application and system events, such as application errors
- *Security Log (SecEvent.Evt)*—Stores audited security events, such as clearing the event log
- *System Log (SysEvent.Evt)*—Stores operating-system-related events, such as creating a new user

These logs are stored in a proprietary binary format and reside in the *%WINDIR%*\System32\Config directory. Although all users can view the application and system logs, only administrators can view and clear the security event log.

NOTE: *The event log files cannot merely be copied and opened on another system. When the system opens the event logs, it modifies the file headers and doesn't reset the header until the file is closed. To copy the event log, use the Save Log As option from the File menu of the Event Viewer.*

The Event Viewer

The Event Viewer is a built-in Windows NT/2000 tool to easily view the three separate event log files (see Figure 11.1). The Event Viewer executable (EVENTVWR.EXE) resides in the *%WINDIR%\System32* directory. To start the Event Viewer, open Administrative Tools and run the Event Viewer. From within the Event Viewer, you can view, delete, archive, or import an entire event log or entry. The most common use of the event log is to troubleshoot system errors, such as service failures.

NOTE: *In Windows 2000, the executable called EVENTVWR.EXE is actually just a pointer to the MMC snap-in EVENTVWR.MSC.*

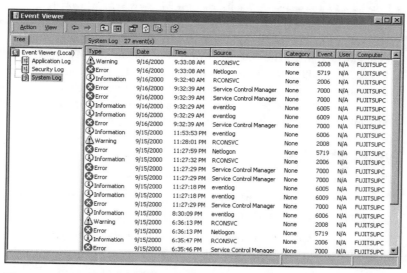

Figure 11.1   The Windows 2000 Event Viewer.

Event Log Entries

Event log entries consist of an event ID that categorizes the type of event, and an event description that is the actual error or event text. The event type specifies the following classification of recorded events:

- *Error*—Indicates critical errors and corruption of data
- *Failure Audit*—Combined with auditing, indicates a failed security event, such as a bad password
- *Information*—Indicates a successful operation, such as a successful driver load
- *Success Audit*—Combined with auditing, indicates a successful security event, such as a successful logon
- *Warning*—Indicates a non-critical warning, such as a failed attempt to obtain a browse list

Other items logged with each event are:

- *Computer*—The name of the target computer
- *Date*—Date the event was written
- *Source Type*—The source of the event
- *Time*—Time the event was written
- *User Name*—The currently logged-on user

Event Log Etiquette

The Windows NT/2000 event log is a logging system that stores critical and important system and application events. The original intent of this log system was only for the system and applications to write events. Some systems might be set up to overwrite events or to crash the system when the event log is full. Storing routine messages like "Logon script completed successfully" might overwrite critical events or cause a system to crash because the event log is full.

Understanding NetBIOS

Logging provides a method to record events, and alerting provides a method to send event messages to users. A common method of sending messages over a network is to use Network Basic Input Output System (NetBIOS). NetBIOS is a non-routable interface that allows various types of computers to communicate over the local area network (LAN). NetBIOS was created by IBM and Sytek during the mid-1980s and has since become an industry standard for network communication. Microsoft Windows currently implements NetBIOS on the following protocols: NetBIOS Enhanced User Interface (NetBEUI), Internetwork Packet Exchange/Sequenced Packet Exchange (IPX/SPX), and Transmission Control Protocol/Internet Protocol (TCP/IP).

NOTE: *A common use of NetBIOS is the Network Neighborhood.*

NetBIOS Communication Modes

NetBIOS contains two modes of communication: session or datagram. Session mode establishes a reliable channel between two systems, and uses error checking to ensure proper data transfer. Datagram mode is a one-way communication method that transmits small messages without error checking. This type of communication is commonly referred to as connectionless communication. A datagram is a container used to transmit data across a network.

NOTE: *The term* datagram *is interchangeable with the term* packet.

Windows includes the ability to send command-line messages to other users or computers through NetBIOS using a utility called NET.EXE. These messages are sent in datagrams to other NetBIOS computer or user names. NetBIOS messages have a restricted size of 128 characters, whereas NetBIOS names are restricted to 15 characters (with a 16th hidden character used by the operating system).

TIP: *Windows NT/2000 monitors these messages through the Messenger Service. If the system experiences errors while transmitting or receiving NetBIOS messages, you should first check the Messenger Service.*

Understanding MAPI

MAPI (Messaging Application Program Interface) is an interface that provides a standard method for applications to send email. MAPI includes a standard set of functions, such as logging on, creating new messages, and reading messages, that developers can call directly in their applications using C or C++. MAPI is a built-in part of Windows $9x$ and Windows NT/2000. Simple MAPI is a slimmed-down version of MAPI that can be accessed using C, C++, Visual Basic, or Visual Basic for Applications (VBA).

Immediate Solutions

Using Logs with Shell Scripting

Currently, shell scripting contains no built-in methods to access the event log. Fortunately, you can create your own text logs or use resource kit utilities to access the event log.

Writing to Text Logs

The simplest way to log events in shell scripting is to append text to a text log. The basic syntax to append text to a text log is as follows:

```
Command >> textlog
```

Here, ***command*** is either an echoed statement or the output of a command, and ***textlog*** is the complete path and file name of the log file. Here is a quick example to send a message to a log file called log.txt:

```
@Echo Off
Echo This is a test to log an event. >> log.txt
```

TIP: *To clear the log, simply delete the file (**DEL textlog**).*

Related solution:	Found on page:
Appending Text Files	54

Writing to Text Logs with the Date and Time

Recording the date and time within a log is essential to determine the exact moment of a particular event. To place the date and time into an environment variable using shell scripting, proceed as follows:

1. Create a new directory to store all files included in this example.

2. Select Start|Run and enter "*scriptfile*.bat".

Here, ***scriptfile*** is the full path and file name of a script file that contains the following:

```
@Echo Off
For /F "Delims= Tokens=1" %%I in ('Date /T')
Do Set Dtime=%%I

For /F "Delims= Tokens=1" %%I in ('Time /T')
Do Set Dtime=%Dtime%%%I
```

NOTE: *The highlighted code above must be placed on one line.*

To log an event using the date and time, proceed as follows:

1. Create a new directory to store all files included in this example.
2. Copy the date time script above to a file called SETDTIME.BAT.
3. Select Start|Run and enter "*scriptfile*.bat".

Here, ***scriptfile*** is the full path and file name of a script file that contains the following:

```
Call setdtime.bat
Echo %Dtime% message >> textlog
```

Here, ***message*** is the alert message to log, and ***textlog*** is the complete path and file name of the log file.

TIP: *To clear the date and time variable (**dtime**), add the following line at the end of your entire script:*

```
SET %Dtime%=
```

Using LOGEVENT to Write to the Event Log

LOGEVENT.EXE is a resource kit utility to write events to the event log from the command line. The basic syntax of LOGEVENT.EXE is as follows:

```
logevent -m \\computer -s type -c category -r source -e id
-t time "message"
```

NOTE: *The code above must be placed on one line.*

Here, ***computer*** is the name of a remote system to connect to; ***source*** specifies the origin of the event; ***id*** indicates the entry ID number (0-65535); ***category*** is the number for the desired category; ***message*** is the text to include in the entry; ***time*** is the amount of seconds the system waits before an exit; and ***type*** specifies one of the following event types:

- **E**—Error
- **F**—Failure
- **I**—Information
- **S**—Success
- **W**—Warning

TIP: *LogEvent will accept either the full name or the first letter of the event type. Example, you can specify **-S ERROR** or **-S E**.*

Here is an example of how to write an event to the event log:

```
logevent -S ERROR -C 3 -E 10 -R ShellScript "Some Event Text"
```

Using Dumpel to Back Up the Event Log

Dumpel is a resource kit utility that allows you to back up an event log in text format from the command line. The basic syntax for using Dumpel is as follows:

```
Dumpel -F textfile -L logtype commands
```

Here, ***textfile*** is the complete path and file name to back up the event log to; ***logtype*** is the type of log to back up (Application, System, or Security); and ***commands*** are any of the following optional commands:

- **-D *days***—Displays only the last number of ***days*** specified where ***days*** must be larger than zero
- **-E *ID***—Displays only the specified event ***ID***s where ***ID*** may be up to ten various event IDs
- **-M *name***—Displays only the events with the ***name*** specified
- **-R**—Specifies to filter by sources of records
- **-S *computer***—Specifies the ***computer*** to connect to
- **-T**—Separates values using tabs as opposed to spaces

To back up security log events from the past ten days using Dumpel, start a command prompt and enter the following:

```
Dumpel -F "C:\DUMP.TXT" -L "Security" -D 10
```

Using Logs with KiXtart

KiXtart provides several methods to write text logs and to access the event log. Through KiXtart, you can write to, back up, and clear the event logs.

Writing to Text Logs

Text logs allow all users, regardless of operating system, to write, modify, and read logged events. To log an event to a text log using KiXtart, proceed as follows:

1. Create a new directory to store all files included in this example.

2. Download and extract the latest version of KiXtart, from **www.microsoft.com**, to the new directory.

3. Select Start|Run and enter "kix32 *scriptfile*".

Here, **scriptfile** is the full path of the new directory from step 1 and file name of a script file that contains the following:

```
$RCODE = Open(1, "textlog", 5)
$RCODE = WriteLine(1, @Date + " " + @Time
+ "message" + Chr(13) + Chr(10))
$RCODE = Close(1)
```

NOTE: *The highlighted code above must be placed on one line.*

Here, **message** is the alert message to log, and **textlog** is the complete path and file name of the log file. Notice that the first line opens and sets the text log to file number 1, the next line writes to file number 1, and then the final line closes file number 1. All three steps are necessary to write to a text file. Failure to include the **close** statement will result in wasted memory space.

TIP: *To clear the log, simply delete the file (**DEL** **textlog**).*

Related solution:	Found on page:
Appending Text Files	58

Writing an Event to the Event Log

LogEvent is a KiXtart command that allows you to write entries to the event log. The basic syntax for using the **LogEvent** command is as follows:

```
LOGEVENT (type, ID, event, computer, source)
```

NOTE: *All events are stored in the application log and cannot be redirected to the system or security logs.*

Here, **ID** is the entry ID number to assign; **event** is the text event entry; **computer** is an optional parameter specifying the name of a remote system to write events to; **source** specifies the event source; and **type** specifies one of the following event types:

- **0**—SUCCESS
- **1**—ERROR
- **2**—WARNING
- **4**—INFORMATION
- **8**—AUDIT_SUCCESS
- **16**—AUDIT_FAILURE

To write an event to the event log using KiXtart, proceed as follows:

1. Create a new directory to store all files included in this example.
2. Download and extract the latest version of KiXtart, from **www.microsoft.com**, to the new directory.
3. Select Start|Run and enter "kix32 *scriptfile*".

Here, **scriptfile** is the full path of the new directory from step 1 and file name of a script file that contains the following:

```
$RCODE = LogEvent(0, 10, "This stuff is easy!",
"", "New Event")
If @ERROR <> 0 or $RCODE <> 0
  ? "Error writing event"
End If
```

NOTE: *The highlighted code above must be placed on one line.*

Backing Up the Event Log

BackUpEventLog is a KiXtart command that allows you to back up the event log in the standard event log binary format. The basic syntax for using the **BackUpEventLog** command is as follows:

```
BackUpEventLog ("logtype", "textfile")
```

Here, *logtype* is the type of log to back up (Application, System, or Security), and *textfile* is the complete path and file name to back up the event log to. To back up the security log to a file called Backup.evt using KiXtart, proceed as follows:

1. Create a new directory to store all files included in this example.

2. Download and extract the latest version of KiXtart, from **www.microsoft.com**, to the new directory.

3. Select Start|Run and enter "kix32 *scriptfile*".

Here, *scriptfile* is the full path of the new directory from step 1 and file name of a script file that contains the following:

```
$RCODE = BackUpEventLog ("Security", "C:\BACKUP.EVT")
If @ERROR <> 0 or $RCODE <> 0
  ? "Error backing up log"
End If
```

Clearing the Event Log

ClearEventLog is a KiXtart command that allows you to clear the contents of an event log. The basic syntax for using the **ClearEventLog** command is as follows:

```
ClearEventLog ("logtype")
```

TIP: *You can clear the event log of a remote computer by including the UNC path before the log type, for example:*

```
ClearEventLog ("\\computer\Security")
```

Here, *logtype* is the type of log to clear (Application, System, or Security). To clear the event log using KiXtart, proceed as follows:

1. Create a new directory to store all files included in this example.

2. Download and extract the latest version of KiXtart, from **www.microsoft.com**, to the new directory.

3. Select Start|Run and enter "kix32 *scriptfile*".

Here, *scriptfile* is the full path of the new directory from step 1 and file name of a script file that contains the following:

```
$RCODE = ClearEventLog ("Security")
If @ERROR <> 0 or $RCODE <> 0
  ? "Error clearing the event log"
End If
```

Using Logs with Windows Script Host

Windows Script Host allows you to write events to a text log and the event log using simple script files. This allows you to store critical events in the event log, while storing less severe events to a text log.

NOTE: *Windows Script Host does not contain any methods to read or modify events in the event log.*

Writing to Text Logs

Text logs provide an easy way to record events and share the file with others, regardless of operating system. To log an event to a text log using Windows Script Host, proceed as follows:

1. Create a new directory to store all files included in this example.

2. Download and install the latest version of Windows Script Host, from **www.microsoft.com**, to the new directory.

3. Select Start|Run and enter "cscript *scriptfile*.vbs".

Here, *scriptfile* is the full path and file name of a script file that contains the following:

```
On Error Resume Next
Set FSO = CreateObject("Scripting.FileSystemObject")
txtlog = "textlog"

If FSO.FileExists(txtlog) Then
  Set LogFile = FSO.OpenTextFile(txtlog, 8)
Else
  Set LogFile = FSO.CreateTextFile(txtlog, True)
End If
```

```
LogFile.WriteLine Date & " " & Time & " message"
LogFile.Close
```

Here, ***message*** is the alert message to log, and ***textlog*** is the complete path and file name of the log file.

Related solution:	Found on page:
Appending Text Files	81

Writing an Event to the Event Log

You can use Wscript.Shell's **LogEvent** method to write events to the event log. The basic syntax for using the **LogEvent** method is as follows:

```
LogEvent(type,event,computer)
```

NOTE: *All events are stored in the application log, and cannot be redirected to the system or security logs.*

Here, ***event*** is the text event entry; ***computer*** is an optional parameter specifying the name of a remote system to write events to; and ***type*** specifies one of the following event types:

- **SUCCESS (0)**
- **ERROR (1)**
- **WARNING (2)**
- **INFORMATION (4)**
- **AUDIT_SUCCESS (8)**
- **AUDIT_FAILURE (16)**

TIP: *You can use the corresponding numbers, as opposed to key words, to specify event types.*

When you use **LogEvent** to create an event log entry, the following is recorded:

- **Category**—Logged as None
- **Computer**—The name of the target computer
- **Date**—Date the event was written
- **Event**—Logged as 0
- **Source Type**—Logged as WSH

- **Time**—Time the event was written
- **Type**—Type of event entry
- **User Name**—Logged as N/A

Here is a subroutine to write an event:

```
Sub WriteLog(Ltype, Ldesc)
  On Error Resume Next
  Set SHELL = CreateObject("WScript.Shell")
  LEvent = SHELL.LogEvent(Ltype, Ldesc)
  If Err.Number <> 0 Or LEvent = False Then
    Wscript.Echo "Error writing event"
  End If
End Sub
```

NOTE: *Because Windows 9x does not contain an event log, all written events will be stored in %WINDIR%\wsh.log.*

Here, *ltype* is the type of event, and *ldesc* is the event text to write. Using the following command combined with the subroutine above will write a success event to the event log:

```
WriteLog 0, "This stuff is cool!"
```

Accessing the Event Log Using WMI

The **Win32_NTLogEvent** class manages the event logs on Windows NT/2000 systems. Through this class, you can view, write, modify, delete, and back up the event log through simple scripts.

Backing Up an Event Log in Binary Mode

The **BackupEventLog** method allows you to back up an event log to a file in standard event log binary format. To create a backup of the event log in standard event log binary format using WMI, proceed as follows:

1. Create a new directory to store all files included in this example.
2. Download and install the latest version of WMI and Windows Script Host, from **www.microsoft.com**, to the new directory.
3. Select Start|Run and enter "cscript *scriptfile*.vbs".

Here, **scriptfile** is the full path and file name of a script file that contains the following:

```
On Error Resume Next
Set FSO = CreateObject("Scripting.FileSystemObject")
LogType = InputBox("Enter the log to backup", "Log Type"
, "application")

BFile = InputBox("Enter file to backup to", "Backup File"
, "C:\BACKUP.LOG")
   If FSO.FileExists(BFile) Then
       FSO.DeleteFile BFile
   End If
Set EventLog = GetObject("winmgmts:{impersonationLevel=
impersonate,(Backup)}").ExecQuery("select * from
Win32_NTEventLogFile where LogfileName='" & LogType & "'")

For each Entry in EventLog
   Entry.BackupEventLog BFile
Next
Wscript.Echo "Done"
```

NOTE: *The highlighted code above must be placed on one line. The **(Backup)** privilege is explicitly included in the example above to allow you to use the **BackUpEventLog** method.*

Here, **LogType** is the event log to back up (application, security, or system), and **Bfile** is the complete path and filename to back up to.

Backing Up the Entire Event Log in Text Mode

In the previous sections, you learned that the **BackUpEventLog** method and the Dumpel utility back up the event log to a text file in binary format. Although this format conforms to the standard event log storage format, it does not allow you to easily view the contents of the backup. To create a backup of the event log in plain-text, tab-delimited format using WMI, proceed as follows:

1. Create a new directory to store all files included in this example.

2. Download and install the latest version of WMI and Windows Script Host, from **www.microsoft.com**, to the new directory.

3. Select Start|Run and enter "cscript *scriptfile*.vbs".

Here, ***scriptfile*** is the full path and file name of a script file that contains the following:

```
On Error Resume Next
Set EventLog = GetObject("winmgmts:{impersonationLevel=
impersonate}").ExecQuery("select * from Win32_NTLogEvent")

Set FSO = CreateObject("Scripting.FileSystemObject")
Set txt = FSO.CreateTextFile("textfile", True)
For each Entry in EventLog
  If Len(Entry.Message) > 0 Then
    For x = 1 to Len(Entry.Message)
      Char = Mid(Entry.Message,x,1)
      If Asc(Char) = 10 Then
        MSG = MSG & " "
      ElseIf Asc(Char) <> 13 Then
        MSG = MSG & Char
      End If
    Next

    EDate = Mid(Entry.TimeGenerated,5,2) & "/" & _
      Mid(Entry.TimeGenerated,7,2) & "/" & _
      Mid(Entry.TimeGenerated,1,4)
    ETime = Mid(Entry.TimeGenerated,9,2) & ":" & _
      Mid(Entry.TimeGenerated,11,2) & ":" & _
      Mid(Entry.TimeGenerated,13,2)
    ETime = FormatDateTime(ETime,3)

    If IsNull(Entry.User) Then
      User = "N/A"
    Else
      User = Entry.User
    End If

    If IsNull(Entry.CategoryString) Then
      Category = "none"
    Else
      Category = Entry.CategoryString
    End If

    EVT = Entry.LogFile & VBtab & _
    Entry.Type & VBtab & _
    EDate & VBtab & _
```

```
        ETime & VBtab & _
        Entry.SourceName & VBtab & _
        Category & VBtab & _
        Entry.EventCode & VBtab & _
        User & VBtab & _
        Entry.ComputerName & VBtab & _
        MSG
        txt.writeline EVT

        EVT = Null
        Char = Null
        MSG = Null
    End If
Next
txt.close
Wscript.echo "Done"
```

NOTE: *The highlighted code above must be placed on one line.*

Here, ***textfile*** is the complete path and file name to back up the event log to.

Clearing an Event Log

The **ClearEventLog** method allows you to clear individual event log entries. To clear the entire contents of an event log using WMI, proceed as follows:

1. Create a new directory to store all files included in this example.

2. Download and install the latest version of WMI and Windows Script Host, from **www.microsoft.com**, to the new directory.

3. Select Start|Run and enter "cscript *scriptfile*.vbs".

Here, ***scriptfile*** is the full path and file name of a script file that contains the following:

```
On Error Resume Next
LogType = InputBox("Enter the log to clear", "Clear Log"
, "application")

Set EventLog = GetObject("winmgmts:{impersonationLevel=
impersonate}").ExecQuery("select * from
Win32_NTEventLogFile where LogfileName='" & LogType & "'")
For each Entry in EventLog
    Entry.ClearEventlog()
```

```
Next
Wscript.Echo "Done"
```

NOTE: *The highlighted code above must be placed on one line.*

Here, ***LogType*** is the event log to clear (Application, Security, or System).

Sending Alerts Using Shell Scripting

Shell scripting does not include a method to send alerts from the command line. Microsoft Windows includes the NET.EXE utility to allow you to send messages to users or computers over the network.

Sending Alerts to a Single User or Computer

To send a message over the network, start a command prompt and enter the following:

```
NET SEND name message
```

NOTE: *NetBIOS messages have a maximum limit of 128 characters.*

Here, ***message*** is the message to send, and ***name*** is the NetBIOS name of a computer or user ID.

Sending Alerts to Multiple Users and Computers

You can also use the asterisk symbol (*) to send messages to all computers on the local network:

```
Net Send * message
```

Here, ***message*** is the message to send. As opposed to specifying a name or asterisk, you can use one of the following commands to send messages to multiple users or computers:

- **/DOMAIN**—Sends a message to the local domain
- **/DOMAIN:*name***—Sends a message to a specified domain
- **/USERS**—Sends messages to users connected to the server

Here is an example to send a *message* to the JESSEWEB domain:

```
Net Send /DOMAIN:JESSEWEB message
```

NOTE: *Sending messages to the entire network or domain will not only utilize a good portion of your network's bandwidth but it is also annoying to all the other users.*

Sending Alerts to Specific Multiple Users and Computers

Although the **Net Send** command contains methods to send messages to multiple users, it does not contain a method to send messages to specific user and computer names. To send an alert to an exact list of user or computer names using shell scripting, proceed as follows:

1. Create a new directory to store all files included in this example.

2. Select Start|Run and enter "*scriptfile*.bat".

Here, *scriptfile* is the full path of the new directory from step 1 and file name of a script file that contains the following:

```
@Echo Off
For /F %%N in (textfile) Do (Echo Sending Message to
%%N... & Net Send %%N Message)
```

NOTE: *The highlighted code above must be placed on one line.*

Here, *textfile* is the name of a text file with each line containing a user or computer name, and *message* is the message to send.

Sending Alerts Using KiXtart

KiXtart includes a command called **SendMessage** that allows you to send NetBIOS messages to users or computers over the network. This command transports messages in a similar fashion to the Microsoft NET.EXE utility.

Sending Alerts to a Single User or Computer

To send an alert to a single user using KiXtart, proceed as follows:

1. Create a new directory to store all files included in this example.

2. Download and extract the latest version of KiXtart, from **www.microsoft.com**, to the new directory.

3. Select Start|Run and enter "kix32 *scriptfile*".

Here, ***scriptfile*** is the full path of the new directory from step 1 and file name of a script file that contains the following:

```
$RCODE = SENDMESSAGE ("name", "message")
If @ERROR <> 0 or $RCODE <> 0
  ? "Error sending message"
End If
```

Here, ***name*** is the user or computer name to send a ***message*** to.

Sending Alerts to Multiple Users or Computers

To send an alert to multiple users using KiXtart, proceed as follows:

1. Create a new directory to store all files included in this example.

2. Download and extract the latest version of KiXtart, from **www.microsoft.com**, to the new directory.

3. Select Start|Run and enter "kix32 *scriptfile*".

Here, ***scriptfile*** is the full path of the new directory from step 1 and file name of a script file that contains the following:

```
$COUNT = 4 ; User Array Count
DIM $NAME[$COUNT] ; User Array
$NAME[0] = "name1"
$NAME[1] = "computer1"
$NAME[2] = "computer2"
$NAME[3] = "name2"

$NETMESSAGE = "This is a test message."

$Index = 0
WHILE $Index <> $COUNT
  $RCODE = SENDMESSAGE ($NAME[$Index], $NETMESSAGE)
  If @ERROR <> 0 or $RCODE <> 0
    ? "Error sending message"
  End If
  $Index = $Index + 1
LOOP
```

Here, ***$count*** is the size of the array. This is the number of users you want to send messages to. This number must exactly match the number of users that you send messages to, or an error will result. **$name** is the array that holds the user or computer names to send messages to, and **$netmessage** is the message to send.

NOTE: *The array size is limited to the amount of memory the system has. Remember, the contents of an array start at 0, not at 1. Using versions older than KiXtart 3.62 will cause a script error when attempting to create an array.*

Sending Alerts Using Windows Script Host

Windows Script Host does not include any methods to send messages to users or computers. Through Windows Script Host, you can call upon the NET.EXE utility or use automation to send messages.

Sending an Alert to a Single User or Computer

To send an alert to a single user or computer using WSH, proceed as follows:

1. Create a new directory to store all files included in this example.

2. Download and install the latest version of Windows Script Host, from **www.microsoft.com**, to the new directory.

3. Select Start|Run and enter "cscript *scriptfile*.vbs".

Here, **scriptfile** is the full path and file name of a script file that contains the following:

```
On Error Resume Next
Set Shell = CreateObject("Wscript.Shell")

RCV = "name"
MSG = "message"

SHELL.Run "Net Send " & Name & " " & MSG, 0, False
```

Here, **RCV** is the user or computer **name** to send a message to, and **MSG** is the **message** to send.

Sending Alerts to Multiple Users or Computers

To send an alert to multiple user or computer names using WSH, proceed as follows:

1. Create a new directory to store all files included in this example.

2. Download and install the latest version of Windows Script Host, from **www.microsoft.com**, to the new directory.

3. Select Start|Run and enter "cscript *scriptfile*.vbs".

Here, ***scriptfile*** is the full path and file name of a script file that contains the following:

```
On Error Resume Next
Set Shell = CreateObject("Wscript.Shell")

Dim Name(2)
Name(0) = "name1"
Name(1) = "name2"

MSG = "message"

For X = 0 to UBound(Name)
   SHELL.Run "Net Send " & Name(X) & " " & MSG, 0, False
Next
```

Here, ***Name*** is the array that holds the user or computer names to send messages to. The size of this array should be equal to the number of users or computers you want to send messages to. ***MSG*** is the ***message*** to send.

Sending an Email Using Outlook Automation

To send an email using Outlook automation, proceed as follows:

1. Create a new directory to store all files included in this example.

2. Download and install the latest version of Windows Script Host, from **www.microsoft.com**, to the new directory.

3. Select Start|Run and enter "cscript *scriptfile*.vbs".

Here, ***scriptfile*** is the full path and file name of a script file that contains the following:

```
On Error Resume Next
RCP = "emailaddress"
SUB = "subject"
MSG = "message"

Set Outlook = CreateObject("Outlook.Application")
Set MAPI = Outlook.GetNameSpace("MAPI")
Set NewMail = Outlook.CreateItem(0)
NewMail.Subject = SUB
NewMail.Body = MSG
NewMail.Recipients.Add RCP

MAPI.Logon "profile", "password"
NewMail.Send
MAPI.Logoff
```

Here, ***RCP*** stores the ***email address*** to email; ***SUB*** is the email ***subject***; ***MSG*** is the ***message*** to send; and ***profile*** and ***password*** are the logon credentials to send the email.

TIP: *You can omit the highlighted lines above if you do not need to log on to a mail server or if your information is cached.*

Sending an Email with Attachments Using Outlook Automation

To send an email to multiple users with attachments using Outlook, proceed as follows:

1. Create a new directory to store all files included in this example.

2. Download and install the latest version of Windows Script Host, from **www.microsoft.com**, to the new directory.

3. Select Start|Run and enter "cscript *scriptfile*.vbs".

Here, ***scriptfile*** is the full path and file name of a script file that contains the following:

```
On Error Resume Next
RCP = "emailaddress"
```

```
Dim File(2)
File(0) = "file1"
File(1) = "file2"

SUB = "subject"
MSG = "message"

Set Outlook = CreateObject("Outlook.Application")
Set MAPI = Outlook.GetNameSpace("MAPI")
Set NewMail = Outlook.CreateItem(0)
NewMail.Subject = SUB
NewMail.Body = MSG
NewMail.Recipients.Add RCP

For X = 0 to (UBound(File)-1)
  NewMail.Attachments.Add(file(X))
Next

MAPI.Logon "profile", "password"
NewMail.Send
MAPI.Logoff
```

Here, *file* is the array that holds the file names to attach to the message; *RCP* stores the *email address* to email; *SUB* is the email *subject*; *MSG* is the *message* to send; and *profile* and *password* are the logon credentials to send the email.

TIP: *You can omit the highlighted lines above if you do not need to log on to a mail server or if your information is cached.*

Sending Emails and Attachments to Multiple Recipients Using Outlook Automation

To send an email to multiple users with attachments using Outlook, proceed as follows:

1. Create a new directory to store all files included in this example.

2. Download and install the latest version of Windows Script Host, from **www.microsoft.com**, to the new directory.

3. Select Start|Run and enter "cscript *scriptfile*.vbs".

Here, ***scriptfile*** is the full path and file name of a script file that contains the following:

```
On Error Resume Next
Dim Name(2)
Name(0) = "emailaddress1"
Name(1) = "emailaddress2"

Dim File(2)
File(0) = "file1"
File(1) = "file2"

SUB = "subject"
MSG = "message"

Set Outlook = CreateObject("Outlook.Application")
Set MAPI = Outlook.GetNameSpace("MAPI")
Set NewMail = Outlook.CreateItem(0)
NewMail.Subject = SUB
NewMail.Body = MSG

For X = 0 to (UBound(Name)-1)
  NewMail.Recipients.Add Name(X)
Next

For X = 0 to (UBound(File)-1)
  NewMail.Attachments.Add(file(X))
Next

MAPI.Logon "profile", "password"
NewMail.Send
MAPI.Logoff
```

Here, ***name*** is the array that holds the ***email addresses*** to email; ***file*** is the array that holds the file names to attach to the message; ***SUB*** is the email ***subject***; ***MSG*** is the ***message*** to send; and ***profile*** and ***password*** are the logon credentials to send the email.

TIP: You can omit the highlighted lines above if you do not need to log on to a mail server or if your information is cached.

Chapter 12

Logon Scripts

In Brief

A logon script is a script that runs automatically each time a user logs on to the network. This script can contain various commands or programs that process on the local station, such as mapping printers or updating the local system time. In this chapter, you will learn how to create logon scripts to easily standardize and update your environment automatically.

TIP: *Although this chapter discusses tasks specifically geared toward logon scripts, you can use any of the scripts within this book in a logon script.*

Common Logon Script Tasks

The difference between a regular script and a logon script is that a logon script performs its functions when the user logs on. Logon scripts are not limited in functionality, but actually contain the same functionality as any other script. Although logon scripts can perform many different tasks, several tasks are commonly performed in logon scripts:

- Synchronize the local time
- Manage network printers and drives
- Update drivers or settings
- Access or modify the registry
- Perform hardware or software inventory
- Set or modify environment variables
- Update antivirus files

Synchronizing the Local Time

Time synchronization is essential when planning to perform enterprise-wide tasks simultaneously, such as remote updates. Windows NT/2000 uses a service called time synchronization to update the local system time with that of a network time source. A time source is any object providing the time to another object.

Time Source Hierarchy

Time synchronization is performed in a hierarchal format (see Figure 12.1). At the top of the hierarchy is the top-level time source that contains the accurate, universal time, such as the Atomic Clock. Primary time sources, usually a PDC or BDC, synchronize their local time with the top-level time source. Below the primary time sources are secondary time sources and clients. Secondary time sources are basically backup primary time sources that obtain their time from a primary time source. Secondary time sources are typically resource domain controllers that obtain their time from the master domain. Underneath the time sources are the clients that synchronize their local time with a secondary or primary time source.

Environment Variables

Environment variables are basically keyword shortcuts that the system and users use to easily access files, directories, and values. You can use these variables in your logon scripts to easily identify the operating system, computer name, domain name, and more. Generally there are two types of environment variables: user and system. User environment variables are set per user, whereas system environment variables are set to the system level and affect all users who log on to the system. These variables are called static variables and are actually stored as registry entries: HKEY_CURRENT_USER\ Environment for user variables and HKEY_LOCAL_MACHINE\ System\CurrentControlSet\Control\Session Manager\Environment for system variables. Dynamic variables, created by the **SET** command,

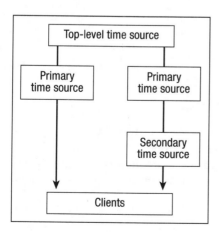

Figure 12.1   The time synchronization heirarchy.

Table 12.1   Registry data types.

Variable Name	Description
ComputerName	Specifies the name of the local system
HomeDrive	Specifies the drive letter to map the user's home directory
HomePath	Specifies the local path to the user's home directory
HomeShare	Specifies the share path to the user's home directory
OS	Specifies the operating system
UserDomain	Specifies the name of the domain the user is currently logged on to
UserName	Specifies the user ID of the currently logged on user
WinDir	Specifies the directory where the operating system is installed

are stored in memory and are applicable for the current command-prompt session. Table 12.1 is a list of common environment variables.

TIP: To see the current environment variables from the command prompt, enter SET.

Norton Antivirus

Although most antivirus products include auto-updating features, updating antivirus files through a logon script provides a backup mechanism to ensure your clients are always up to date. Norton Antivirus is an advanced antivirus utility from Symantec (**www.symantec.com**), designed for both home and corporate use. This utility's antivirus signature files can be easily updated with an executable called Intelligent Updater. This executable supports the following command-line switches:

- **/EXTRACT** *location*—Extracts files from the executable to the *location* specified

- **/Q**—Undocumented switch, specifies to install the update silently

- **/TEMP=***path*—Specifies the temporary directory to use

McAfee VirusScan

McAfee VirusScan is a popular antivirus utility from NAI (**www.nai.com**), for both home and corporate use. NAI releases updates to their antivirus engine and signature files (.DAT extension) in a self-extracting executable (for example, sdat9999.exe) called SuperDAT. They also release a version of the SuperDAT without the engine update (for example, 9999xdat.exe) to reduce the size of the update file and to supply updated signature files simply. These files provide an easy way to update antivirus software because they first stop running antivirus services, update the antivirus files, and then restart the antivirus services.

The two executables just described support the following command-line switches:

- **/E** *location*—Extracts files from the executable to the specified *location*
- **/F**—Forces an updating of existing files
- **/LOGFILE** *textfile*—Logs the status to a *text file*
- **/PROMPT**—Displays a prompt dialog before reboot
- **/REBOOT**—Reboots if necessary
- **/SILENT**—Runs the executable in silent mode, with no prompting
- **/V**—Displays information about the executable

The Windows NT Logon Process

The logon sequence is initiated on a Windows NT machine when the user enters the secure command sequence (SCS), better known as Ctrl+Alt+Del. The WINLOGON.EXE awakes and displays the logon dialog box through the Microsoft Graphical Identification and Authentication library (MSGINA), stored in *%windir%*\system32\msgina.dll. Windows NT allows you to create or purchase a third-party GINA to customize the logon dialog box to meet your needs. The user then enters the username, password, and domain name, and GINA passes it to the Local Security Authority Subsystem (LSASS), stored in *%windir%*\system32\lsass.exe.

The user's password is doubly encrypted through a one-way function (OWF) and stored in the user's section of the registry (HKEY_USERS*SID*). The first method of encryption uses the DES (Data Encryption Standard)algorithm, and is used for compatibility with LAN Manager. The second method of encryption uses the RSA MD-4 algorithm (Rivest Shamir Adelman Message Digest 4), and is the default method for Windows NT. The user's relative ID (RID) is also encrypted.

The LSASS then checks the domain name and determines whether to log on locally or to find a domain controller. Once the authenticating machine has been located, it passes that request to the SAM. If the logon request is for a domain controller, the DC confirms whether the local system has a computer account in that domain. Once authentication has been approved, the user is granted a security access token, describing the rights and groups of the specified user.

The Windows 2000 Logon Process

The logon sequence is initiated on a Windows 2000 machine when the user enters the secure command sequence (SCS), better known as Ctrl+Alt+Del. After the user enters the username and password, the Kerberos client encrypts the password through a one-way function (OWF) using the DES-CBC-MD5 algorithm (Data Encryption Standard Cipher Block Channel Message Digest 5). The client then converts the password to an encryption key.

The Kerberos client then sends the encryption key, username, a time stamp, and the authentication request to the Key Distribution Center (KDC), which is a service running on the authenticating server. The user name is then checked for a valid name stored in the active directory database, the password is verified, and the time stamp is checked to ensure the request is not old or falsified.

Once the user account has been validated, the KDC then sends back a Kerberos authentication response. This response is called a ticket granting number (TGT) and includes an encrypted copy of the KDC's encryption key. The client finally stores this ticket into memory and is allowed into the domain.

Windows NT/2000 Replication

Replication helps to easily distribute logon scripts to all your servers based on a regular schedule. The purpose of replication is to synchronize the contents of one file location with the contents of another. Replication is a service that performs one-way transfers, ensuring that all child locations are synchronized with the parent location. This synchronization includes file additions, modifications, and deletions.

Windows NT

Windows NT uses a replication engine called LAN Manager replication to replicate system policies and logon scripts among other network servers. This replication engine replicates files on a regular schedule, usually set to five minutes. When a user logs on, he or she connects to the NETLOGON share, which is mapped to the %*windir*%\system32\repl\import\scripts directory. This is the default

12. Logon Scripts

replication location for logon scripts. These scripts are replicated to this directory from the master replication server's %*windir*%\system32 \repl\export\scripts directory. Although the LAN Manager replication engine works well for logon scripts and policies, it was not intended and does not work well with regular data replication.

NOTE: *The master replication server replicates files to itself, from the export to the import directory.*

Windows 2000

Windows 2000 no longer supports the LAN Manager replication engine, and alternately uses the file replication service (FRS) to perform file replication. FRS is a replication service that is used to replicate system policies and logon scripts to the System Volume directory (SYSVOL). FRS is a more robust replication engine and can be used to replicate files in addition to policies and logon scripts. Unlike the LAN Manager replication engine, the FRS synchronizes immediately within sites and synchronizes on a schedule between sites. File replication service is a robust replication service that works well for all types of data files.

Immediate Solutions

Creating Logon Scripts with Shell Scripting

Shell scripting is the original source of logon scripting for Windows. Although it may lack some of the more complex features of other scripting languages, its main advantage is compatibility. Unlike KiXtart or Windows Script Host, shell scripting does not require any installed client files to run (other than the operating system). Shell scripting provides a simple, logon script solution for quick and easy deployment.

Setting the Window Title

Windows NT/2000 supports the **title** command to change the title of a shell prompt window. The basic syntax of the **title** command is as follows:

```
Title name
```

Here, **name** is the name to give the current command-prompt window. Here is an example to change the shell prompt title to "Logon Script":

```
If "%OS%"=="Windows_NT" Title Logon Script
```

Here, **%OS%** is an environment variable that indicates the operating system type.

Changing the Background and Foreground Colors

Windows NT/2000 supports the **color** command to change the background and foreground in a shell prompt. The basic syntax of the **color** command is as follows:

```
COLOR BF
```

Here, **B** is the background color value and **F** is the foreground color value. The **color** command supports the following color values:

- **0**—Black
- **1**—Blue
- **2**—Green
- **3**—Aqua

- **4**—Red
- **5**—Purple
- **6**—Yellow
- **7**—White
- **8**—Gray
- **9**—Light Blue
- **A**—Light Green
- **B**—Light Aqua
- **C**—Light Red
- **D**—Light Purple
- **E**—Light Yellow
- **F**—Bright White

Here is an example to change the shell prompt colors to bright white text on a blue background:

```
IF "%OS%"=="Windows_NT" COLOR 1F
```

Here, **%*OS*%** is an environment variable that indicates the operating system type.

Synchronizing the Local System Time

Synchronizing the local system to a central time source allows you to perform enterprise-wide tasks simultaneously. The basic syntax to synchronize the local clock with a specified time source is as follows:

```
Net Time \\server /commands
```

Here, ***server*** is the name of the time source server to sync with. This parameter is only necessary when syncing with a specific server. If this parameter is omitted (**Net Time**), the system will search the local domain for a time source server. **/*commands*** are any of the following parameters:

- **/SET**—Sets the local time to the time source server
- **/Y**—Forces to sync the time with the server specified, regardless of whether the server is a time source server or not
- **/DOMAIN:*domainname***—Searches the specified domain for a time source server

The following script attempts to sync the local system time with the server named ***servername***. If this fails, the domain will be searched for a time source to sync with. To execute this script, proceed as follows:

1. Create a new directory to store all files included in this example.

2. Select Start|Run and enter "*scriptfile*.bat".

Here, ***scriptfile*** is the full path and file name of a script file that contains the following:

```
@Echo Off
CLS ; Clears the screen
Set TServer=ServerName

Echo Syncing the time with %TServer%...
Net Time \\%TServer% /set /yes
If %errorlevel% NEQ 0 CLS && Goto Domain
CLS && Echo Sync Successful
Goto End

:Domain
Echo Searching the local domain for a time-server...
Net Time /set /yes
If %errorlevel% EQU 0 CLS && Echo Sync Successful && Goto End
CLS && Echo Time Sync Error

:End
```

Here, ***tserver*** is a variable containing the name of the time source server; **NEQ** is the "not equal to" operator; and **&&** allows you to run a second command after the first has completed.

Mapping Universal Drives

Mapping common drives for all users allows you to present a central resource location for applications or data. In Chapter 7, you learned how to map network drives from within Windows and the command prompt. To map a network drive and display the status from the command prompt, proceed as follows:

1. Create a new directory to store all files included in this example.

2. Select Start|Run and enter "*scriptfile*.bat".

Here, ***scriptfile*** is the full path and file name of a script file that contains the following:

```
@Echo Off
CLS ; Clears the screen
```

12. Logon Scripts

```
Set Drive=DriveLetter
Set Share=\\server\sharename

Echo Mapping drive %Drive% to %Share%
Net Use %Drive%: /Delete && CLS
Net Use %Drive%: %Share%
If %errorlevel% EQU 0 CLS && Echo Map Successful && Goto End
CLS && Echo Error mapping drive %Drive% to %Share%

:End
```

Here, **driveletter** is the **drive** letter to map a **share** to, and **server** contains the **sharename** you want to map to.

Mapping Drives by Group

Mapping drives by group membership allows you to control which drives and resources will be available to which users. The resource kit utility IfMember allows you to determine a user's group membership from the command line. The basic syntax of the IfMember utility is as follows:

```
IfMember /Commands Groups
```

Here, **Groups** are any group, separated by spaces, whose membership you want to check. An errorlevel of 1 indicates the user is a member of the specified group. The available **commands** are as follows:

• **/List**—Lists all groups the user belongs to

• **/Verbose**—Displays all group matches

To map a network drive according to group membership and display the status from the command prompt, proceed as follows:

1. Create a new directory to store all files included in this example.

2. Select Start|Run and enter "*scriptfile*.bat".

Here, **scriptfile** is the full path and file name of a script file that contains the following:

```
@Echo Off
CLS ; Clears the screen
Fullpath\IfMember GroupName > Nul

If Not %errorlevel% EQU 1 Goto End
Set Drive=DriveLetter
Set Share=\\server\sharename
```

```
Echo Mapping drive %Drive% to %Share%
Net Use %Drive%: /Delete && CLS
Net Use %Drive%: %Share%
If %errorlevel% EQU 0 CLS && Echo Map Successful && Goto End
CLS && Echo Error mapping drive %Drive% to %Share%

:End
```

Here, *fullpath* is the full path where the IfMember utility is located; *GroupName* is the name of the group to check membership; *driveletter* is the *drive* letter to map a *share* to; **NEQ** is the "not equal to" operator; **EQU** is the "equal to" operator; *server* contains the *sharename* you want to map to; and **&&** allows you to run a second command after the first has completed.

Mapping Printers Using Con2PRT

Mapping printers through a logon script provides an easy method to remotely update printer connections. Con2PRT (Connect To Port) is a utility, found in the Zero Administration Kit (ZAK) and Windows 2000 Resource Kit, to control printer connections from the command line. The basic syntax of the con2PRT utility is as follows:

```
Con2prt /commands \\server\printer
```

Here, *server* is the name of the printer server containing the shared *printer* to map. The available *commands* are:

- **/F**—Removes all printer connections
- **/C**—Connects to the *printer* specified
- **/CD**—Connects to the *printer* specified and marks it as the default printer

To remove all current printer connections and map a default printer using con2PRT, proceed as follows:

1. Create a new directory to store all files included in this example.

2. Select Start|Run and enter "*scriptfile*.bat".

Here, *scriptfile* is the full path and file name of a script file that contains the following:

```
@Echo Off
Set Pserver=server
Set DPrinter=Printer
```

```
fullpath\con2prt /F
fullpath\con2prt /CD \\%server%\%printer%
```

Here, **pserver** is the variable holding the printer **server** name; **dprinter** is the variable holding the name of the **printer** share; and **fullpath** is the full path where con2prt is located.

Checking for Remote Access

Determining whether a client is logging in through the network or remote access helps you specify which parts of the script to run. CheckRAS is a command-line, SMS resource kit utility to determine whether a user is using remote access. To determine whether the current user is using remote access during a logon script, proceed as follows:

1. Create a new directory to store all files included in this example.

2. Select Start|Run and enter "*scriptfile*.bat".

Here, **scriptfile** is the full path and file name of a script file that contains the following:

```
@Echo Off
CLS ; Clears the screen
Set RAS=NO
fullpath\CheckRAS > Nul
If %errorlevel% EQU 1 Set RAS=YES
```

Here, **fullpath** is the full path where the CheckRAS utility is located, and **RAS** indicates whether the current user is using remote access or not.

Displaying Time-Based Greetings

Although it's not essential, many administrators like to display a greeting to the user depending on the time of day. To display a time-based greeting from the command line, proceed as follows:

1. Create a new directory to store all files included in this example.

2. Select Start|Run and enter "*scriptfile*.bat".

Here, **scriptfile** is the full path and file name of a script file that contains the following:

```
@Echo Off
CLS
For /F "Delims=: Tokens=1" %%I in ('Time /T') Do Set Hour=%%I
```

```
For /F "Delims=: Tokens=2" %%I in ('Time /T') Do Set Min=%%I
For /F "Delims=0,1,2,3,4,5,6,7,8,9 Tokens=2" %%I in
('Set Min') Do Set AP=%%I

If %AP% EQU p Goto PM
Set Greet=Good Morning
Goto End

:PM
If %Hour% EQU 12 Set Hour=0
If %Hour% LSS 12 Set Greet=Good Evening
If %Hour% LSS 6 Set Greet=Good Afternoon

:End
Echo %Greet%
Set Hour=
Set Min=
Set AP=
```

NOTE: *The highlighted code above should be placed on one line.*

Here, the **Time /T** command indicates the local system time.

Updating McAfee Antivirus Files

To update your McAfee antivirus engine and/or signature files with shell scripting, proceed as follows:

1. Create a new directory to store all files included in this example.

2. Select Start|Run and enter "*scriptfile*.bat".

Here, *scriptfile* is the full path and file name of a script file that contains the following:

```
@Echo Off
CLS
Set SDAT="superdat"
Set DAT="datfile"
Set NAILOG="textlog"
Set DDAY="DOTW"

For /F "Tokens=1" %%I in ('Date /T') Do Set Day=%%I

If %DAY% EQU %DDAY% Goto UENGINE
%DAT% /F /PROMPT /REBOOT /SILENT /LOGFILE %NAILOG%
GOTO END
```

```
:UENGINE
%SDAT% /F /PROMPT /REBOOT /SILENT /LOGFILE %NAILOG%
GOTO END

:END
Set SDAT=
Set DAT=
Set NAILOG=
Set DAY=
```

Here, **SDAT** is a variable containing the complete path and file name of the SuperDAT executable; **DAT** is a variable containing the complete path and file name of the DAT executable; **NAILOG** is a variable containing the complete path and file name of the status log text file; and **DDAY** is the day of the week (Mon, Tue, Wed, Thu, Fri, Sat, Sun) to run the SuperDAT as opposed to the daily DAT file.

Updating Norton Antivirus Files

To update your Norton antivirus files with shell scripting, proceed as follows:

1. Create a new directory to store all files included in this example.

2. Download the latest Intelligent Updater file from **www.symantec.com** to the new directory.

3. Select Start|Run and enter "*scriptfile*.bat".

Here, **scriptfile** is the full path and file name of a script file that contains the following:

```
@Echo Off
Set IUPDATER=iufile

%IUPDATER% /Q > Nul
```

Here, **IUPDATER** is a variable containing the complete path and file name of the Intelligent Updater executable.

Creating Logon Scripts with KiXtart

KiXtart is a powerful scripting tool primarily focused and used for logon scripts. KiXtart contains many built-in methods and macros to retrieve quick information; other scripting languages would require external tools or extensive scripting to retrieve the same information.

Setting Up the Environment

When creating a logon script, it is important to make sure the script looks and feels as it was intended. KiXtart includes several commands to customize the logon script environment. To set up a customized logon script environment using KiXtart, proceed as follows:

1. Create a new directory to store all files included in this example.

2. Download and extract the latest version of KiXtart, from **www.microsoft.com**, to the new directory.

3. Select Start|Run and enter "kix32 *scriptfile*".

Here, **scriptfile** is the full path of the new directory from step 1 and file name of a script file that contains the following:

```
CLS ; Clear screen
BREAK OFF ; Logoff user when attempt to close logon box
$RCODE = SETCONSOLE("ALWAYSONTOP") ; Set box on top
$RCODE = SETASCII("ON") ; Turn on ASCII characters
```

This script first clears the screen (CLS) and sets the logon script box to log off the current user if he/she attempts to close the box. The logon script box is then set to be on top of all other windows. The final command turns on ASCII characters. This is a new feature included with KiXtart 3.62 and higher that allows you to change the look of text by turning ASCII on or off.

Changing the Background and Foreground Colors

KiXtart supports the **color** command to change the background and foreground in a shell prompt. The basic syntax of the **color** command is as follows:

```
COLOR Fx/By
```

Here, **F** is the foreground color value, **x** is an optional indicator to increase the color intensity if a plus sign (+) is specified, **B** is the background color value, and **y** is an optional indicator that causes the background to blink if a plus sign (+) is specified. The **color** command supports the following color values:

- **N**—Black
- **B**—Blue
- **G**—Green
- **C**—Cyan

- **R**—Red
- **M**—Magenta
- **Y**—Yellow/Brown
- **W**—White

Here is an example to change the shell prompt colors to bright white text on a blue background:

```
COLOR W+/B
```

Synchronizing the Local System Time

Synchronizing the local system to a central time source allows you to perform enterprise-wide tasks simultaneously. KiXtart includes the **SetTime** command to synchronize the local system time to a time source. The basic syntax of the **SetTime** command is as follows:

```
SetTime source
```

Here, *source* is any one of the following types:

- **\\Server**—Specifies the name of a time source *server*
- *DomainName*—Searches the specified domain for a time source
- "***"—Specifies to search the local domain for a time source

The following script attempts to sync the local system time with the logon server. If this fails, the domain will be searched for a time source to sync with. To execute this script, proceed as follows:

1. Create a new directory to store all files included in this example.

2. Download and extract the latest version of KiXtart, from **www.microsoft.com**, to the new directory.

3. Select Start|Run and enter "kix32 *scriptfile*".

Here, *scriptfile* is the full path of the new directory from step 1 and file name of a script file that contains the following:

```
? "Syncing the time with @LSERVER..."
SETTIME "@LSERVER"
If @ERROR <> 0
  ? "Searching the local domain for a time-server..."
  SETTIME "*"
  If @ERROR <> 0
    ? "Time Sync Error"
  Else
```

```
    ? "Sync Successful"
  EndIf
EndIf
```

Mapping Universal Drives

Mapping common drives for all users allows you to present a central resource location for applications or data. In Chapter 7, you learned how to map network drives from within Windows and the command prompt. KiXtart includes the **use** command, similar to the **Net Use** command, to attach a drive letter to a network share. To map a network drive and display the status using KiXtart, proceed as follows:

1. Create a new directory to store all files included in this example.

2. Download and extract the latest version of KiXtart, from **www.microsoft.com**, to the new directory.

3. Select Start|Run and enter "kix32 *scriptfile*".

Here, *scriptfile* is the full path of the new directory from step 1 and file name of a script file that contains the following:

```
$Drive="DriveLetter"
$Share="\\server\sharename"

? " Mapping drive $Drive to $Share"
Use " $Drive: " /Delete
Use " $Drive: " $Share
If @Error = 0
  ? " Map Successful"
Else
  ? " Error mapping drive $Drive to $Share"
EndIf
```

Here, *driveletter* is the *drive* letter to map a *share* to, and *server* contains the *sharename* you want to map to.

Mapping Drives by Group

Mapping drives by group membership allows you to control which drives and resources will be available to which users. KiXtart includes the **InGroup** command, similar to the IfMember resource kit utility, to determine group membership. To map a network drive according to group membership and display the status using KiXtart, proceed as follows:

1. Create a new directory to store all files included in this example.

2. Download and extract the latest version of KiXtart, from
   www.microsoft.com, to the new directory.

3. Select Start|Run and enter "kix32 *scriptfile*".

Here, ***scriptfile*** is the full path of the new directory from step 1 and
file name of a script file that contains the following:

```
$Drive="DriveLetter"
$Share="\\server\sharename"

If InGroup("GroupName")
  ? "Mapping drive $Drive to $Share"
  Use "$Drive: "/Delete
  Use "$Drive: "$Share
  If @Error = 0
    ? "Map Successful"
  Else
    ? "Error mapping drive $Drive to $Share"
  EndIf
EndIf
```

Here, ***GroupName*** is the name of the group to check membership;
driveletter is the ***drive*** letter to map a ***share*** to; and ***server*** contains the ***sharename*** you want to map to.

Mapping Printers

Mapping printers through a logon script provides an easy method to
remotely update printer connections. KiXtart contains several commands to add, remove, and set default printers. To map a printer using KiXtart, proceed as follows:

1. Create a new directory to store all files included in this example.

2. Download and extract the latest version of KiXtart, from
   www.microsoft.com, to the new directory.

3. Select Start|Run and enter "kix32 *scriptfile*".

Here, ***scriptfile*** is the full path of the new directory from step 1 and
file name of a script file that contains the following:

```
$Pserver="Server"
$DPrinter="Printer"

If AddPrinterConnection("\\$PServer\$DPrinter") = 0
  ? "Added printer $DPrinter"
```

```
Else
  ? "Error adding $DPrinter"
EndIf
```

Here, **pserver** is the variable holding the printer **server** name, and **dprinter** is the variable holding the name of the **printer** share.

Checking for Remote Access

Determining whether a client is logging in through the network or remote access helps you specify which parts of the script to run. KiXtart includes the @RAS macro to the number of remote access connections. To determine whether a user is logging on through remote access using KiXtart, proceed as follows:

1. Create a new directory to store all files included in this example.

2. Download and extract the latest version of KiXtart, from **www.microsoft.com**, to the new directory.

3. Select Start|Run and enter "kix32 *scriptfile*".

Here, **scriptfile** is the full path of the new directory from step 1 and file name of a script file that contains the following:

```
If @RAS = 0
  ? " You are logging in through the local network. "
Else
  ? "You are logging on through remote access"
EndIf
```

Displaying Time-Based Greetings

Although it's not essential, many administrators like to display a greeting to the user depending on the time of day. To display a time-based greeting using KiXtart, proceed as follows:

1. Create a new directory to store all files included in this example.

2. Download and extract the latest version of KiXtart, from **www.microsoft.com**, to the new directory.

3. Select Start|Run and enter "kix32 *scriptfile*".

Here, **scriptfile** is the full path of the new directory from step 1 and file name of a script file that contains the following:

```
SELECT
  CASE ((@TIME > "00:00:00") AND (@TIME < "12:00:00"))
    ? "Good Morning @FULLNAME"
```

```
CASE ((@TIME > "12:00:00") AND (@TIME < "18:00:00"))
  ? "Good Afternoon @FULLNAME"
CASE 1
  ? "Good Evening @FULLNAME"
ENDSELECT
```

Here, the **@TIME** macro indicates the current time, and **@FULLNAME** indicates the full name of the current user.

Updating McAfee Antivirus Files

To update your McAfee antivirus engine and/or signature files with KiXtart, proceed as follows:

1. Create a new directory to store all files included in this example.

2. Download and extract the latest version of KiXtart, from **www.microsoft.com**, to the new directory.

3. Select Start|Run and enter "kix32 *scriptfile*".

Here, *scriptfile* is the full path of the new directory from step 1 and file name of a script file that contains the following:

```
$SDAT="superdat"
$DAT="datfile"
$NAILOG="textlog"
$DDAY="DOTW"

If @DAY = $DDAY
  SHELL "%COMSPEC% /C $SDAT /F /PROMPT /REBOOT /SILENT
  /LOGFILE $NAILOG"
Else
  SHELL "%COMSPEC% /C $DAT /F /PROMPT /REBOOT /SILENT
  /LOGFILE $NAILOG"
EndIf
```

Here, **SDAT** is a variable containing the complete path and file name of the SuperDAT executable; **DAT** is a variable containing the complete path and file name of the DAT executable; **NAILOG** is a variable containing the complete path and file name of the status log text file; and **DDAY** is the day of the week (Monday-Sunday) to run the SuperDAT as opposed to the daily DAT file.

Updating Norton Antivirus Files

To update your Norton antivirus files with KiXtart, proceed as follows:

1. Create a new directory to store all files included in this example.

2. Download the latest Intelligent Updater file from www.symantec.com to the new directory.

3. Download and extract the latest version of KiXtart, from **www.microsoft.com**, to the new directory.

4. Select Start|Run and enter "kix32 *scriptfile*".

Here, *scriptfile* is the full path of the new directory from step 1 and file name of a script file that contains the following:

```
$IUPDATER = "iufile"
SHELL "%COMSPEC% /C $IUPDATER /Q"
```

Here, *IUPDATER* is a variable containing the complete path and file name of the Intelligent Updater executable.

Creating Logon Scripts with Windows Script Host

Windows Script Host is a relatively new scripting language and is rather limited with logon scripts. Although you can call external functions or custom COM objects to perform specific logon script tasks, WSH does not contain many of the standard logon script functions other scripting languages may have, such as a time synchronization command.

Synchronizing the Local System Time

Windows Script Host does not have a time synchronization command to sync the local system time with a network time source. You can use the shell **run** command to call external commands, such as the **Net Time** command, and use a return variable to indicate whether the command was successful. The following script attempts to sync the local system time with the server named *servername* using the Net Time command. If this synchronization fails, the domain will be searched for a time source to sync with. To execute this script, proceed as follows:

1. Create a new directory to store all files included in this example.

2. Download and install the latest version of Windows Script Host, from **www.microsoft.com**, to the new directory.

3. Select Start|Run and enter "cscript *scriptfile*.vbs".

Here, ***scriptfile*** is the full path and file name of a script file that contains the following:

```
On Error Resume Next
Set SHELL = CreateObject("WScript.Shell")
TServer="ServerName"

Wscript.Echo "Syncing the time with " & TServer & "..."
ELevel = Shell.Run("Net Time \\" & TServer & "
/Set /Yes",0,True)

If (ELevel <> 0) Then
  Wscript.Echo "Searching the local domain for a " & _
    time-server..."
  ELevel = Shell.Run("Net Time /Set /Yes",0,True)
  If (ELevel = 0) Then
    Wscript.Echo "Sync Successful"
  Else
    Wscript.Echo "Time Sync Error"
  End If
Else
  Wscript.Echo "Sync Successful"
End If
```

NOTE: *The highlighted code above must be placed on one line.*

Mapping Universal Drives

Mapping common drives for all users allows you to present a central resource location for applications or data. In Chapter 7, you learned how to map network drives from within Windows and the command prompt. You can use the Windows Script Host network object to attach a drive letter to a network share. To map a network drive and display the status using Windows Script Host, proceed as follows:

1. Create a new directory to store all files included in this example.

2. Download and install the latest version of Windows Script Host, from **www.microsoft.com**, to the new directory.

3. Select Start|Run and enter "cscript *scriptfile*.vbs".

Here, ***scriptfile*** is the full path and file name of a script file that contains the following:

```
On Error Resume Next
Set Network = CreateObject("WScript.Network")
```

```
Drive = "DriveLetter:"
Share = "\\server\sharename"

Wscript.Echo "Mapping drive " & Drive & " to " & Share
Network.MapNetworkDrive Drive, Share
If Err.Number = 0 Then
  Wscript.Echo "Map Successful"
Else
  Wscript.Echo "Error mapping drive " & Drive & " to " & _
    Share
End If
```

Here, *driveletter* is the *drive* letter to map a *share* to, and *server* contains the *sharename* you want to map to.

Mapping Drives by Group

Mapping drives by group membership allows you to control which drives and resources will be available to which users. Windows Script Host does contain a method to determine group membership. Although you can use the ADSI IfMember method, this method can be slow on larger networks. Alternatively, you can use the WSH shell run command to call external commands, such as the IfMember resource kit utility, and use a return variable to indicate whether the command was successful. To map a network drive according to group membership and display the status using Windows Script Host, proceed as follows:

1. Create a new directory to store all files included in this example.

2. Download and install the latest version of Windows Script Host, from **www.microsoft.com**, to the new directory.

3. Select Start|Run and enter "cscript *scriptfile*.vbs".

Here, *scriptfile* is the full path and file name of a script file that contains the following:

```
On Error Resume Next
Set SHELL = CreateObject("WScript.Shell")
Set Network = CreateObject("WScript.Network")
Drive = "DriveLetter:"
Share = "\\server\sharename"
DGroup = "groupname"

ELevel = Shell.Run("fullpath\IfMember " & DGroup,0,True)
If (ELevel = 1) Then
  Wscript.Echo "Mapping drive " & Drive & " to " & Share
  Network.MapNetworkDrive Drive, Share
```

12. Logon Scripts

```
       If Err.Number = 0 Then
         Wscript.Echo "Map Successful"
       Else
         Wscript.Echo "Error mapping drive " & Drive & " to " & _
         Share
       End If
End If
```

Here, *fullpath* is the full path where the IfMember utility is located; *GroupName* is the name of the group to check membership; *driveletter* is the *drive* letter to map a *share* to; and *server* contains the *sharename* you want to map to.

Mapping Printers

Mapping printers through a logon script provides an easy method to remotely update printer connections. Starting with version 2, Windows Script Host provides several commands to add, remove, and set default printers. To map a printer using Windows Script Host, proceed as follows:

1. Create a new directory to store all files included in this example.

2. Download and install the latest version of Windows Script Host, from **www.microsoft.com**, to the new directory.

3. Select Start|Run and enter "cscript *scriptfile*.vbs".

Here, *scriptfile* is the full path and file name of a script file that contains the following:

```
On Error Resume Next
PServer = "Server"
DPrinter = "Printer"
Port = "LPT1"
Set Network = CreateObject("Wscript.Network")

Network.AddPrinterConnection Port, "\\" & PServer &
"\" & Printer
If Err.Number <> 0 Then
  Wscript.Echo "Added printer " & Printer
Else
  Wscript.Echo "Error adding printer " & Printer
End If
```

NOTE: *The highlighted code above must be placed on one line.*

Here, ***pserver*** is the variable holding the printer ***server*** name, and ***dprinter*** is the variable holding the name of the ***printer*** share.

---

*TIP: You can use the **AddWindowsPrinterConnection** method to add printers to Windows NT/2000 systems without having to supply a port.*

Checking for Remote Access

Determining whether a client is logging in through the network or remote access helps you specify which parts of the script to run. Windows Script Host does not contain a method to detect remote access connections. CheckRAS is a command-line, SMS resource kit utility to determine whether a user is using remote access. To determine whether the current user is using remote access during a logon script using Windows Script Host, proceed as follows:

1. Create a new directory to store all files included in this example.

2. Download and install the latest version of Windows Script Host, from **www.microsoft.com**, to the new directory.

3. Select Start|Run and enter "cscript *scriptfile*.vbs".

Here, ***scriptfile*** is the full path and file name of a script file that contains the following:

```
On Error Resume Next
Set SHELL = CreateObject("WScript.Shell")

ELevel = Shell.Run("fullpath\CheckRAS",0,True)
If (ELevel = 0) Then
  RAS = "YES"
Else
  RAS = "NO"
End If
```

Here, ***fullpath*** is the full path where the CheckRAS utility is located, and ***RAS*** indicates whether the current user is using remote access or not.

Displaying Time-Based Greetings

Although it's not essential, many administrators like to display a greeting to the user depending on the time of day. To display a time-based greeting using Windows Script Host, proceed as follows:

1. Create a new directory to store all files included in this example.

2. Download and install the latest version of Windows Script Host, from **www.microsoft.com**, to the new directory.

3. Select Start|Run and enter "cscript *scriptfile*.vbs".

Here, *scriptfile* is the full path and file name of a script file that contains the following:

```
On Error Resume Next
If Hour(Now) < 12 Then
  Wscript.Echo "Good Morning"
ElseIf Hour(Now) < 18 Then
  Wscript.Echo "Good Afternoon"
Else
  Wscript.Echo "Good Evening"
End If
```

Updating McAfee Antivirus Files

To update your McAfee antivirus engine and/or signature files with shell scripting, proceed as follows:

1. Create a new directory to store all files included in this example.

2. Download and install the latest version of Windows Script Host from **www.microsoft.com** to the new directory.

3. Select Start|Run and enter "cscript *scriptfile*.vbs".

Here, *scriptfile* is the full path and file name of a script file that contains the following:

```
On Error Resume Next
Set SHELL = CreateObject("WScript.Shell")

SDAT="superdat"
DAT="datfile"
NAILOG="textlog"
DDAY="DOTW"

If WeekDayName(WeekDay(Date)) = DDAY
  Shell.Run CHR(34) & SDAT & CHR(34) & " /F /PROMPT /REBOOT
  /SILENT /LOGFILE NAILOG",1,True
Else
  Shell.Run CHR(34) & DAT & CHR(34) & " /F /PROMPT /REBOOT
  /SILENT /LOGFILE NAILOG",1,True
EndIf
```

The left margin shows a vertical black tab with white text "12. Logon Scripts".

NOTE: *Chr(34) translates the ASCII code character 34 into a quotation mark ("). This is necessary when using the Shell.Run command with long file names.*

Here, **SDAT** is a variable containing the complete path and file name of the SuperDAT executable; **DAT** is a variable containing the complete path and file name of the DAT executable; **NAILOG** is a variable containing the complete path and file name of the status log text file; and **DDAY** is the day of the week (Monday-Sunday) to run the SuperDAT as opposed to the daily DAT file.

Updating Norton Antivirus Files

To update your Norton antivirus files with Windows Script Host, proceed as follows:

1. Create a new directory to store all files included in this example.

2. Download the latest Intelligent Updater file from www.symantec.com to the new directory.

3. Download and install the latest version of Windows Script Host, from **www.microsoft.com**, to the new directory.

4. Select Start|Run and enter "cscript *scriptfile*.vbs".

Here, **scriptfile** is the full path and file name of a script file that contains the following:

```
On Error Resume Next
Set SHELL = CreateObject("WScript.Shell")

IUPDATER = "iufile"
Shell.Run CHR(34) & IUPDATER & CHR(34) & " /Q",1,True
```

NOTE: *Chr(34) translates the ASCII code character 34 into a quotation ("). This is necessary when using the Shell.Run command with long file names.*

Here, **IUPDATER** is a variable containing the complete path and file name of the Intelligent Updater executable.

Using Microsoft Internet Explorer as a Logon Script Box

Through Automation, you can use Internet Explorer to display logon script status to the user. To use Internet Explorer as a logon script box using the previous WSH logon scripts, proceed as follows:

1. Create a new directory to store all files included in this example.

2. Download and install the latest version of Windows Script Host, from **www.microsoft.com**, to the new directory.

3. Select Start|Run and enter "cscript *scriptfile*.vbs".

Here, ***scriptfile*** is the full path and file name of a script file that contains the following:

```
On Error Resume Next
Set Network = CreateObject("WScript.Network")
Set MSIE = CreateObject("InternetExplorer.Application")
sTITLE = "Processing Logon Script, please wait..."
Drive = "DriveLetter:"
Share = "\\server\sharename"

SetupMSIE
MSIE.Document.Write "<HTML><TITLE>" & sTitle & _
  "</TITLE><BODY bgcolor=#C0C0C0><FONT FACE=ARIAL>"

If Hour(Now) < 12 Then
  MSIE.Document.Write "<B>Good Morning " & _
    Network.UserName & "</B><BR><BR>"
ElseIf Hour(Now) < 18 Then
  MSIE.Document.Write "<B>Good Afternoon " & _
    Network.UserName & "</B><BR><BR>"
Else
  MSIE.Document.Write "<B>Good Evening " & _
    Network.UserName & "</B><BR><BR>"
End If

MSIE.Document.Write "<B>Mapping drive " & Drive & " to " & _
  Share & "...</B><BR>"

Network.MapNetworkDrive Drive, Share
If Err.Number = 0 Then
  MSIE.Document.Write "  Mapping Successful<BR>"
Else
  MSIE.Document.Write "  Error mapping drive " & Drive & _
    " to " & Share & "<BR>"
End If

MSIE.Document.Write "<BR><B>Closing in 3 seconds</B><BR>"
Wscript.Sleep 3000
MSIE.Quit

Sub SetupMSIE
  MSIE.Navigate "About:Blank"
```

```
MSIE.ToolBar = False
MSIE.StatusBar = False
MSIE.Resizable = False

Do
Loop While MSIE.Busy

SWidth = MSIE.Document.ParentWindow.Screen.AvailWidth
SHeight = MSIE.Document.ParentWindow.Screen.AvailHeight
MSIE.Width = SWidth/2
MSIE.Height = SHeight/2
MSIE.Left = (SWidth - MSIE.Width)/2
MSIE.Top = (SHeight - MSIE.Height)/2

MSIE.Visible = True
End Sub
```

Here, *driveletter* is the *drive* letter to map a *share* to, and *server* contains the *sharename* you want to map to.

Related solution:	Found on page:
Using Microsoft Internet Explorer as a Display Tool	96

12. Logon Scripts

Chapter 13

Backups and Scheduling

In Brief

Most companies and people couldn't continue to be in business or do their work if all their data were lost. Backups provide an easy method to restore a system or a set of files after some corruption, deletion, or hardware failure has taken place. Backups are an extremely important part of your task as an administrator—something that no one likes to do, but everyone appreciates when needed. Although many third-party backup tools are available, a limited budget or compatibility issues might prevent you from using them.

In previous chapters, you learned how to back up files and the registry using simple scripts. In this chapter, you will learn how to automate backups and ERDs (Emergency Repair Disks). You will also learn how to schedule your backups and scripts to run automatically.

Backups under Windows NT/2000

NTBackup (New Technology Backup) is a Windows NT/2000 utility that allows you to back up your registry and data files. These backups are stored using the Microsoft Tape Format (MTF). NTBackup can read and restore any backup stored in this format. This includes many of today's third-party backup programs that comply to this format, such as Veritas Backup Exec. Before performing any backup, you should decide which type of backup you would like to perform. NTBackup supports the following backup types:

- *Full*—Also called a normal backup, backs up all the files specified. The archive bit is cleared for all files backed up. This provides the most complete backup but also takes the most time and occupies the greatest amount of storage space on the backup media. This backup type provides the quickest restore method.

- *Incremental*—Only backs up files that have changed since the last full and incremental backup. The archive bit is cleared for all files backed up. This backup type requires marginal time and backup space but provides the longest restore method because the full backup and all other incremental backups must be restored sequentially.

- *Differential*—Only backs up files that have changed since the last full backup. The archive bit is not cleared for any files. This is the most common backup method used and provides an average restore time because the full backup must be restored before a differential backup can be restored.

- *Daily*—Only backs up files modified on the day the backup is performed. The archive bit is not modified.

- *Custom*—Allows you to specify which files to back up. This method is most commonly used on an on-demand basis when a small number of files are to be backed up.

- *Copy*—Copies files to the backup media. The archive bit is not cleared because you are merely copying files. This method is best used when you want to perform backups in combination with other backup utilities, and do not want the archive bit to be modified.

NOTE: *An archive bit is a file attribute that is cleared when a file is modified. This is a signal to all backup programs that this file needs to be backed up.*

The Drawbacks of the NTBackup Utility for Windows NT

Although NTBackup is a useful backup utility for basic backups, it does not contain many of the advanced features of the Windows 2000 NTBackup or third-party programs. One major drawback of NTBackup is its inability to back up files that are open, in use, or locked. This makes it unsuitable for servers running Microsoft SQL Server (Structured Query Language Server), Windows Internet Naming Service (WINS), Dynamic Host Configuration Protocol (DHCP), or other applications that constantly have open files. NTBackup does not support the universal naming convention (UNC) and cannot back up remote files without first connecting a mapped drive. Further, NTBackup does not back up temporary system files, such as the page file (pagefile.sys); does not support scheduling; does not back up remote registries; and only supports tape devices.

TIP: *You can perform a live backup of the Exchange information store and directory using the EDBBCLI.DLL, found on the Exchange Server CD.*

The NTBackup Utility for Windows 2000

The version of NTBackup that ships with Windows 2000 supports many new features, such as scheduling and UNC support. In addition to tape devices, Windows 2000 NTBackup can now back up data to removable media, such as a Jaz or Zip drive, using Remote Storage Management (RSM). You can back up to any removable media that RSM supports and that does not require special formatting at the time of backup. RSM cannot back up to CD-R (Compact Disc Recordable), CD-RW (Compact Disc ReWritable), or DVD-RAM (Digital Versatile Disc Random Access Memory) because it sees these devices as read-only. As with both versions of NTBackup, a major drawback to this backup utility is that you can only back up folders, not files.

NOTE: *You cannot restore files from the command line using Windows 2000 NTBackup.*

Best Backup Practices

The following list describes the best backup practices to help protect your data:

- *Secure your backups.* Many companies protect their servers and yet leave their backup tapes in an open cabinet. If an intruder can access your backup tapes, he or she can access your data.

- *Perform backup verifies.* Verify compares the contents of the backup media with the targeted files backed up, and reports any corruption or differences.

- *Test your backups and hardware regularly.* Although your backup software may state that your backups are successfully running, there is no real indication of this until you perform a restore.

- *Rotate your backups offsite.* If something happens to your office building or location where you store your backups, you'll be glad you stored more tapes in another location.

- *Store your backups in a fire/water-proof container.* Tapes are very sensitive to corruption, especially heat. Storing your tapes in fire/water-proof containers helps protect your backups from damage.

- *Remember that backups can be subpoenaed.* Only back up files you wouldn't mind discussing in court.

- *Establish a written backup policy and stick to it.* This helps ensure that all the backup practices mentioned here, and many others, are clearly understood and followed daily.

Emergency Repair Disks

Emergency Repair Disks (ERDs) allow you to easily back up critical system files and registry entries to a floppy disk. The purpose of an ERD is not to perform backups, but to help return your system to a bootable state when corruption or boot errors prevent it. Once you have your system up and running again, you can perform a backup restore to replace corrupted files. You should create or update an ERD whenever a system change has taken place, such as adding hardware.

Under Windows NT, the utility to create ERDs is called RDISK.EXE, stored in the *%windir%*\system32 directory. When you run this utility, it copies the critical data to the *%windir%*\repair folder and then onto a floppy disk. Windows 2000 no longer includes the RDISK utility. Instead, you can create an ERD through NTBackup. This ERD does not contain any registry information because of the size of the Windows 2000 registry.

NOTE: *Windows 2000 NTBackup does not contain the ability to script an ERD. You must manually create ERDs under Windows 2000.*

Scheduling Windows NT/2000 Tasks

The **AT** command is a Windows NT/2000 command-line utility that allows you to schedule applications to run based on a predetermined schedule. You can use this command to automatically launch your backups, scripts, or any other tasks you can think of. The **AT** command works with the schedule service to monitor the system time, start tasks, and run the programs under the security context of the specified account.

The Evolution of the AT Command

Originally, the **AT** command worked with a service called schedule (ATSVC.EXE) that, by default, was configured as a system service. You could later configure this service to run under a specific administrative domain account, allowing your tasks to run for all users regardless of user privilege.

The New and Improved Task Scheduler

If you have Windows 2000 or at least Microsoft Internet Explorer 4, the schedule service is replaced with the Task Scheduler service (MSTASK.EXE). This service does not need to be configured with a specific account because you can now specify these credentials with each new task you create. For backward compatibility with tasks created by the **AT** command, you can still set the Task Scheduler service to run under a specified account.

The new task scheduler also adds a control panel applet called Scheduled Tasks, that provides a graphical interface to create, view, and modify scheduled tasks created by the **AT** command or task scheduler. These tasks are stored in the *%WINDIR%*\tasks directory. Although you can view and modify tasks under the Scheduled Tasks applet, the **AT** command does not recognize tasks created by the new task scheduler. This is because tasks created by the task scheduler can use additional features and require a specific user account to run. Any task created by the **AT** command will be converted to a task created by the task scheduler if a specific user account is specified or if any of the task scheduler's additional features are used, such as power management.

Immediate Solutions

Managing Windows NT's NTBackup

The Windows NT NTBackup utility supports multiple switches for performing backups from the command line. Here is a list of the available switches:

- **/A**—Appends backups

- **/B**—Performs a local registry backup

- **/D** *"text"*—Sets a backup comment

- **/E**—Logs only exceptions to the backup log

- **/HC:***x*—Controls hardware compression where *x* is **ON** or **OFF**

- **/L** *"filename"*—Sets the backup log file name

- **/NoPoll**—Used for troubleshooting; erases the tape and disables the DAT scan function when starting NTBackup (not to be used with other parameters)

- **/MISSINGTAPE**—Used for troubleshooting; instructs NTBackup to only work with the current tape regardless of whether it belongs to a multiple tape backup set

- **/R**—Restricts tape access to the tape owner or administrators

- **/T** *x*—Specifies the backup type where *x* is:

  - **copy**—Back up files and do not clear their archive flag

  - **daily**—Back up today's changed files and do not clear their archive flag

  - **differential**—Back up changed files and do not clear their archive flag

  - **incremental**—Back up changed files then clear their archive flag

  - **normal**—Back up files then clear their archive flag

- **/TAPE:***x*—Sets the destination tape drive where *x* is the device number

- **/V**—Performs backup verification

Running Windows NT NTBackup with Shell Scripting

To perform a full backup to tape drive 1 using shell scripting, proceed as follows:

1. Create a new directory to store all files included in this example.

2. Select Start|Run and enter "*scriptfile*.bat".

Here, **scriptfile** is the full path and file name of a script file that contains the following:

```
@Echo Off
Set BList=folders
Set BFile=backupfile
Set BComment=BackupComment

fullpath\NTBACKUP.EXE Backup %BList% /d "%BComment%"
/l logfile /T normal "%BFile%" /V:YES

Set BList=
Set BFile=
Set BComment=
```

NOTE: *The highlighted code above must be placed on one line.*

Here, **folders** are the folders to back up; **backupfile** is the complete path and file name of the backup file to create (typically stored with a BKS extension); **BackupComment** is the comment to give the backup; **logfile** is the complete path and file name of the backup log file; and **fullpath** is the complete path to the NTBackup utility.

Managing Windows 2000's NTBackup

The Windows 2000 NTBackup utility supports multiple switches for performing backups from the command line. Some of these switches are additional or have been modified from the Windows NT version of NTBackup. Here is a list of the available switches:

- **/A**—Appends backups
- **/D "label"**—Specifies a backup set **label**
- **/DS "server"**—Backs up the Microsoft Exchange directory service for the specified **server** name
- **/F "name"**—Specifies full path and file **name** of the backup file

- **/G "*tapeID*"**—Specifies to overwrite or append to the tape based on the specified *tape id*
- **/HC:*x***—Controls hardware compression where *x* is **ON** or **OFF**
- **/IS "*server*"**—Backs up the Microsoft Exchange information store for the specified *server* name
- **/J "*job*"**—Specifies a descriptive job name to record in the log file
- **/L:*x***—specifies the type of log file where *x* is:
  - **F**—Complete logging
  - **S**—Summary logging
  - **N**—No logging
- **/M *x***—Specifies the backup type where *x* is:
  - **copy**—Back up files and do not clear their archive flag
  - **daily**—Back up today's changed files and do not clear their archive flag
  - **differential**—Back up changed files and do not clear their archive flag
  - **incremental**—Back up changed files then clear their archive flag
  - **normal**—Back up files then clear their archive flag
- **/N "*name*"**—Specifies a new *name* to give the tape
- **/P "*name*"**—Specifies the *name* of the media pool to use
- **/R:*x***—Restricts tape access to the tape owner or administrators, where *x* is **YES** or **NO**
- **/RS *x***—Specifies to back up the removable storage database, where *x* is **YES** or **NO**
- **/T "*tapename*"**—Specifies to overwrite or append to the tape based on the specified *tape name*
- **/UM**—Specifies to find and format the find media available
- **/V:*x***—Performs backup verification, where *x* is **YES** or **NO**

Running Windows 2000 NTBackup with Shell Scripting

To automate a full backup using NTBackup and shell scripting, proceed as follows:

1. Create a new directory to store all files included in this example.
2. Select Start|Run and enter "*scriptfile*.bat".

Here, ***scriptfile*** is the full path and file name of a script file that contains the following:

```
@Echo Off
Set BList=folders
Set BFile=backupfile
Set BComment=BackupComment

fullpath\NTBACKUP.EXE Backup %BList% /d "%BComment%" /l:F
/F "%BFile%" /V:YES

Set BList=
Set BFile=
Set BComment=
```

NOTE: *The highlighted code above must be placed on one line.*

Here, ***folders*** are the folders to back up; ***backupfile*** is the complete path and file name of the backup file to create (typically stored with a BKS extension); ***BackupComment*** is the comment to give the backup; and ***fullpath*** is the complete path to the NTBackup utility.

Running Windows 2000 NTBackup with KiXtart

To automate a full backup using NTBackup and KiXtart, proceed as follows:

1. Create a new directory to store all files included in this example.

2. Download and extract the latest version of KiXtart, from **www.microsoft.com**, to the new directory.

3. Select Start|Run and enter "kix32 *scriptfile*".

Here, ***scriptfile*** is the full path of the new directory from step 1 and file name of a script file that contains the following:

```
$BList = "folders"
$BFile = "backupfile"
$BComment = "BackupComment"

$BCommand = "fullpath\NTBACKUP.EXE Backup $BList /d " +
  chr(34) + "$BComment" + chr(34) + " /l:F /F " +
  chr(34) + "$BFile" + chr(34) + " /V:YES"
Run $Bcommand
```

Here, *folders* are the folders to back up; *backupfile* is the complete path and file name of the backup file to create (typically stored with a BKS extension); *BackupComment* is the comment to give the backup; and *fullpath* is the complete path to the NTBackup utility.

Running Windows 2000 NTBackup with Windows Script Host

To automate a full backup using NTBackup and Windows Script Host, proceed as follows:

1. Create a new directory to store all files included in this example.

2. Download and install the latest version of Windows Script Host, from **www.microsoft.com**, to the new directory.

3. Select Start|Run and enter "cscript *scriptfile*.vbs".

Here, *scriptfile* is the full path and file name of a script file that contains the following:

```
On Error Resume Next
Set Shell = CreateObject("Wscript.Shell")

BList = "folders"
BFile = "backupfile "
BComment = "BackupComment"

BCommand = "fullpath\NTBACKUP.EXE Backup " & _
    BList & " /d " & chr(34) & BComment & chr(34) & _
    " /l:F /F " & chr(34) & BFile & chr(34) & " /V:YES"

Shell.Run BCommand, 0, TRUE
```

Here, *folders* are the folders to back up; *backupfile* is the complete path and file name of the backup file to create (typically stored with a BKS extension); *BackupComment* is the comment to give the backup; and *fullpath* is the complete path to the NTBackup utility.

Controlling Backup Exec from the Command Line

Backup Exec is a complete backup solution from Veritas (**www.veritas.com**) that includes advanced backup functionality, such as virus scanning. The BackupExec executable (BKUPEXEC.EXE) allows you to run a scheduled job from the command line. The basic syntax of BKUPEXEC is as follows:

```
BkupExec /J:"jobname"
```

Here, **/J** indicates to run BackupExec in command-line mode, and *jobname* is the name of the scheduled backup job.

NOTE: *If the BackupExec program is running or the* **jobname** *does not exist, the* **BkupExec** *command will not work.*

Consolidating BackUp Exec Logs

Whenever BackUp Exec performs a task, it records the progress in an individual log file stored in the program's data directory. Call me lazy, but I hate having to go to the server room, log onto multiple servers, and then check the job status. To remotely consolidate these log files to a central Excel spreadsheet (right from your desk), proceed as follows:

1. Create a new directory to store all files included in this example.

2. Download and install the latest version of Windows Script Host, from **www.microsoft.com**, to the new directory.

3. Select Start|Run and enter "cscript *scriptfile*.vbs".

Here, *scriptfile* is the full path and file name of a script file that contains the following:

```
On Error Resume Next
Set FSO = CreateObject("Scripting.FileSystemObject")
Set objXL = CreateObject("Excel.Application")

BEPath = "logpath"
Server = "servername"
```

```
SDays = InputBox("Please enter the number of days to report")
SDays = Int(SDays) - 1

Column = 1
Row = 1
SetupXL 'Setup Excel Sheet

BEFolder = "\\" & Server & "\" & BEPath
ChkBkUp BEFolder

Wscript.Echo "Complete."
Wscript.Quit

Sub SetupXL 'Setup and format Excel Sheet
  objXL.Workbooks.Add
  objXL.Columns(1).ColumnWidth = 20
  objXL.Columns(2).ColumnWidth = 10
  objXL.Columns(3).ColumnWidth = 15
  objXL.Columns(4).ColumnWidth = 10
  objXL.Columns(5).ColumnWidth = 15
  objXL.Columns(6).ColumnWidth = 10
  objXL.Cells(1,Column).Value = "Server"
  objXL.Cells(1,Column+1).Value = "Job"
  objXL.Cells(1,Column+2).Value = "Type"
  objXL.Cells(1,Column+3).Value = "Start Date"
  objXL.Cells(1,Column+4).Value = "Start Time"
  objXL.Cells(1,Column+5).Value = "Status"
  objXL.Cells(1,Column+6).Value = "Size"
  objXL.Range("A1:K1").Select
  objXL.Selection.Font.Bold = True 'Bold top row
  objXL.Selection.Interior.ColorIndex = 1
  objXL.Selection.Interior.Pattern = 1
  objXL.Selection.Font.ColorIndex = 2
End Sub

Sub ChkBkUp(BEFolder) 'Check if log folder exists
  If FSO.FolderExists(BEFolder) Then
    Set objDirectory = FSO.GetFolder(BEFolder)
    Set DirFiles = objDirectory.Files
    ExcelSheet(DirFiles)
  Else
    Wscript.echo "Could not access folder: " & BEFolder
  End If
End Sub
```

```
Sub ExcelSheet(DirFiles) 'Enter info to Excel sheet
  For Each objFile in DirFiles
    objXL.Visible = True
    FEXT = FSO.GetExtensionName(objFile.Path)
    fDate = DateDiff("d", objFile.DateCreated, Date)
    'Check if log date is within the search days specified
    If (LCase(FEXT) = "txt") AND ((fDate <= SDays) AND _
    (fDate > 0)) Then
      Verify = 0
      strSize = 0
      'Open log and transfer data to Excel sheet
      Set ts = FSO.OpenTextFile(objFile, 1)
      Do while ts.AtEndOfStream <> true
      s = ts.ReadLine
      If InStr(s, "Job server: ") <> 0 Then
        Row = Row + 1
        objXL.Cells(Row,Column).Value = Mid(s, 13)
      ElseIf InStr(s, "Job type: ") <> 0 Then
        objXL.Cells(Row,Column+1).Value = Mid(s, 11)
      ElseIf InStr(s, "Job name: ") <> 0 Then
        objXL.Cells(Row,Column+2).Value = Mid(s, 11)
      ElseIf InStr(s, "Job started: ") <> 0 Then
        dTemp = InStr(s, ", ")
        tTemp = InStr(s, " at ")
      dTemp = dTemp + 2
      dEnd = tTemp - dTemp
        objXL.Cells(Row,Column+3).Value = Mid(s, dTemp,dEnd)
      tTemp = tTemp + 4
        objXL.Cells(Row,Column+4).Value = Mid(s, tTemp)
      ElseIf S = "Job Operation - Verify" Then
        Verify = 1
      ElseIf (Verify = 1) AND _
      InStr(s, "Processed ") <> 0 Then
        myarray = Split(s)
        If IsNumeric(myarray(1)) Then
          strSize = strSize + _
          (LEFT((myarray(1)/1073741824),6))/1
      End If
      ElseIf InStr(s, "Job completion status: ") <> 0
      Verify = 0
        objXL.Cells(Row,Column+6).Value = strSize
        objXL.Cells(Row,Column+5).Value = Mid(s, 24)
        'If backup failed, bold and highlight red
        If LCase(Mid(s, 24)) = LCase("Failed") Then
          tRange = "A" & Row & ":G" & Row
        objXL.Range(tRange).Select
          objXL.Selection.Font.Bold = True
```

```
            objXL.Selection.Font.ColorIndex = 3
         'If backup not successful, bold
         ElseIf LCase(Mid(s, 24)) <> LCase("Successful") Then
            tRange = "A" & Row & ":G" & Row
         objXL.Range(tRange).Select
            objXL.Selection.Font.Bold = True
      End If
        End If
    Loop
    ts.Close 'Close log file
      End If
  Next
End Sub
```

Here, ***servername*** is the name of the server to connect to, and ***logpath*** is the administrative share and complete path where the logs are stored (typically c$\Program Files\Veritas\Backup Exec\NT\Data).

Related solution:	Found on page:
Creating Detailed Spreadsheets in Microsoft Excel	100

Controlling ARCserve 2000 from the Command Line

ARCserve 2000 is an advanced backup utility from Computer Associates (**www.cai.com**). ARCbatch, included with ARCserve, is a command-line utility that runs backup script files or templates. The basic syntax of the ARCbatch command is as follows:

```
ARCbatch /H=server /S=script
```

Here, ***server*** is the name of the server to run the specified ***script***. ***Script*** is the full name and path to the ARCbatch script or template file. ARCbatch scripts have an ASX extension and are created with the ARCserve manager. ARCbatch templates are INI files you can create to perform or schedule backups and restores. To immediately run a full backup using ARCbatch, proceed as follows:

1. Create a new directory to store all files included in this example.

2. Start a command prompt and enter "*fullpath*\ARCbatch /H=*server* /S=*template*".

Here, *fullpath* is the full path to the ARCbatch utility; *server* is the name of the server to run the specified *script*; and *template* is the full path and file name of a template file that contains the following:

```
[GENERAL]
HOST=*
JOBTYPE=BACKUP
JOBDESCRIPTION=description

[SOURCE_BACKUP]
NODE_NUM=1
BKMETHOD=1
VERIFICATION=2

[NODE_1]
DOMAINNAME=*
NODENAME=$HOST$
NODETYPE=NTAGENT

[DESTINATION_BACKUP]
TAPENAME=tape
GROUPNAME=group

[MEDIA_OPTIONS]
FIRSTTAPEOPTIONS=2
```

Here, *description* is the comment to add to the job; *tape* is the name of the tape; and *group* is the name of the device group.

---

*TIP: ARCbatch templates support numerous entries. Visit **www.cai.com** for more information.*

Updating Emergency Repair Disk Information

An Emergency Repair Disk (ERD) contains a copy of critical system files for a particular machine. These files are stored in *%windir%* \repair and are copied to the ERD whenever one is updated or created. Unfortunately, floppy disks are small in size, prone to corruption, and easily misplaced. To update these files without creating an ERD, start a command prompt and enter the following:

```
RDISK /S-
```

Here, the **/S** option specifies to skip the main dialog and copy the complete SAM (Security Account Manager) and SECURITY database files to the repair directory. The - specifies to bypass creating an ERD.

WARNING! You should only use the /S option when updating ERD information or creating an ERD on a system with a small number of users and groups. Systems such as a primary domain controller (PDC) have a large SAM that could not possibly fit on an ERD.

Archiving Daily ERD Information to a Central Share

To automatically store ERD information to a central network share on a daily basis, proceed as follows:

1. Create a new directory to store all files included in this example.

2. Select Start|Run and enter "*scriptfile*.bat".

Here, **scriptfile** is the full path and file name of a script file that contains the following:

```
@Echo Off
Set Server=%ComputerName%
Set Share=cshare
Set Drive=driveletter
Set RDrive=%Drive%\%ComputerName%\ERD
Set RLog=%RDrive%\ERD.log

NET USE %Drive% /DELETE > Nul
NET USE %Drive% \\%Server%\%Share% > Nul
If errorlevel 1 Goto End

REM *Create a time stamp variable to use in logs
For /F "Delims= Tokens=1" %%I in ('Date /T') Do Set Dtime=%%I
For /F "Delims= Tokens=1" %%I in ('Time /T')
Do Set Dtime=%Dtime%%%I

REM *Create a date variable to name new folders
For /F "Tokens=2" %%I in ('Date /t') Do Set DTemp=%%I
For /F "Delims=/,= Tokens=2" %%I in ('Set DTemp')
Do Set TDate=%%I

For /F "Delims=/,= Tokens=3" %%I in ('Set DTemp')
Do Set TDate=%TDate%%%I
```

```
For /F "Delims=/,- Tokens=4" %%I in ('Set DTemp')
Do Set TDate=%TDate%%%I
Set RDrive=%RDrive%\%TDate%
Set DTemp=
Set TDate=

Echo %Dtime%: Starting ERD Archving Process >> %RLog%
Set DTime=

If Exist %RDrive% Goto MKERD
MD %RDrive%

:MKERD
Echo - Updating ERD Information >> %RLog%
%windir%\system32\rdisk.exe /s- > Nul
If %errorlevel% EQU 0 Goto Copy
Echo - Error running RDISK >> %RLog%
Goto End

:Copy
Echo - Copying ERD Information >> %RLog%
Copy %windir%\Repair\*.* %RDrive% > Nul
Echo - Archiving ERD Information Complete >> %RLog%
NET USE %Drive% /DELETE > Nul

:End
Set Server=
Set Share=
Set Drive=
Set RDrive=
Set RLog=
```

NOTE: *The highlighted code above must be placed on one line.*

TIP: *You can schedule this script to run regularly by calling with the code from the next example.*

Here, **cshare** is the central share to store archived ERD information, and **driveletter** is the temporary letter to use while transferring ERD information.

Scheduling Tasks with the **AT** Command

The **AT** command allows you to schedule tasks from the command line. The basic syntax of the **AT** command is as follows:

```
AT \\remote ID /COMMANDS "fullpath"
```

TIP: To display a list of schedule tasks from the command line, start a command prompt and enter "AT".

Here, *remote* is an optional name of a remote system of which tasks to control; *ID* specifies a task ID to modify; *fullpath* is the complete path and file name of the item to schedule; and the available *commands* are as follows:

- **/DELETE**—Removes a scheduled job.

- **/YES**—Combined with **/DELETE**, suppresses all jobs cancellation prompt.

- **/INTERACTIVE**—Sets the job to interact with the desktop. This switch must be set if you want the user to have any interactivity with the scheduled task.

- **/EVERY:*x***—Recurrently runs the command on the specified day (*x*).

- **/NEXT:*x***—Runs the command on the next specified date (*x*).

To schedule a script file to run at a specified time every work day, start a command prompt and enter the following:

```
AT  \\remote time /interactive /every:M,T,W,TH,F scriptfile
```

Here, *remote* is the name of the system to store the scheduled task; *time* is the time to run the task; and *scriptfile* is the full path and name of the script to run.

TIP: You can use the Resource Kit Utility WINAT to graphically control and view scheduled tasks.

Creating Tasks with WMI

The **Win32_ScheduledJob** class allows you to create, delete, or view scheduled tasks. This class is extremely limited in functionality, incorrectly documented, and difficult to work with. There is no method

13. Backups and Scheduling

to modify an existing task and there are only a few available parameters when creating a task. This class also only recognizes and can create tasks compatible with the **AT** command. For whatever reason, to create a scheduled task using WMI, proceed as follows:

1. Create a new directory to store all files included in this example.

2. Download and install the latest version of WMI and Windows Script Host, from **www.microsoft.com**, to the new directory.

3. Select Start|Run and enter "cscript *scriptfile*.vbs".

Here, ***scriptfile*** is the full path and file name of a script file that contains the following:

```
On Error Resume Next
DTime = MilTime

Set TZone = GetObject("winmgmts:{impersonationLevel=
impersonate}!\\computer\root\cimv2").ExecQuery
("select * from Win32_TimeZone")

For each Zone in TZone
   TBias = Zone.bias + 60 'Compensates for daylight savings
Next

STime = "********" & DTime & "00.000000" & TBias

Set ScheduledJob = GetObject("winmgmts:{impersonationLevel=
impersonate}!\\computer\root\cimv2:Win32_ScheduledJob")
   Set method = ScheduledJob.Methods_("Create")
   Set inParam = method.inParameters.SpawnInstance_()
      inParam.Command = "fullpath "
      inParam.StartTime = STime
      inParam.RunRepeatedly = rp
      inParam.DaysOfWeek = dow
   Set outParam = ScheduledJob.ExecMethod_("Create", inParam)
```

NOTE: *The highlighted code above must be placed on one line.*

Here, ***miltime*** is the time to schedule a task to run (in military format); ***fullpath*** is the full path and file name of the program to execute; ***rp*** is a binary entry (0 or 1) that specifies whether to create a reoccurring task; and ***dow*** are the days of the week to run the task. ***Dow*** does not accept abbreviated day names (M,T,W,...), but must be entered in binary format where the days of the week are as follows:

- *Monday*—1
- *Tuesday*—2
- *Wednesday*—4
- *Thursday*—8
- *Friday*—16
- *Saturday*—32
- *Sunday*—64

To schedule a task to run on a specific day, simply add up the day values and enter the total. For example, to run a task on Tuesday, Friday, and Saturday, you would enter 50 (2+16+32).

Listing Tasks in Internet Explorer Using WMI

The **Win32_ScheduledJob** class can retrieve and display information on any task previously created using the **Win32_ScheduledJob** class or **AT** command. To list these scheduled tasks within a formatted Internet Explorer window, proceed as follows:

1. Create a new directory to store all files included in this example.
2. Download and install the latest version of WMI and Windows Script Host, from **www.microsoft.com**, to the new directory.
3. Select Start|Run and enter "cscript *scriptfile*.vbs".

Here, **scriptfile** is the full path and file name of a script file that contains the following:

```
On Error Resume Next
Set FSO = CreateObject("Scripting.FileSystemObject")
Set MSIE = CreateObject("InternetExplorer.Application")
Set ScheduledJob = GetObject("winmgmts:{impersonationLevel=
impersonate}!\\computer\root\cimv2").ExecQuery("select *
from Win32_ScheduledJob")

SetupMSIE
MSIE.Document.Write "<HTML><TITLE>Scheduled Jobs" & _
  "</TITLE><BODY bgcolor=#ffffff><FONT FACE=ARIAL>"
MSIE.Document.Write "<B>Displaying tasks created " & _
  "with WMI or the AT command:</B><BR><BR>" & _
```

```
        "<table border=0 width=100% cellspacing=0 " & _
        "cellpadding=0>"

For each ejob in ScheduledJob
    IEWrite "Caption", EJob.Caption
    IEWrite "Command", EJob.Command
    IEWrite "Days Of Month", EJob.DaysOfMonth
    IEWrite "Days Of Week", EJob.DaysOfWeek
    IEWrite "Description", EJob.Description
    IEWrite "Install Date" ,EJob.InstallDate
    IEWrite "Interact With Desktop", EJob.InteractWithDesktop
    IEWrite "Job ID", EJob.JobID
    IEWrite "Job Status", EJob.JobStatus
    IEWrite "Name", EJob.Name
    IEWrite "Notify", EJob.Notify
    IEWrite "Owner", EJob.Owner
    IEWrite "Priority", EJob.Priority
    IEWrite "Run Repeatedly", EJob.RunRepeatedly
    IEWrite "Start Time", EJob.StartTime
    IEWrite "Status", EJob.Status
    IEWrite "Time Submitted", EJob.TimeSubmitted
    IEWrite "Until Time", EJob.UntilTime
    IEWrite " ", " "
Next

MSIE.Document.Write "</table><BR><B>End of List</B>" & _
    "</FONT></BODY>"

Sub SetupMSIE
    MSIE.Navigate "About:Blank"
    MSIE.ToolBar = False
    MSIE.StatusBar = False
    MSIE.Resizable = False

    Do
    Loop While MSIE.Busy

    SWidth = MSIE.Document.ParentWindow.Screen.AvailWidth
    SHeight = MSIE.Document.ParentWindow.Screen.AvailHeight
    MSIE.Width = SWidth/2
    MSIE.Height = SHeight/2
    MSIE.Left = (SWidth - MSIE.Width)/2
    MSIE.Top = (SHeight - MSIE.Height)/2

    MSIE.Visible = True
End Sub
```

```
Sub IEWrite(Caption,Prop)
    MSIE.Document.Write "<tr><td>" & Caption & "</td>" & _
    "<td> </td><td align=right>" & Prop & _
    "</td></tr>"
End Sub
```

NOTE: *The highlighted code above must be placed on one line.*

Here, **computer** is the name of the computer containing the tasks to list.

Related solution:	Found on page:
Using Microsoft Internet Explorer as a Display Tool	96

Deleting Tasks Using WMI

The **Win32_ScheduledJob** class can delete any task previously created with the **Win32_ScheduledJob** class or **AT** command. To delete all of these scheduled tasks using WMI, proceed as follows:

1. Create a new directory to store all files included in this example.
2. Download and install the latest version of WMI and Windows Script Host, from **www.microsoft.com**, to the new directory.
3. Select Start|Run and enter "cscript *scriptfile*.vbs".

Here, **scriptfile** is the full path and file name of a script file that contains the following:

```
On Error Resume Next
Set ScheduledJob = GetObject("winmgmts:{impersonationLevel=
impersonate}!\\computer\root\cimv2").ExecQuery
("select * from Win32_ScheduledJob")

For each ejob in ScheduledJob
  ejob.Delete()
Next
```

NOTE: *The highlighted code above must be placed on one line.*

Here, **computer** is the name of the computer containing the tasks to delete.

Chapter 14

Fun with Multimedia

In Brief

If you're not having complete and utter fun yet, this chapter is for you. In this chapter, you will learn how to use simple scripts to play and control multimedia files. You will also learn how to script the Office Assistant and Microsoft Agent characters to interact with your users.

The Dreaded Office Assistant

Office assistants are animated characters designed to help and entertain users of Microsoft Office. These characters provide tips, accept natural language queries (such as "How do I hide the Office Assistant?"), and perform animations based on the actions of the user. In theory, these assistants sound like a good idea. However, soon after the release of these assistants with Office 97, a flood of complaints followed denouncing them. The main problem was the overinteraction of these assistants.

To turn on the Office Assistant, choose Help|Show the Office Assistant. Once the assistant is visible, right-click on it and choose Options. Under the Options tab, you can disable the Office Assistant by unchecking Use the Office Assistant. Under the Gallery tab, you can choose which assistant you want to use. The default assistant is called Clippit, a hyperactive paper clip that doesn't know when to be quiet.

The Office Assistant Object Model

The Office Assistant object model is a limited one. At the top of the model is the assistant object. An instance of the Office Assistant object model is created whenever an instance of an office application is created. Once the instance is created, you can make the assistant visible by setting the **Visible** property to **True**:

```
officeapp.Assistant.Visible = True
```

Once the assistant is visible, you can move, resize, or animate the assistant:

```
officeapp.Assistant.Left = 500
officeapp.Assistant.Top = 500
```

Office assistants display messages to users through the **Balloon** object. You can use the **NewBalloon** property to create an instance of the **Balloon** object:

```
Set Balloon = officeapp.Assistant.NewBalloon
```

Once an instance of the **Balloon** object has been created, you can create text messages and check boxes, and then show these messages using the **Show** property:

```
Balloon.Heading = "Some Text Heading"
Balloon.Text = "Some Body Text"
Balloon.CheckBoxes(1).Text = "An example check box"
Balloon.Show
```

TIP: *If you have Microsoft Office 2000 with the VBA help files installed, the complete Office Assistant object model can be found in the file VBAOFF9.CHM.*

Under Office 97, office assistants are stored in actor files, with an ACT (Actor) extension (typically located in C:\Program Files\Microsoft Office\Office). Office 2000 uses the Microsoft Agent ActiveX technology and stores its assistants in ACS (Agent Character) files, allowing for more animations and interaction with the user.

Microsoft Agent

Microsoft Agent, originally called Microsoft Interactive Agent, is an ActiveX technology that allows you to display and animate characters to interact with the computer user. Agent characters are cartoon-like animations stored in agent character (ACS) files. Each character contains its own set of animations and voice patterns. You can use Microsoft Agent within Microsoft Office, script files, Web pages, and applications.

The Microsoft Agent Support Files

In order to run Microsoft Agent, you need to download and install the following items:

- *Microsoft Agent core components*—These are the core components that allow you to access and control a Microsoft Agent character.

- *Microsoft Agent character files*—These are the agent characters you can use to interact with the computer user.

- *Text-to-speech engines*—These engines allow the Microsoft Agent characters to translate text to speech, giving these characters the ability to "speak."

You can obtain these components from the Microsoft Agent Web site, **msdn.microsoft.com/workshop/imedia/agent/**.

The Microsoft Agent Process

All agent character commands and requests are exposed through the agent object model, MSAgent.ocx. After you create an instance of the object model, the character can be loaded and is ready to receive requests. When a request for a character animation is made, the data provider (AgentDPV.dll) decompresses the graphic and audio files, and passes them to the automation server (AgentSvr.exe). The automation server renders the files to use transparent backgrounds and borders, giving them the appearance of hovering on top of the screen.

Scripting the Microsoft Agent Using Windows Script Host

The first step to accessing the Microsoft Agent character methods is to create an instance of the Microsoft Agent Control:

```
Set ACTL = CreateObject("Agent.Control.2")
```

Once a connection has been established, you can load one of the preinstalled Microsoft Agent characters and set a reference to it:

```
ACTL.Characters.Load charactername, "charactername.acs"
Set CREF = ACTL.Characters(charactername)
```

Here, *charactername* is the name of the Microsoft Agent character, such as Merlin or Peedy. After the character has been loaded, you can make the character visible using the **Show** method:

```
CREF.Show
```

Once the character is visible, you can call on any of the character's methods to perform an animation or to speak. Each agent contains a set of unique animations. To make a character use a specific animation, you use the **Play** method:

```
CREF.Play "animation"
```

NOTE: *For a complete list of animations, consult the character's animation reference file.*

Here, ***animation*** is the type of animation to perform, such as greet or sad. You can use the **Speak** method to make the character say a specific phrase:

```
CREF.Speak "text"
```

Finally, you can cause the character to move to a specific location using the **MoveTo** method:

```
CREF.MoveTo x,y
```

Here, ***x*** is the horizontal pixel location, and ***y*** is the vertical pixel location.

TIP: *Specifying 0,0 will move the characters to the upper left corner of the screen.*

Immediate Solutions

Playing an Audio File Using KiXtart

KiXtart has the built-in ability to play a WAV or SPK file using the **Play** command. To play an audio file using KiXtart, proceed as follows:

1. Create a new directory to store all files included in this example.

2. Download and extract the latest version of KiXtart, from **www.microsoft.com**, to the new directory.

3. Select Start|Run and enter "kix32 *scriptfile*".

Here, *scriptfile* is the full path of the new directory from step 1 and file name of a script file that contains the following:

```
$Aud = "filename"
Play File $Aud
```

Here, *filename* is the full path and file name of the WAV or SPK file to play.

Scripting the Microsoft Media Player

Windows NT/2000 includes a free application called Media Player, designed to play audio and video files. Mplay32.exe is the 32-bit version of the standard Media Player, and this utility can play audio, video, and DirectShow files. This utility supports a limited amount of command-line switches.

Microsoft Media Player 7 is a Windows add-on that provides extremely enhanced functionality when compared to the older Windows multimedia players. Some of these features include media rights, MP3 (Motion Pictures Expert Group Layer 3 Audio) support, video streaming, radio tuners, and play list support. This player is intended to be the core Windows multimedia player and manager while replacing the older, built-in multimedia players, such as CDPlayer.exe and Mplay32.exe. This utility has limited support for Windows Script Host.

Playing a Media File from the Command Line

To play and then close a media file using Mplay32.exe and shell scripting, proceed as follows:

1. Create a new directory to store all files included in this example.

2. Select Start|Run and enter "*scriptfile*.bat".

Here, *scriptfile* is the full path and file name of a script file that contains the following:

```
@Echo Off
MPLAY32 /PLAY /CLOSE "filename"
```

Here, *filename* is the full path and file name to play.

Playing a Media File Using Windows Script Host

To play and then close a media file using Mplay32.exe and Windows Script Host, proceed as follows:

1. Create a new directory to store all files included in this example.

2. Download and install the latest version of Windows Script Host, from **www.microsoft.com**, to the new directory.

3. Select Start|Run and enter "cscript *scriptfile*.vbs".

Here, *scriptfile* is the full path and file name of a script file that contains the following:

```
On Error Resume Next
Set SHELL = CreateObject("wscript.shell")

SHELL.Run "MPLAY32 /PLAY /CLOSE filename",0
```

Here, *filename* is the full path and file name to play. The value **0** within the **Run** command causes the media player to be hidden.

Playing Multiple Media Files Using a Play List

Many new audio players (for example, winamp) utilize play lists to play one audio file after another. To play multiple media files using a play list, Mplay32.exe, and Windows Script Host, proceed as follows:

1. Create a new directory to store all files included in this example.

2. Download and install the latest version of Windows Script Host, from **www.microsoft.com**, to the new directory.

3. Select Start|Run and enter "cscript *scriptfile*.vbs".

Here, ***scriptfile*** is the full path and file name of a script file that contains the following:

```
On Error Resume Next
PlayList ("playlist")

SUB PlayList(TXTfile)
  Set SHELL = CreateObject("wscript.shell")
  Set FSO = CreateObject("Scripting.FileSystemObject")
  Set readfile = FSO.OpenTextFile(TXTfile, 1, false)

  Do while readfile.AtEndOfStream <> true
    contents = Trim(readfile.Readline)
      If contents <> "" Then
          SHELL.RUN "MPLAY32 /PLAY /CLOSE " & contents,3,True
      End If
  Loop
End Sub
```

Here, ***playlist*** is the full path and file name of a playlist file. Each line of this file contains the full path and file name of an audio file to play.

TIP: *The value **3** within the **SHELL.RUN** command specifies to maximize the player. You can change this value to **0** if you would like the player hidden.*

Ejecting a CD Using Windows Script Host

Microsoft Media Player 7 does not currently support access through Windows Script Host. You can, however, use the Media Player 7 object model to display information and control the CD player. To eject a CD using the Media Player 7 object model and Windows Script Host, proceed as follows:

1. Create a new directory to store all files included in this example.

2. Download and install Microsoft Media Player 7 and the latest version of Windows Script Host, from **www.microsoft.com**, to the new directory.

3. Select Start|Run and enter "cscript *scriptfile*.vbs".

Here, ***scriptfile*** is the full path and file name of a script file that contains the following:

```
On Error Resume Next
Set MPlayer = CreateObject("WMPlayer.OCX.7")
```

```
MPlayer.cdromCollection.item(x).eject()
```

Here, *x* is the number of the CD-ROM drive (starting at 0).

Ejecting All CDs Using Windows Script Host

To eject all CDs using the Media Player 7 object model and Windows Script Host, proceed as follows:

1. Create a new directory to store all files included in this example.

2. Download and install Microsoft Media Player 7 and the latest version of Windows Script Host, from **www.microsoft.com**, to the new directory.

3. Select Start|Run and enter "cscript *scriptfile*.vbs".

Here, ***scriptfile*** is the full path and file name of a script file that contains the following:

```
On Error Resume Next
Set MPlayer = CreateObject("WMPlayer.OCX.7")
Set FSO = CreateObject("Scripting.FileSystemObject")
Count=-1

For Each Drive in FSO.Drives
  If Drive.DriveType = 4 Then
    Count=Count+1
  End If
Next

If Count > -1 Then
  For x = 0 to Count
    MPlayer.cdromCollection.item(x).eject()
  Next
End If
```

Here, a **DriveType** value of **4** indicates a CD-ROM player.

Scripting RealPlayer G2

RealPlayer G2 is an advanced multimedia player from Real Networks (**www.real.com**). Although this player is commonly used to play streaming media on the Internet, you can use these same ActiveX control calls to script RealPlayer using Windows Script Host.

Playing an Audio File

To play an audio file using the RealPlayer ActiveX control and Windows Script Host, proceed as follows:

1. Create a new directory to store all files included in this example.

2. Download and install the latest version of Windows Script Host, from **www.microsoft.com**, to the new directory.

3. Download and install the latest version of RealPlayer G2, from **www.real.com**, to the new directory.

4. Select Start|Run and enter "cscript *scriptfile*.vbs".

Here, ***scriptfile*** is the full path and file name of a script file that contains the following:

```
On Error Resume Next
Set RPlayer = CreateObject("rmocx.RealPlayer G2 Control.1")

RPlayer.SetSource "file:filename"
RPlayer.DoPlay

Wscript.Echo "Press OK to end."
```

Here, ***filename*** is the full path and file name to play.

Playing an Audio File with Windows Script Host Controls

To play an audio file with basic controls using the RealPlayer ActiveX control and Windows Script Host, proceed as follows:

1. Create a new directory to store all files included in this example.

2. Download and install the latest version of Windows Script Host, from **www.microsoft.com**, to the new directory.

3. Download and install the latest version of RealPlayer G2, from **www.real.com**, to the new directory.

4. Select Start|Run and enter "cscript *scriptfile*.vbs".

Here, ***scriptfile*** is the full path and file name of a script file that contains the following:

```
On Error Resume Next
Set RPlayer = CreateObject("rmocx.RealPlayer G2 Control.1")
```

```
CMD = 2

Do While CMD <> 10
  Select Case CMD
    Case 0
      RPlayer.DoPlay
    Case 1
      RPlayer.DoPause
    Case 2
      If AUD = "" Then AUD = "filename"
      AUD = InputBox("Please enter the name of the audio file
        to play", "Audio File", AUD)
      RPlayer.SetSource "file:" & AUD
    Case 3
      WScript.Quit
  End Select
    Message = "Choose a command:" & vblf & vblf & _
    "0: Play file" & vblf & _
    "1: Pause file" & vblf & _
    "2: Choose file" & vblf & _
    "3: Quit" & vblf
  CMD = InputBox(Message, "RealPlayer Commands", "0")
Loop
```

NOTE: *The highlighted code above must be entered as one paragraph.*

Here, *filename* is the full path and file name to play.

Playing Multiple Audio Files Using a Play List

Many new audio players (for example, winamp) utilize play lists to play one audio file after another. To play multiple media files using a play list, the RealPlayer ActiveX control, and Windows Script Host, proceed as follows:

1. Create a new directory to store all files included in this example.

2. Download and install the latest version of Windows Script Host, from **www.microsoft.com**, to the new directory.

3. Download and install the latest version of RealPlayer G2, from **www.real.com**, to the new directory.

4. Select Start|Run and enter "cscript *scriptfile*.vbs".

Here, ***scriptfile*** is the full path and file name of a script file that contains the following:

```
On Error Resume Next
Set RPlayer = CreateObject("rmocx.RealPlayer G2 Control.1")
Set FSO = CreateObject("Scripting.FileSystemObject")
Set readfile = FSO.OpenTextFile(TXTfile, 1, false)

PlayList ("playlist")
Wscript.Echo "Press OK to end."

SUB PlayList(TXTfile)
  Do while readfile.AtEndOfStream <> true
    filename = Trim(readfile.Readline)
      If filename <> "" Then
        RPlayer.SetSource "file:filename"
        RPlayer.DoPlay
      End If
  Loop
End Sub
```

Here, ***filename*** is the full path and file name to play.

Scripting the Office Assistant

The Office Assistant is an interactive animated character used to help and entertain users of Microsoft Office. You can only access the assistant object model through an Office application object model. This means that you must have an Office application installed in order to automate an office assistant. To script the Office Assistant in Excel using Windows Script Host, proceed as follows:

1. Create a new directory to store all files included in this example.
2. Install the latest version of Microsoft Excel.
3. Download and install the latest version of Windows Script Host, from **www.microsoft.com**, to the new directory.
4. Select Start|Run and enter "cscript *scriptfile*.vbs".

Here, ***scriptfile*** is the full path and file name of a script file that contains the following:

```
On Error Resume Next
Set FSO = CreateObject("Scripting.FileSystemObject")
```

```
Set objXL = CreateObject("Excel.Application")

objXL.Workbooks.Add
objXL.Visible = False
objXL.Assistant.Visible = True

With objXL.Assistant
  .Reduced = True
  .Left = 300
  .Top = 300
  .MoveWhenInTheWay = True
End With

Set Balloon = objXL.Assistant.NewBalloon

Balloon.Heading = "Multiple Selections"
Balloon.Text = "Please make a selection"
Balloon.CheckBoxes(1).Text = "Selection 1"
Balloon.CheckBoxes(2).Text = "Selection 2"
Balloon.Show

If Balloon.CheckBoxes(1).Checked Then
  Wscript.Echo "You selected check box 1."
End If
If Balloon.CheckBoxes(2).Checked Then
  Wscript.Echo "You selected check box 2."
End If

objXL.quit
```

Related solution:	Found on page:
Automating Applications through an Application Object	96

Scripting Microsoft Agent Using Windows Script Host

Microsoft Agent is an ActiveX technology that allows you to use animated characters to present information to your users. This technology can be used in presentations, logon scripts, new user setups, and any other situation where an interaction is needed.

Scripting a Character to Speak

Many developers use Microsoft Agent to entertain, educate, or guide their users through a process. To script a Microsoft Agent character to speak using Windows Script Host, proceed as follows:

1. Create a new directory to store all files included in this example.

2. Download and install the latest version of Microsoft Agent, a text-to-speech engine, a Microsoft Agent character, and Windows Script Host, from **www.microsoft.com**, to the new directory.

3. Select Start|Run and enter "cscript *scriptfile*.vbs".

Here, **scriptfile** is the full path and file name of a script file that contains the following:

```
On Error Resume Next
Set SHELL = CreateObject("wscript.shell")
Set FSO = CreateObject("Scripting.FileSystemObject")
aCHAR = "charname"

Set ACTL = CreateObject("Agent.Control.2")
  ACTL.Connected = True
  If Not IsObject(ACTL) Then
    Wscript.Echo "Microsoft Agent was not found on your " & _
      "system." & vblf & "Please install and try again."
    Wscript.Quit
  End If
ACTL.Connected = True

ACTL.Characters.Load aCHAR, aCHAR & ".acs"
If Err.Number <> 0 Then
  Wscript.Echo "Could not locate the Agent called " & aCHAR
  Wscript.Quit
End If

Set CREF = ACTL.Characters(aCHAR)
CREF.Show
CREF.Speak "Hello there!"

WScript.Echo "Press OK to close"
```

Here, **charname** is the name of the agent character to use.

14. Fun with Multimedia

Scripting a Character to Speak a WAV File

Microsoft Agent has the ability to accept a WAV (WAVeform Audio) file and appear to speak it based on the gaps of silence detected. This allows you to use a real voice, as opposed to a synthesized voice, to speak to your users. To use Microsoft Agent to speak a WAV file, proceed as follows:

1. Create a new directory to store all files included in this example.

2. Download and install the latest version of Microsoft Agent, a text-to-speech engine, a Microsoft Agent character, and Windows Script Host, from **www.microsoft.com**, to the new directory.

3. Select Start|Run and enter "cscript *scriptfile*.vbs".

Here, ***scriptfile*** is the full path and file name of a script file that contains the following:

```
On Error Resume Next
Set SHELL = CreateObject("wscript.shell")
Set FSO = CreateObject("Scripting.FileSystemObject")
aCHAR = "charname"

Set ACTL = CreateObject("Agent.Control.2")
  ACTL.Connected = True
  If Not IsObject(ACTL) Then
    Wscript.Echo "Microsoft Agent was not found on your " & _
      "system." & vblf & "Please install and try again."
    Wscript.Quit
  End If
ACTL.Connected = True

ACTL.Characters.Load aCHAR, aCHAR & ".acs"
If Err.Number <> 0 Then
  Wscript.Echo "Could not locate the Agent called " & aCHAR
  Wscript.Quit
End If

Set CREF = ACTL.Characters(aCHAR)
CREF.Show
CREF.Speak "", "WAVFile"

WScript.Echo "Press OK to close"
```

Here, **charname** is the name of the agent character to use, and **WAVFile** is the full path and file name of the WAV file to use.

Scripting a Character to Sing

You can make the Microsoft Agent appear to sing by modifying the pitch and speed of the agent's voice. To make a Microsoft Agent character sing the Imperial March from Star Wars, proceed as follows:

1. Create a new directory to store all files included in this example.

2. Download and install the latest version of Microsoft Agent, a text-to-speech engine, a Microsoft Agent character, and Windows Script Host, from **www.microsoft.com**, to the new directory.

3. Select Start|Run and enter "cscript *scriptfile*.vbs".

Here, **scriptfile** is the full path and file name of a script file that contains the following:

```
On Error Resume Next
Set SHELL = CreateObject("wscript.shell")
Set FSO = CreateObject("Scripting.FileSystemObject")
aCHAR = "charname"

Set ACTL = CreateObject("Agent.Control.2")
  ACTL.Connected = True
  If Not IsObject(ACTL) Then
    Wscript.Echo "Microsoft Agent was not found on your " & _
      "system." & vblf & "Please install and try again."
    Wscript.Quit
  End If
ACTL.Connected = True


ACTL.Characters.Load aCHAR, aCHAR & ".acs"
If Err.Number <> 0 Then
  Wscript.Echo "Could not locate the Agent called " & aCHAR
  Wscript.Quit
End If


Set CREF = ACTL.Characters(aCHAR)
CREF.Show
CREF.Speak "\Chr=""Monotone""\\Map=""\Pit=98\\Spd=50\DUN DUN
\Spd=134\DUN \Spd=50\DUN \Pit=78\DUN \Pit=117\\Spd=200\DUN
\Pit=98\\Spd=50\DUN \Pit=78\DUN \Pit=117\\Spd=150\DUN
\Pit=98\\Spd=50\DUN""=""""\"
```

```
CREF.Speak "\Chr=""Monotone""\\Map=""\Pit=147\\Spd=50\DUN
DUN DUN \Pit=156\\Spd=67\DUN \Pit=117\\Spd=134\DUN
\Pit=92\\Spd=67\DUN \Pit=78\\Spd=80\DUN \Pit=117
\\Spd=77\DUN \Pit=98\\Spd=67\DUN""=""""\"
```

```
Wscript.Echo "Press OK to end the show"
```

NOTE: *The highlighted code above must be placed on one line.*

Here, *charname* is the name of the agent character to use.

Scripting a Character to Read

You can make the Microsoft Agent speak any text that you can inter-
pret in Windows Script Host. To make a Microsoft Agent character
read a text file using Windows Script Host, proceed as follows:

1. Create a new directory to store all files included in this example.

2. Download and install the latest version of Microsoft Agent, a
   text-to-speech engine, a Microsoft Agent character, and Windows Script Host, from **www.microsoft.com**, to the new
   directory.

3. Select Start|Run and enter "cscript *scriptfile*.vbs".

Here, *scriptfile* is the full path and file name of a script file that contains the following:

```
On Error Resume Next
Set SHELL = CreateObject("wscript.shell")
Set FSO = CreateObject("Scripting.FileSystemObject")
aCHAR = "charname"

Set ACTL = CreateObject("Agent.Control.2")
  ACTL.Connected = True
  If Not IsObject(ACTL) Then
    Wscript.Echo "Microsoft Agent was not found on your " & _
      "system." & vblf & "Please install and try again."
    Wscript.Quit
  End If
ACTL.Connected = True

ACTL.Characters.Load aCHAR, aCHAR & ".acs"
If Err.Number <> 0 Then
  Wscript.Echo "Could not locate the Agent called " & aCHAR
  Wscript.Quit
End If
```

```
Set CREF = ACTL.Characters(aCHAR)
CREF.Show
ReadTXT ("textfile")

WScript.Echo "Press OK to close"

SUB ReadTXT(TXTfile)
  Set FSO = CreateObject("Scripting.FileSystemObject")
  Set readfile = FSO.OpenTextFile(TXTfile, 1, false)
  Do while readfile.AtEndOfStream <> true
    contents = readfile.Readline
    If contents <> "" THEN
      CREF.Speak contents
    End IF
  Loop

  contents = NULL
  readfile.close
End Sub
```

Here, **charname** is the name of the agent character to use, and **textfile** is the full path and file name of the text file to read.

Scripting a Character to Check for Events

In Chapter 7, you learned how to check for events using Windows Management Instrumentation. To make a Microsoft Agent character notify you of events using WMI and Windows Script Host, proceed as follows:

1. Create a new directory to store all files included in this example.

2. Download and install the latest version of Microsoft Agent, a text-to-speech engine, the Merlin Microsoft Agent character, WMI, and Windows Script Host, from **www.microsoft.com**, to the new directory.

3. Select Start|Run and enter "cscript *scriptfile*.vbs".

Here, **scriptfile** is the full path and file name of a script file that contains the following:

```
On Error Resume Next
Set SHELL = CreateObject("wscript.shell")
Set FSO = CreateObject("Scripting.FileSystemObject")
aCHAR = "Merlin"
```

```
Set ACTL = CreateObject("Agent.Control.2")
  ACTL.Connected = True
  If Not IsObject(ACTL) Then
    Wscript.Echo "Microsoft Agent was not found on your " & _
      "system." & vblf & "Please install and try again."
    Wscript.Quit
  End If
ACTL.Connected = True

ACTL.Characters.Load aCHAR, aCHAR & ".acs"
If Err.Number <> 0 Then
  Wscript.Echo "Could not locate the Agent called " & aCHAR
  Wscript.Quit
End If

Wscript.Echo "Press CTRL+C to end this script."

Set CREF = ACTL.Characters(aCHAR)
CREF.MoveTo 200,200
CREF.Show
CREF.Play "Wave"
CREF.Play "Restpose"
CREF.Speak "Hello, my name is Merlin!"
CREF.Play "Greet"
CREF.Play "Restpose"
CREF.Speak "I am your personal CPU monitoring assistant!"
CREF.Play "Announce"
CREF.Play "Restpose"
CREF.MoveTo 0,0
CREF.Speak "I will now monitor your CPU usage and notify " & _
  "you when an overload occurs."
CREF.Play "StartListening"

Computer = InputBox("Enter the computer name",
"CPU Monitor", "localhost")

CPULoad = InputBox("Enter the CPU overload threshhold",
"CPU threshhold", "75")

Poll = InputBox("Enter the polling interval",
"Poll Interval", "5")

If Computer = "" Then Computer = "Localhost"
If CPULoad = "" Then CPULoad = 75
If Poll = "" Then Poll = 5
```

14. Fun with Multimedia

```
Set ProLoad = GetObject("winmgmts:{impersonationLevel=
impersonate}!\\" & Computer & "\root\cimv2")
.ExecNotificationQuery("SELECT * FROM
__InstanceModificationEvent WITHIN " & Poll & " WHERE
TargetInstance ISA 'Win32_Processor' and
TargetInstance .LoadPercentage > " & CPULoad)
If Err.Number <> 0 then
  WScript.Echo Err.Description, Err.Number, Err.Source
End If

Do
  Set ILoad = ProLoad.nextevent
  If Err.Number <> 0 then
    WScript.Echo Err.Number, Err.Description, Err.Source
    Exit Do
  Else
    AMessage = ILoad.TargetInstance.DeviceID & _
    " is overloaded at " & _
    ILoad.TargetInstance.LoadPercentage & "%!"
    CREF.Stop
    CREF.Show
    CREF.Play "GetAttention"
    CREF.Play "GetAttentionContinued"
    CREF.Play "GetAttentionReturn"
    CREF.Speak AMessage
    RandomAction
  End If
Loop

Sub RandomAction()
  ulimit = 5.0
  llimit = 1.0

  Randomize
  X = Int((ulimit - llimit)*Rnd() + llimit)
  Select Case X
    Case 1
      CREF.Play "Acknowledge"
    Case 2
      CREF.Play "Alert"
    Case 3
      CREF.Play "Explain"
    Case 4
```

```
        CREF.Play "Sad"
      Case 5
        CREF.Play "Uncertain"
  End Select
End Sub
```

NOTE: *The highlighted code above must be placed on one line.*

Here, **computer** is the name of the system to monitor; **CPULoad** is the CPU utilization threshold to monitor for (1-100); and **poll** is the number of seconds to set as the polling interval to check for events. The subprocedure **RandomAction** creates a random number and then specifies an animation based on that number.

WARNING! *If you run this script with WSCRIPT, you will only be able to terminate the script by ending the WSCRIPT.EXE process through the Task Manager.*

Related solution:	Found on page:
Monitoring CPU Utilization	186

14. Fun with Multimedia

Resources

This appendix lists various Web sites and newsgroups where you can gather more information or download some of the tools used in this book.

ADSI

The following sites provide information on Active Directory Services Interface (ADSI):

msdn.microsoft.com/library/psdk/adsi/adsistartpage_7wrp.htm
www.15seconds.com/focus/ADSI.htm

Newsgroups

microsoft.public.adsi.general
microsoft.public.platformsdk.adsi

Antivirus

The following sites provide information on antivirus:

www.mcafeeb2b.com/avert/avert-research-center/
www.symantec.com/avcenter/

Newsgroups

alt.comp.virus
alt.comp.virus.source.code
microsoft.public.scripting.virus.discussion
symantec.support.winnt.nortonantivirus.general

KiXtart

The sites on the following page provide information on KiXtart.

KiXtart.org

KiXtart.org, formerly **kixtart.to**, is the premiere Web site for KiXtart scripting. The heart of this site is its bulletin board where you can find hundreds of KiXtart tips, tricks, facts, and scripts.

Site: **www.KiXtart.org**

Visual KiXtart Editor

Visual KiXtart Editor, by Version Zero Software, is a compact script editor designed just for KiXtart scripting. Although it lacks some of the advanced features of other editors, this program provides for fast editing and little overhead at a reasonable price.

Site: **versionzero.romanweb.com**

Microsoft Agent

The following sites provide information on Microsoft Agent.

The Agentry

The Agentry is the Web's core location for everything that is Microsoft Agent. Here you will find the Net's largest collection of Microsoft Agent characters, along with tools, book links, newsgroups, applications, and more.

Site: **agentry.net**

MASH (Microsoft Agent Scripting Helper)

MASH, by BellCraft Technologies, is the easiest and quickest way to script Microsoft Agent. This advanced tool allows you to browse through character animations and create complex script files with absolutely no prior scripting or programming experience.

Site: **www.bellcraft.com**

Microsoft Agent Web Ring

The Microsoft Agent Web Ring is the one place on the Web that tries to bring all Microsoft Agent Web sites together. This site is full of examples, applications, characters, and links to other Microsoft Agent Web sites.

Site: **www.msagentring.org**

MSDN Online Web Workshop

This is the official site for Microsoft Agent. Here you will find the latest news and downloads regarding Microsoft Agent.

Site: **msdn.microsoft.com/workshop/imedia/agent/**

Newsgroups

microsoft.public.msagent

Other

The following sites provide information on other helpful sites.

ActiveWin.com

This site is truly an Internet resource center for the Windows platform. Here you will find all sorts of information, drivers, articles, tools, tips, and tricks for the Windows operating system of your choice.

Site: **www.activewin.com**

Dave G. Thomas

Although small in size, this site contains several utilities that can prove real handy when other methods of scripting fail.

Site: **www.mindspring.com/~dgthomas/**

JesseWeb

This is my own personal Web site. Here you will find updates and support material for the book, scripts, tricks, tips, security documents, music, and more. If you visit any site on this page, this should be the place to start.

Site: **www.jesseweb.com**

JSIInc

Glad to see that this site is still alive and well. JSIInc contains an extensive amount of registry tips, tricks, and hacks. The site also contains administrative utilities, tips, and tricks for almost anything you can think of. A definite bookmark.

Site: **www.jsiinc.com/reghack.htm**

Sysinternals

The site for the true Windows administrator. From the guys that brought you NTFSDOS, ERD Commander, and FAT32 for Windows NT (**www.wininternals.com**), this site contains many free and invaluable utilities that you may find yourself using on a daily basis.

Site: **www.sysinternals.com**

Windows 2000 FAQ

Formerly Windows NT FAQ, this site contains the answers to hundreds of Windows NT/2000 questions on just about every topic. A good site for quick questions and answers.

Site: **www.windows2000faq.com**

Shell Scripting

The following sites provide information on shell scripting.

BatFiles

It's amazing that with the growth of all the other scripting languages, a site like this could still exist. BatFiles is a Web site purely devoted to the DOS shell scripter. Here you will find tons of examples, tricks, FAQs, links, and downloads.

Site: **bigfoot.com/~batfiles/**

DOS Batch Programming

A simple site full of tips, tricks, and techniques. There's even a section purely devoted to NT shell scripting.

Site: **www.calweb.com/~webspace/batch/**

The DOS Command Index

This site contains a comprehensive list of shell scripting commands and their usage.

Site: **www.easydos.com/dosindex.html**

Newsgroups

alt.msdos.batch
alt.msdos.batch.nt

Scripting: General

The following sites provide information on scripting in general.

AutoIt

AutoIt is a 59K free automation tool to send key presses, manipulate the mouse, modify files and the registry, control dialog boxes and more.

Site: **www.hiddensoft.com/AutoIt/**

Brainbuzz

Dubbed "The Mother of All Tech Sites," the Brainbuzz site truly lives up to its name. Filled with IT news, products, tools, jobs, links, and more, this site has a section purely devoted to scripting.

Site: **www.brainbuzz.com**

DevGuru

DevGuru is an Internet learning center providing downloads, tutorials, and references for scripters and ASP developers.

Site: **www.devguru.com**

Microsoft ScriptIt

Microsoft ScriptIt is an advanced macro utility used to send key commands to Windows objects. ScriptIt detects window titles and text and sends commands to specific windows based on that information.

Site: **www.microsoft.com/NTServer/nts/deployment/custguide/scriptit3.asp**

Microsoft Windows Script Technologies

This Web site is Microsoft's central location to obtain scripting downloads, documentation, news, and support. Here you can download the latest versions of Windows Script Host, Microsoft Script Encoder, and the complete VBScript documentation.

Site: **msdn.microsoft.com/scripting/**

PrimalSCRIPT

PrimalSCRIPT, by Sapien Technologies, is by far the leader of script editors. Packed with advanced features and providing support for more than 20 scripting languages, PrimalSCRIPT is the tool of choice for scripting professionals.

Site: **www.sapien.com**

UltraEdit-32

UltraEdit-32, by IDM Computer Solutions, Inc., is an award-winning script editor that provides for quick and painless editing. This compact editing tool contains many of the advanced features of other editors, at a fraction of the cost. With features like project management, macros, keyboard mapping, automatic backup, and unlimited file sizes, this little tool packs a big punch.

Site: **www.ultraedit.com**

Win32 Scripting

Win32 Scripting is the Web center for the serious scripter. Packed with code and custom tools for all types of scripting languages, this site proves that nothing is unscriptable.

Site: **cwashington.netreach.net**

Win32 Scripting Journal

Windows 2000 Magazine's Win32 Scripting Journal is a 15-page monthly publication focused on task automation for the Windows administrator. The site is generally restricted to its publication subscribers, but is full of scripting articles and examples.

Site: **www.win32scripting.com**

Newsgroups

microsoft.public.scripting.vbscript
microsoft.public.scripting.jscript
microsoft.public.scripting.remote
microsoft.public.scripting.scriptlets

Windows Management Instrumentation

The following sites provide information on Windows Management Instrumentation (WMI):

msdn.microsoft.com/downloads/sdks/wmi/default.asp
www.microsoft.com/NTServer/management/Techdetails/
   ProdArchitect/WMIScripting.asp
msdn.microsoft.com/library/backgrnd/html/wmicim.htm
www.microsoft.com/WINDOWS2000/library/technologies
   /management/
www.microsoft.com/HWDEV/WMI/default.htm

Newsgroups

microsoft.public.wbem

Windows Script Host

The following sites provide information on Windows Script Host.

Windows Script Host Bazaar

Günter Born's Windows Script Host Bazaar is packed with samples, ActiveX controls, book reviews, newsletters, tools, links, and more.

Site: **www.borncity.de/WSHBazaar/**

Windows Script Host FAQ

This site is an excellent resource for anyone interested in Windows Script Host. This site is loaded with information, tutorials, FAQs, links, reviews, and more. A definite starting point for the new WSH scripter.

Site: **wsh.glazier.co.nz/**

WinScripter

Although most of the scripts at this site are written in Jscript (and the scripts in this book were written in VBScript), this site is an excellent resource for articles, tutorials, and examples.

Site: **www.winscripter.com**

Newsgroups

Microsoft.Public.Scripting.wsh

Appendix: Resources

Security

The following sites provide information on security issues.

Microsoft Security

Microsoft's official security site providing the latest security news, fixes, and links.

Site: **www.microsoft.com/security/**

RootShell

A site purely devoted to security and hacker exploits.

Site: **rootshell.com**

SANS (System Administration, Networking, and Security)

SANS is a research community, composed of over 96,000 security personnel and system administrators. Here you'll find the latest security news, events, resources, and more.

Site: **www.sans.org**

Technotronic

Technotronic is a Wb site and mailing listing dedicated to sharing and archiving security information for all types of operating systems. This site has many security utilities available.

Site: **www.technotronic.com**

Windows IT Security

Windows 2000 Magazine's central site for IT security news, FAQS, files, articles, and more.

Site: **www.ntsecurity.net**

Newsgroups

microsoft.public.win2000.security

VBA

The following sites provide information on Visual Basic for Applications (VBA).

OfficeVBA.com

OfficeVBA.com is the official site to the monthly publication "Microsoft Office Visual Basic for Applications Developer." This site is packed with VBA articles, book and product reviews, news, case studies, and more.

Site: **www.officevba.com**

Newsgroups

microsoft.public.word.vba.beginners
microsoft.public.word.vba.customization
microsoft.public.word.vba.general

Index

A

ACEs (access control entries), 142–143
ACLs (access control lists), 142
Active Directory Services Interfaces.
  See ADSI.
ActiveX control, AutoIt, 88
AddProgramGroup function, 153
AddProgramItem command, 153
ADDUSERS utility, 199–200
  managing groups with, 202
Administrative shares, 164–166
  removing, 254–255
Administrative tools, locking down, 255–256
Administrator account, renaming the, 267–268
ADSI (Active Directory Services Interfaces), 192–194, 203–214
  adding a user account to a group with, 210
  changing the local administrator password with, 206–207
  creating computer accounts with, 205
  creating groups with, 209–210
  creating shares with, 204
  creating user accounts with, 207–208
  deleting computer accounts with, 206
  deleting groups with, 210
  deleting shares with, 205
  deleting user accounts with, 208
  disabling user accounts with, 209
  listing shares with, 203–204
  removing a user account from a group with, 211
  resources, 375
  security and, 264–269
    account lockout policy, 266–267
    minimum password length, 264–265
    password age, 265
    renaming the administrator account, 267–268

    searching for locked-out accounts, 267
    searching for unused accounts, 268–269
    unique password changes, 266
  setting a user's domain password with, 206
  silent installation of, 32
  unlocking user accounts with, 208
ADSI client, 193
Advertising, Microsoft Office 2000, 40–41
Alerts, sending
  with KiXtart, 290–292
  with shell scripting, 289–290
  with Windows Script Host, 292–296
Antivirus. *See also* McAfee VirusScan;
  Norton AntiVirus 2000
  resources, 375
APIs (Application Programming Interfaces), 48
Appending text files
  with KiXtart, 58
  with shell scripting, 54
  with Windows Script Host, 81
Application objects
  accessing, 85–86
  automating applications through, 96–109
    Microsoft Internet Explorer as a display tool, 96–99
  changing the visibility of, 86
  closing, 86
ARCserve 2000, 343–344
Arguments, 51
AT command, 333–334, 347
Attaching to shares, 164–165
Attributes
  file
    displaying, 56–57
    getting, 79
    setting, 57–58, 80–81

S

X